INTERNATIONAL LONGSHORE & WAREHOUSE UNION

CANADA

Longshoring on the Fraser

LONGSHORING on the Fraser

Stories and History of ILWU Local 502

ILWU Local 502
Chris M.V. Madsen
Liam O'Flaherty
Michelle La

GRANVILLE ISLAND
PUBLISHING

www.granvilleislandpublishing.com

Library and Archives Canada Cataloguing in Publication

Madsen, C. M. V. (Chris Mark Vedel), 1968–, author
Longshoring on the Fraser : stories and history of ILWU Local 502 / ILWU Local 502, Chris M.V. Madsen, Liam O'Flaherty, Michelle La.

Includes bibliographical references and index.
ISBN 978-1-926991-83-2 (hardback). — ISBN 978-1-926991-69-6 (paperback). — ISBN 978-1-926991-70-2 (pdf)

1. International Longshore and Warehouse Union. Local 502 (New Westminster, B.C.) — History. 2. Stevedores — British Columbia — History. 3. Labor unions — British Columbia — History. I. La, Michelle, author II. O'Flaherty, Liam, 1984–, author III. International Longshore and Warehouse Union. Local 502 (New Westminster, B.C.), author IV. Title.

HD8039.L82C353 2016   331.7'613875440971133   C2016-901287-5
                                                          C2016-901288-3

Editor: Kyle Hawke
Proofreader and Indexer: Bookmark: Editing & Indexing
Cover designer: Omar Gallegos
Text designer: Victor Daniel Colmont
Cover image: Bill Smillie, photographer

Granville Island Publishing Ltd.
604-688-0320 / 1-877-688-0320
www.granvilleislandpublishing.com

First published in May 2016
Printed in Canada on recycled paper

Printed by Thunderbird Press

*To the men and women who built
the Union and to those who lost
their lives working in the industry*

Contents

Introduction
In New Westminster and on the Fraser River

Peter Hall

This book tells the story of ILWU Local 502 and its relationship to the City of New Westminster and the Fraser River. Local 502 was officially chartered as part of the International Longshoremen's and Warehousemen's Union in 1944, but the first efforts to organize longshore workers in this port go back to early part of the 20th Century. In becoming a 'local' of the ILWU, New Westminster longshoremen had joined the 'international' union that has represented dockworkers along the entire west coast of Canada and the United States, including Alaska and Hawaii, since the 1930s. It's easy to forget that New Westminster was once an important upriver port providing access to the BC interior, and allowing for the export of Canadian resources and products. It's also easy to forget that there are still industrial activities on the Fraser riverfront, and to forget that there are still working people in all those waterfront businesses, restaurants, parks, and condominiums. The Local 502 story reminds us that the waterfront always was, and still is, a place where community members go to work. When we forget the working people of the waterfront, we paint a pretty picture, but not something that is socially just and sustainable in a true sense of the words. The story of ILWU Local 502 is important because it reminds us that the waterfront is still valuable as a place of work.

Across the world, most organizations which represent working people are under attack. They are increasingly blamed by some corporations and politicians for raising costs and for being inflexible. Dockworkers know what it means to provide low-cost and flexible labour to an industry which is subject to ever-changing demand — it means a shape-up, where workers are picked for jobs through bribes and favouritism, where they are paid poverty wages, and where they are discarded when they become injured, sick, or too old. For this reason, dockworkers and longshoremen have a tradition of building unions which are amongst the most militant and best organized in any economic sector. In many of the world's largest ports, they have secured excellent working conditions, good wages, and strong safety records. They have embraced new technologies, positioning maritime shipping to drive the global economy.

Still, it's also true that in many places, waterfront unions and jobs have simply disappeared due to changes in the industry. With bigger ships, there are fewer ports and only those with deep water, wide terminals, and good connections have thrived. Technology has also eliminated many jobs, and changed the skills required from longshoremen. The longshoremen who built Local 502 could have been put out of work as the New Westminster terminals became obsolete, and as port activity moved across the Fraser River and to Roberts Bank. So the story of the men and women of ILWU Local 502 and the hard decisions they took is important: this union successfully navigated the restructuring forces of globalization, and unlike many other unions in developed countries, it has survived and grown.

Telling the story of Local 502 is one goal of this book, the other being to place ILWU Local 502 in the context of the city where it began. Because of its location on the Fraser River, New Westminster was a key meeting point for warring First Nations people and then selected for settlement by early British Columbia colonists. It is at the head of the river's delta, the first place going inland where the river could be crossed in one voyage. The main channel of the river is deep here, overlooking the defensible and desirable neighbourhoods that comprise the city today, including Sapperton, Queen's Park, and Brow of the Hill. It was a great place to develop a settlement, and it was a great place to develop a port. The construction of successive land-based transportation routes reinforced the choice of this fortunate location: North Road, Kingsway, the continental railroads, and the Pattullo Bridge. As a port city, as a commercial hub, and as an administrative centre, New Westminster was and remains a good place to work and live. Although the river and city remain closely connected, New Westminster's port activity declined and relocated.

New Westminster is not alone in this. Port facilities and port cities all across the world have experienced such changes. Through this painful process, the nature and locations of waterfront work has changed. Port terminals have become more technologically complex and they require larger cranes and more land to service larger ships. All over the world, ports have consolidated and major cargo-handling terminals have been moved away from urban riverfronts to deepwater oceanfront locations. Ports, once governed by authorities representing local business and political interests, are now corporatized and subject to fragmented ownership by large multinational corporations. These global processes have played out in New Westminster and along the Fraser River over the past fifty years. However, while the port activities have changed and moved away the core waterfront of the city, Local 502 has survived and thrived.

There are problems when we focus only on the negative story of loss in port cities. We tend to tell the story of waterfront change as a simple shift from male industrial work to non-work — this is not correct. The simplified story presents the waterfront as a much less diverse place than it was and than it is. It ignores the actual non-industrial work of the past and the presence of diverse workers including women, aboriginal people, and immigrants from the four corners of the world. The longshoremen of Local 502 were never the only industrial workers on the waterfront — there were also, and still are in many places, mill workers, tug boat operators, fishery and cannery workers, ship-builders, and more. Most of these workers were men, but not all of them. Even in traditional industrial waterfronts, there were office workers, secretaries, restaurant servers, and other non-industrial workers, just as there are today.

In recognition of the changing gender composition of the membership, in 1997 the official name of the ILWU was changed from 'International Longshoremen's and Warehousemen's Union' to

'International Longshore and Warehouse Union'. In this book, we use the official name as it applied in each time period, and we also shift from the term 'longshoremen' to 'longshore workers' in Chapter 5. We recognize that some ILWU members (of both genders) prefer to be called 'longshoremen' while others prefer to be called 'longshore workers'.

In this book, we tell a realistic and inclusive story about Local 502 and the many ways that the waterfront was, and still is, connected to its hosting community. Waterfront workers often lived in the City of New Westminster, although this changed over time as the location of the work changed. They frequented bars, restaurants, and shops in the city. Other residents of the city likewise frequented restaurants, markets, and retailers on the waterfront, even long before the decline of port activity. Even though the city no longer has any major marine terminals, it is still affected every day by port activity, whether by trucks and trains moving on the land or by barges and log booms on the river.

Finally, if we were to focus only on the global forces that restructured the port industry from the outside, we would be ignoring the role of working people and worker's organizations in shaping those changes. This book shows workers as active, highlighting how they and their organizations can shape the outcomes, whether for good and bad. If we ignore the role of workers and worker's organizations in shaping the world around us, we ignore the subtle but important differences between and solidarity amongst workers. Telling the history of Local 502 is important because it shows how the union has both responded to and influenced the changes in port activity on the Fraser River.

This book grew out of a research partnership between retired members of ILWU Local 502, the New Westminster Museum and Archives, students and faculty from Simon Fraser University, and academics at other institutions. Funded by the Social Sciences and Humanities Research Council of Canada, the (Re)Claiming the New Westminster Waterfront partnership aimed at understanding the complex history of work on the waterfront from the perspective of actual workers, past and present. Other partners include New Westminster schools and individual residents of New Westminster.

Today's retired longshoremen began their working lives on the docks in New Westminster. One of the things that the partnership has made clear is that the history of Local 502 is much more than an evolving set of labour–management agreements. Waterfront workers constitute a principal, but often ignored, point of connection between the docks and the communities where ports are located. Rank-and-file members are important actors in the networks of globalization. In the past, and this may still be the case, longshore workers served as 'ambassadors' between international seafarers and local communities. Thus a goal of the research partnership was to use oral history to document the changes in waterfront work in New Westminster from 1945 to the present.

Organization of the book

The chapters of this book follow the history of Local 502 in New Westminster and on the Fraser River in a timeline. The story begins before World War II, when dockworkers faced harsh working conditions and suffered defeats when they went on strike to improve their working conditions. These struggles laid the ground for the chartering of the local in 1944 within the International Longshoremen's and Warehousemen's Union. The contents of the chapters are summarized below, but cutting across these chapters are six themes. The themes are important, demarcating what makes the story of Local 502 and the story of New Westminster as a unique port, not quite the same as anywhere else in the world.

These themes are:

1. Union activities
Local 502 is a member of ILWU Canada and through this, it is connected to other locals in the BC Lower Mainland and all along the west coast of North America. So the history of ILWU Local 502 is part of the history of ILWU Canada, of the ILWU International, and indeed of longshore unions all around the world.

Still, it is a distinct history because Local 502 is a distinct organization within that larger movement. It is its own independent organization and differences result from that matter. For example, Local 502 has control of its own dispatch hall and, until the three port authorities in the Lower Mainland amalgamated in 2008 to form Port Metro Vancouver, it represented its members at terminals across these Port Authority jurisdiction boundaries. This is because Local 502's charter included the waters south of the mouth of the Fraser River, all the way to the United States border. Indeed, there are even important currents and trends within Local 502, such as the distinction between those who work at Westshore Terminal and those who work at Deltaport and along the Fraser River. Keeping the union together and using these differences as a source of strength is an important theme in the history of the local.

2. Global trends in longshoring and ports

Ports have always been about connecting widely dispersed places, but there is a sense that the flows between places are more intense today. This ties New Westminster to the many other industrial upriver ports in the developed world that have experienced the painful process of restructuring. From a local economy with many cargo terminals and lumber mills, the city is now increasingly post-industrial with many commercial and residential developments on the waterfront. Concepts such as globalization and restructuring are used to understand this process.

In Western Canada, globalization has not eliminated the resource economy but has diversified its markets for lumber and other commodities, mostly towards Asia. Manufacturing in places such as BC's Lower Mainland has declined precipitously, replaced by containerized imports. Much of the history of the Fraser River told in this book shows increasing imports of cars and manufactured goods from Asia. Ports have been made larger and more corporate to manage these new and intensified flows of goods. We can see how this process has played out in New Westminster and on the Fraser River, but the closer we look, the more we can see that the story here is unique. For some members of Local 502, especially veterans of World War II, the turn to Asia was difficult. For others, it was an opportunity to participate in trade missions which accelerated the process.

3. Geography of work

In the period covered in this book, the work of handling cargo moved from terminals in New Westminster, first across the river to Surrey, then leapfrogging down the Fraser River to Robert's Bank. However, because of Local 502's jurisdiction, even as the geography of work changed, the members of the local continued to handle cargo.

The ability of these longshore workers to follow and benefit from the changing geography of work is a potent lesson for workers in restructuring industries everywhere. Still, the changing geography of work does present its own challenges. As the prime site of work moved away from the City of New Westminster and became more widely spread out, it has been important to make sure that all the members of the union have a chance to get to know and understand each other.

4. Technology changes

Local 502 members have experienced many of the same technology changes as port workers elsewhere. This is not only because of the introduction of containers, but also because of changes in other modes of transport. New Westminster itself never had a container port terminal and the container terminal at Fraser Surrey Docks has never been very successful. However, the container terminal at Deltaport — which only opened in 1997 — is now as important as the two Burrard container terminals combined.

Containerization was not the only technological change that directly affected Local 502 and the City of New Westminster. Lumber handling, which was always a core activity in New Westminster and on the Fraser River, began to change as early as the 1950s. Whereas before, most lumber was delivered from nearby mills by barge or scow for hand-stowing, by the 1960s most lumber was delivered by truck as packaged lumber. This necessitated new technologies such as the forklift and, for a brief period, the assassinator.

Also by the 1960s, the fleet of Victory and other World War II-era ships was aging out, being replaced by more specialized and larger ships. The newer ships were not as well-suited to the berthing arrangements in New Westminster — Fraser Surrey Docks and Annacis Island were better locations. Such early experiences with changing technology were not easy, but probably prepared Local 502 member for subsequent changes.

5. Social life at work and connection to community

Changes in the organization, technologies, and geography of waterfront work have big implications for the social relationships between workers at work and in their communities. One challenge is that longshoremen are increasingly working alone, operating specialized equipment and travelling to different terminals.

The hiring hall, regular member meetings, and social functions are important to maintaining solidarity at work. As well, in the past, many members of Local 502 used to live in New Westminster. While some still do, the combined effects of the relocation of port work to the south side of the Fraser and to Roberts Bank, along with the development of suburbs in Surrey, Delta, and beyond, mean that today most members do not live in New Westminster. This has heightened some of the sense of separation between the resident community and the waterfront workers of Local 502.

6. International solidarity

Longshoremen the world over are some of the most informed and highly-organized workers. In part, this is because they are exposed to new ideas, products, and people on a daily basis.

The history of Local 502 has many examples of the connections and relationships between seamen and dockworkers. These include acts of solidarity that range from parties and personal friendships to support for strikers and acts of international solidarity. Although daily contact between seamen and dockers continues, it is increasingly difficult for workers in the supply chain to maintain their understanding of each other's lives and work. This is because changes in the port and logistics industry are separating workers into technology-intensive jobs on the waterfront, but less desirable jobs elsewhere in the supply chain.

Together, these themes in the book help remind us about the global forces confronting Local 502 and the port and City of New Westminster, but also about what is unique and special about these people and this place. The themes highlight the challenges, but also the possibilities to address them.

Chapter contents

Chapter 1 describes the history of New Westminster from the first colonial settlement until the 1920s. Before the ILWU established a presence in New Westminster, port workers in the city either had no collective institution to protect their rights at work or were represented by one of the competing worker organizations, such as the International Longshoremen's Association or the Canadian Longshoremen's Association. For different reasons, none of these early unions were particularly effective at protecting port workers from harsh and uncertain working conditions.

The grounds were ripe for the growth of the kind of coastwise, worker-controlled unionism provided by the ILWU, but still it was not easy in coming. Chapter 2 records the tumultuous events of the 1930s and '40s. At the height of the Great Depression, longshoremen along the west coast of North America joined in the efforts to create the ILWU. Under the leadership of Harry Bridges, this union forged a new model of coastwise solidarity amongst dockworkers. In New Westminster, it was only as World War II was coming to an end that ILWU Local 502 was chartered on 3 October 1944. This timing was both ideal and, in many ways, not a surprise. Demobilized soldiers and workers who had toiled under harsh wartime conditions were strong unionists.

Chapter 3 describes what many now recognize as the heyday of the City of New Westminster being involved with the ILWU. The decade and a half after the end of the war was a boom period for trade on the Fraser River. At the same time, New Westminster enjoyed a boom as the retail centre for the emerging suburbs of greater Vancouver.

The good times, however, were not to last forever. Chapter 4 examines the 1960s and 1970s, a period of painful technological, organizational, and geographic restructuring in ports across the world — especially so in New Westminster. Technological changes began in the late 1950s, but their effects only became apparent in later years. Prime amongst these was the commercial adoption of the ocean shipping container. New Westminster's small port was never able to join this wave and thus went into decline.

However, the cargo did not disappear. Chapter 5 examines the surprising period that brings us to the present. One might have expected Local 502 to have withered away given the changes in the 1960s and 1970s, or that it might have been absorbed by some other part of ILWU Canada. This did not happen because, by the late 1990s, the local was playing an active role in supporting the new patterns of trade focused around Deltaport.

Today, the future of Local 502 is promising, with growth in cargo handling on, alongside, and at the mouth of the Fraser River. But the challenges of maintaining union solidarity in the face of changing technology and work organization remain. The concluding Chapter 6 looks to the future in two sections; first, some reflections on the future prospects for Local 502 and second, a description of an intergenerational arts project in New Westminster schools. Both of these sections emphasize a key message of the whole book: namely, the importance of education of members, casuals, and the wider community about the history, value and importance of good jobs on the waterfront.

Bringing Back the First ILWU Charter in British Columbia

As featured in the centennial edition of the *ILWU Canada Waterfront News* in November 1971, retirees Leo Labinsky, Frank Parker, and Jack Remple present Don Garcia with a copy of the first ILWU charter given to longshore workers in New Westminster in 1937. Labinsky was president of ILWU Local 502 for the better part of the 1950s and elected ILWU Canadian Area president 1962–63. Garcia was first elected ILWU Local 502 president in 1963, lost badly to Robert Crane the next year, returned again in 1965, and subsequently served long tenures back and forth as ILWU Canadian Area president and ILWU Local 502 president. Parker and Remple found the original charter in San Francisco at the ILWU Anne Rand Library.

From left to right: Leo Labinsky — instrumental in bringing the ILWU to New Westminster, Don Garcia — Canadian Area president and past president of Local 502, Frank Parker and Jack Remple — charter members of Local 502 in 1944.
Source: Fisher Photo Studio

*Dedicated to the memory of
Joe Miranda, eight years old*

Chapter 1
Unionism on the Waterfront 1859–1928

Chris Madsen

As a recognized labour union of long standing serving the interests of member longshore workers, ILWU Local 502 has a long history on the Fraser River waterfront. That history goes back to the establishment and growth of New Westminster as Western Canada's busiest freshwater port when men loaded ships of sail and steam with lumber, agricultural produce, and other commodities for export. The individual stories of longshoremen during those early years tell of struggle and hard work for modest wages, of one-sided relations with private employers, and of the beginning of collective association and action amongst those who toiled on the waterfront.

Life was difficult before formal unions arrived. Why does a strong union matter to every longshore worker? That central question, as important today as back then, can only be answered by knowing the history and the full scope of the shared experience by those members who came before, now retired or long dead. ILWU Local 502 is the sum of its accumulated relations with each other, leadership in the face of employer expectations, and interaction with broader communities.

A union performs certain basic functions. Most of all, it ensures that a worker is not alone, but part of a broader group connected by skill, trade, and type of work. Persons identify with those around them working in a similar way and at the same locations. The workplace provides fraternity, friendship, and fellowship.

Upon joining the union, members accept the requirements for qualification and remaining in good standing, such as regular attendance and payment of dues, in return for a sense of belonging and advancement of shared interests. The union is a legally-constituted body that enjoys protections and rights under federal and provincial laws applied to labour relations and affiliated by charter with larger labour organizations — in the case of Local 502, the Canadian and American ILWU down the Pacific coast. Unions also belong to a broader tradition of labour and progressive politics in the province of British Columbia. On this basis, the union negotiates the terms of employment such as wages, hours of work, work conditions, and other matters with employers and any association representing them. Collective agreements covering specified periods of time are signed to govern those terms and how they affect members of the union.

The union lives by the collective agreement in place at any given time and always prepares for negotiation toward the next one. Should disputes or disagreements occur, the union may resort to corrective measures up to and including withholding the performance of work by its members in the form of strike, walkout, or slowdown. In those situations, members respond together with solidarity and common purpose. Even then, some of the big strikes taken on by longshoremen in the past, in 1923 and 1935, for instance, did not go well for the union. That the struggle was lost on those occasions only strengthened the resolve of longshoremen to achieve a truly unionized waterfront in and around New Westminster on the Fraser River.

The goal was to move away from the fractured and uneven environment created by the employers toward better arrangements that looked after all longshore workers and furthered the advancement of common concerns and interests. Longshore workers sought better pay and work conditions, control over the workplace through the dispatch, recognition of legitimate labour association, and most importantly, respect from employers for the work done. The gains enjoyed today were won yesterday.

Longshore Work During the Sail Era

Employment on the Fraser River waterfront evolved with the emergence of New Westminster as an administrative centre and harbour of standing in British Columbia. On 14 December 1859, the wooden-mast schooner *D.L. Clinch*, captained by George Bunker, left New Westminster bound for San Francisco loaded with 60,000 feet of cut cabinet wood and fifty barrels of cranberries.[1] This commercial cargo is believed to be the first registered by an ocean-going ship from the province to a foreign port and the first from the Fraser River. During the first six months of 1860, one hundred and four vessels, mostly riverboat steamers, called at New Westminster, its name changed from the original Queensborough by proclamation and becoming an incorporated city with the blessing of Queen Victoria. By 1861, a wooden quay shown on a contemporary map ran the entire length of the main waterfront between Ellice Street (now Tenth Street) and Albert Crescent.[2] During the Gold Rush period, large numbers of miners arrived by ship, either from Victoria on the southern tip of Vancouver Island or direct from San Francisco, eager for transport to stake claims far away in gold fields upriver. In 1872, the city applied to the federal government through the provincial legislature for transfer of waterfront lands within city limits to municipal ownership on the understanding that any wharves in private hands be acquired by payment of fair compensation.[3] New Westminster became home to fish canneries and a number of large sawmills that processed rough logs into cut lumber of fixed lengths available for export. These industries brought trade to the outside world. Sailing ships, in varying numbers from year to year, came directly into the Fraser River to pick up cargo from the main waterfront and wharves at mills and canneries.

The loading and unloading of the large ships was a complex operation involving back-breaking work and long hours. An ocean-going sailing ship typically took several weeks to take on a cargo of milled lumber at sawmill wharves. Rocks and gravel carried as ballast first had to be removed and discarded, then the lumber lengths carefully put into holds to maximize available space, prevent shifting during voyage, and maintain the ship's load integrity in terms of stability. Horses and barges were used to bring lumber to the wharves.

Longshoreman Danny Amero, whose grandfather worked sailing ships at New Westminster, remarked on the physical strength required by the men:

> . . . *they used to load these sail ships. They used to come from overseas. They used to pack timbers in, from one end to the other.*
> *. . . It was crazy. And they thought it was all good jobs. They were happy. God, they lived to their '90s. They were big guys. My uncles and my cousins — a whole bunch of us down here . . .*[4]

Special openings on the sides allowed larger pieces and bundled lumber to be passed directly into some ships. The lumber was loaded manually from one end to the other.

People undertaking this work generally fell into three broad categories: riggers who handled lines and ropes for lifting and placing the heavy lumber, experienced stevedores acting as foremen and supervisors, and longshoremen providing the general labour drawn from seamen and local populations.

The term 'longshoreman' comes literally from the practice of hiring 'Men Along the Shore' to work the ships. The wharves attached to fish canneries and lumber mills in New Westminster and nearby Burrard Inlet supported a large casual workforce of men drawn from various backgrounds.[5] Stevedoring companies picked and retained individuals according to willingness to accept offered pay and ability to perform heavy physical tasks intensively over extended periods of time. Each day, men hung about or lined up waiting to be chosen for work on the waterfront, making the 'shape-up' commonplace. Most longshoremen hated the shape-up. They worked for small wages because many men competed for the same job. There was no guarantee of placement for work, while favouritism and arbitrary selection by foremen and bosses ruled the day. It was demeaning and unfair.

Work on the lumber wharves occurred from dawn to dusk until the job was done. Owners and shippers were under pressure to get cargo loaded and sent off to destinations as quickly as possible, conveying the same sense of urgency to those persons working the wharves and ships. Most lumber shipped from New Westminster went to Australia, the United States, South America, and later, the United Kingdom. In the interval between arrival and departure of sailing ships — a period of time that might involve weeks or months of waiting — individuals were compelled to find other employment suited to skills and abilities. Men working on the waterfront typically had two or three other jobs to support themselves.

Early longshore work on the Fraser River in the time of sail ships
A picked gang of men use hand tools to load huge lumber timbers onto a barque clipper at Brunette Sawmills in Sapperton. These ships generally came from San Francisco, with larger ones from Australia and other parts of the Pacific Rim. The opening of the the Panama Canal in 1914 shortened travel times and created new markets for British Columbia's export commodities in Europe.
Source: City of Vancouver Archives, AM 54-S4 Bo P51

In the early days, work on New Westminster's wharves was hardly a regular occupation for most persons without special skills and attracted large numbers of transient labourers and older seamen. The modes of hiring and nature of the work generally prevented close association in regular gangs. Accidents were frequent and those unfortunate enough to suffer one risked lost limbs or permanent injury that could deny further work and employment prospects for fields involving heavy labour. Getting on the bad side of owners or foremen, whether through carelessness, sloppiness, or drunkenness, was another way to be quickly out of work on the wharves.

The city's bars and taverns — once the haunts of gold-seekers — counted new clientele amongst wharf men with some cash in their pockets and an insatiable thirst after a long day's work. More respectable longshoremen, the most experienced who enjoyed first choice of employment under the shape-up, bought houses with monies saved, and joined pockets of working-class communities sprouting around places of major employment in or near New Westminster.[6] Prices fluctuated for exported lumber as competition grew from nearby sawmills on the north and south shores of Burrard Inlet. These factors determined the levels of business and, in turn, opportunities for employment on New Westminster's wharves, which was in direct relation to the number of ships coming up the Fraser River.

**The staging of lumber for loading onto sail ships
at Brunette Sawmill Company in 1895**

The long planks were popular during this time period in the balloon framing of houses, which favoured fast and cheap construction and buildings. Sawmills in New Westminster were a major provider of milled lumber for export from the province of British Columbia.

Source: City of Vancouver Archives , AM 54-S4 Mi P59

Unlike nearby Burrard Inlet or even Victoria, New Westminster was not a natural harbour blessed with easy access to the sea, being thirty-four kilometres upriver from the mouth of the Fraser River at a point wide and deep enough for ocean-going sail ships to turn. The distance between the two riverbanks was less than a kilometre. The water depth ranged from six metres at low level to ten metres at high, depending on tides, river currents, and seasonal ice-melt. The Pacific coast's moderate weather and climate, however, allowed year-round shipping with the interference of ice buildup only happening rarely. The Fraser River's fresh waters also reduced the effects of the destructive Teredo worm to wooden-hulled ships, a favourable consideration for ship captains and owners as well as a major advantage over other competitor seaports in the region.

Pilots with local knowledge of the river and its conditions guided ships venturing into and farther up the Fraser River, either by way of the narrowing north arm or the semi-impassable south arm. Navigation up the Fraser River to wharves at New Westminster was difficult and posed considerable risk until the Yale and New Westminster pilotage authority was created in 1879.[7] Sandbanks in the river constantly shifted and changed causing problems with depth and passage. The main impediment was the river itself, which had to be tamed and better improved in terms of navigation on the lower reaches.

Port of Importance

New Westminster possessed ambitions to be a port of preference, taking advantage of the export trade for the province's basic commodities and accessibility to the Pacific and, by virtue of that, other oceans of the world beyond. The city's steady economic activity and population growth compared favourably to rival Victoria — in fact, outpaced it — and preceded tiny Granville (soon renamed Vancouver). Orders-in-council in 1880 proclaimed the port of New Westminster, appointed a harbour master, and set harbour limits from where the Pitt River joined at Douglas Island down to the Fraser's mouth, effectively the extent of the tidal river.[8] However, it was the coming of the railways that determined New Westminster's destiny because, unlike Vancouver where the Canadian Pacific Railway bought up virtually all waterfront lands, the Fraser riverfront was mostly city-owned. Deliberate efforts to attract rail connections running through New Westminster eventually resulted in construction of a dual railway-road steel bridge across to Brownsville (today in Surrey) on the river's south shore — a big project at the time and colloquially known as the 'one million dollar bridge'.[9] This structure gave New Westminster a competitive advantage over rival plans to develop port and docking facilities farther up the river at Port Coquitlam and Port Mann (Surrey). Despite the setback of a major fire that destroyed much of the New Westminster waterfront, the business centre in the downtown core on Columbia Street and whole city blocks in September 1898, New Westminster's aspirations to develop its port continued. The large sawmills, from whose wharves ocean-going sailing ships loaded and unloaded lumber, were outside the radius of the great fire and survived.

Sailing ships progressively gave way to cargo steamships and motor ships of deeper draft powered by coal and diesel fuel. The four leading sawmills in the vicinity — Fraser Mills, Brunette, British Columbia Mills, and Small & Bucklin — jointly concluded that foreign trade in lumber required a channel sufficiently wide and deep enough to allow both forms of maritime conveyance, sail and steam.[10] Mayor John Lee, a prominent retailer of dry goods and owner of the city's largest department store, on Columbia Street, and his city council believed that New Westminster deserved at least as much attention as Montreal — another river-based port in eastern Canada, which was given much political patronage — and worried about keeping up with the rise of Vancouver and its expanding waterfront facilities for handling cargo. To be competitive, the Fraser River-based port had to make some critical investment in harbour infrastructure and channel improvements or risk being left behind.

At the same time, technology began changing the nature of waterfront work. Hand trucks and cargo slings, old stand-bys, supplemented human power. Longshoremen still used the ubiquitous cargo hook to hold and move lumber and other bulky items. The use of modern aids such as steam donkey engines, powered winches and lifts, and electrical cranes was increasingly common and aided enormously the speed and efficiency of loading. Ocean-going ships possessed their own loading equipment, which longshoremen used in port. What was novel in the first decade of the 20th Century progressively became a regular feature of work. A ship could be filled by the new methods in a matter of days or weeks rather than months.

A dependable and trained waterfront workforce was integral to the ambitions of New Westminster emerging as a major shipping port with the latest technological devices. On occasion, freight handlers and deck hands in New Westminster stopped work for hours or a day or two to protest working conditions and unilateral attempts by employers to limit wages paid for the work done. The workforce began to think and act collectively. Individuals engaged in longshore work, prey to the shape-up and held in relatively low standing by other ranks of skilled labour until that time, were getting organized.[11] It was no longer sufficient to engage just any 'man from along the shore'.

Organizing Work on the Waterfront

Identification with occupation-based mutual associations and unions on New Westminster's waterfront happened gradually compared to other locales along the Pacific coast. Various labour groupings, including the Knights of Labor and an independent Stevedores Union, had attempted early organizing amongst longshoremen. By the turn of the century, the International Longshoremen's Association, renamed from the National Longshoremen's Association originating on the Great Lakes in 1892, emerged with the broadest membership and numerous chartered locals.[12] In Seattle, Vancouver, and Victoria, longshoremen joining or supporting International Longshoremen's Association locals confronted indifference from fellow workers, hostility from employing shipping companies, and competition from rival factions and independent unions.

The Victoria Longshoremen's Union, one hundred twenty strong, and headed by president William Murphy, sought affiliation with the International Longshoremen's Association (alternately known then as the International Longshoremen, Marine and Transport Workers' Association), in March 1901. It encompassed all longshoremen working in Victoria and its vicinity.[13] Members met regularly on Monday evenings in a room above a cigar store. The local sought agreements with the principal stevedoring companies operating in the port that purposefully promoted union recognition and membership as well as higher wage rates.[14]

It is mutually agreed between the Victoria and Vancouver Stevedoring and Contracting Company, Limited, and the International Longshoremen, Marine and Transportworkers' Association, Local 227, of Victoria, that the party of the first part agrees to pay as a scale of wages thirty cents and forty cents (30¢ and 40¢) on all sailing vessels, thirty-five and forty cents (35¢ and 40¢) on all steamers, thirty-five and forty cents (35¢ and 40¢) on all coal vessels sail or steam.

The party of the first part also agrees to urge and influence the Longshoremen now employed by them to become members of the Union.

And the party of the second part agrees to admit such employees to membership in the Union, provided that the said employee comply with the rules governing the initiation fees and dues of the Union. And whenever such employee is denied membership in the Union, the name of such employee shall be submitted to the party of the first part, in order that a conference may be mutually held for adjustment.

The party of the first part further agrees that they will from date, employ at least one-half of all men employed from the union. It is mutually agreed that this agreement remain in force for twelve (12) months from February 3, 1903.

At the expiration of 12 months, the party of the first part agrees to pay as a scale of wages, on all vessels, 40 and 50 cents per hour.

For the faithful performance of this agreement it is mutually agreed that the party of the first part and the party of the second part each deposit the sum of one hundred ($100.00) or a satisfactory bond for that amount, with a disinterested body or committee, who will act as the arbitrators in the event of any further dispute.

Source: "Proceedings of the Tenth Annual Convention of the International Longshoremen's Association, Toledo, Ohio, July 8th to 13th, inclusive, 1901", 26–27; "Longshoremen's Wages", Daily Colonist (7 March 1901)

Six months later, longshoremen in ILA Local 227 were on strike against those companies still paying less.

After a personal trip to British Columbia, international president Daniel Keefe reported on the state of organizing:

On Wednesday, October 15th I left Seattle for Vancouver, B.C., and on Thursday, the 16th, I attended a large meeting of Local 211. This local was getting along very nicely and had little or no friction with the steamboat agents or stevedores and their relations were pleasant.

On Friday, October 17th, I left Vancouver for Victoria, B.C., where I attended a meeting of Local 227. This was perhaps the best attended that I had the pleasure of being present at while on the [Pacific] coast. All the members were in attendance. This Local had a strike on with one of the Stevedores for the purpose of trying to bring about some kind of an understanding. This was not a success. However, on Sunday the 19th, we had another meeting where arrangements were made for a future conference. On the same evening, I attended a meeting of Local 163 and advised that they invest their committee with full power to bring about the best settlement they could.

The rosy picture was also changing in Vancouver. ILA Local 211 dated from a union, established on 17 November 1888, that became affiliated with Terence Powderly's Knights of Labor until December 1896 and thereafter joined the competing International Longshoremen's Association.[15] After some initial gains, ILA Local 211 invoked a strong reaction from waterfront employers after a lockout of waterfront workers by a steamship company in February 1900. A visiting international official tried to find some positives.[16] But these were few and far-between. Organizational problems, uneven leadership, and a strike in sympathy with Canadian Pacific Railway western branch employees led to the demise of ILA Local 211 and reversion back to independent unions. Some of these coalesced into the Longshoremen's Union of the Pacific, which encompassed major Canadian and American ports on both sides of the international boundary.

Alex Nyman, a longshoreman who worked in New Westminster, remembered:

When I first started longshoring, we had unions and we didn't have unions. We had several different things. At first, we had nothing. It was a shipside pick . . . Those that wanted a job would go down there and stand on the dock. Foreman would come along or, if it was a steamer, there would be two foremen, one for the forward end and one for the after end. They would size up the bunch on the dock. The senior man was in charge and he would say that he would take that end of the lineup and the other guy would get the other end. There was a lot of cutting one another's throat in that too. The first guy would take the best and leave the scraps for the other guy. Well, anyway, that is the way they started. We had a union with the general cargo people, a long time ago.[17]

The waterfront workplace comprised a mixture of affiliated-union and non-union men because not all longshoremen were required to belong to organized labour organizations. For today's unionized longshore workers with an exclusive collective agreement governing employment, it is important to remember that at one time work on the waterfront was done by men predominantly outside any recognized unions.

In fact, recognition and payment of consistent and fair wages posed a constant struggle on the part of waterfront workers. In May 1907, two hundred fifty striking Vancouver longshoremen won a five-cent increase to forty cents per hour for day work and forty-five cents for night work.[18] Many Vancouver longshoremen were sent to New Westminster to work on the lumber mill wharves, though individual companies determined the rates paid, which averaged only twenty-five cents for day work and thirty cents for night work. In contrast to general cargo, handling lumber was considered tough, demanding, and sometimes dangerous. Despite the lower pay, men accepted regular work in gangs when they could because the alternative was the uncertainty of the shape-up or shipside pick.

The shipping companies, for the most part, considered the International Longshoremen's Association as a threat and took advantage of every opportunity to limit its influence and press the principle of an open shop. The open shop meant no preference was given to any union, even if one existed. Longshoremen in Seattle and Vancouver seeking advances in wages to the higher standard by striking non-complying companies faced a united front from employers that included refusal of employment and actual reductions to proffered rates. A major walkout in Seattle ceased on 19 October 1908, with little to show for the effort. Prevailing wage rates fell back to twenty-seven-and-a-half cents per hour for day work and five cents additional for night work.

When two hundred twenty-five longshoremen in Vancouver stopped work in April 1909, demanding forty cents for regular time and fifty cents for overtime, the shipping and stevedoring companies brought in strikebreakers from Winnipeg to unload and load idle ships on the waterfront. The Deputy Minister of Labour in Ottawa was informed, "Longshoremen's strike declared off and lost".[19] These setbacks, far from weakening the drive toward collective action, galvanized men working on the waterfront to seek out unions that could steadfastly stand up to the employers.

In September 1909, the international president, Thomas Ventry O'Connor, travelled to San Francisco and invited twenty-seven locals of the Longshoremen's Union of the Pacific to re-affiliate with his union on the assurance of autonomy and provision of effective organizers.[20] Unionized longshoremen along the Pacific coast were again united under a single labour body pushing for improvements to wages and conditions with waterfront employers. Members of the International Longshoremen's Association who vocally accused the shipping companies of trying to undermine or 'bust' the union were specifically targeted. Belonging to a union on the waterfront was sometimes a risky proposition that could affect continued employment.

The International Longshoremen's Association chartered four locals in Canada during 1910, three in the province of Ontario and one at Prince Rupert, ILA Local 38-41. Victoria's Local 38-46 followed early the next year. During this second rebuilding phase, O'Connor and the international union organized smaller and medium-size ports on the Pacific coast and the Great Lakes before turning attention to the three major ones — Vancouver, Montreal, and Halifax.

The first real breakthrough in British Columbia came in Victoria. George Leckey from ILA Local 38-46 convinced a leading stevedoring company to only employ members belonging to the International Longshoremen's Association.[21] As well, longshoremen in Vancouver were well along in organizing their own chartered local, with sixty men meeting in the labour hall to elect provisional executive officers and form a committee for the purpose.

By May 1912, two hundred fifty-two men had joined the new ILA Local 38-52 because many were working ten hour days at thirty-five cents per hour and they looked toward improvements.[22] Three previous longshore unions had been affiliated with the Vancouver Trades and Labour Council before the coming of ILA Local 38-52. Members met Friday evenings at 133 Water Street, between Cambie and Abbott. The Vancouver local's first elected president was Benjamin Hughes, who also represented the longshore union on the Vancouver Trades and Labour Council. Thomas Nixon was secretary. The International Longshoremen's Association counted twenty-four chartered union locals across Canada, as well as eighteen hundred longshoremen in Montreal and eight hundred in Halifax, belonging to large independent unions.[23] Besides the existing ILA locals in Prince Rupert and Victoria, ILA Local 38-57, comprising lumbermen and freight handlers, joined ILA Local 38-52 in Vancouver.

The International Longshoremen's Association foothold in New Westminster at the beginning was never large, no more than the committed few persons who were strong in the belief that association and collective action stood higher than exploitation and individualistic gain. Convincing others of this simple rule was the hardest task. Victoria delegates from ILA Local 38-46 put forward a resolution to the International Longshoremen's Association Pacific District convention meeting in Tacoma:

> Whereas. As long as the port of New Westminster remains unorganized, it must of necessity have a tendency to retard progress in organizing, especially in British Columbia ports on the Pacific coast, therefore be it Resolved, That this Convention bring pressure to bear upon the I.L.A. to take some steps to remedy the same.[24]

The New Westminster Trades and Labour Council, the central body in the city representing most established unions, included the teamsters who wanted more work on the waterfront. The city's longshoremen were as yet without an organized union ready to join the International

Longshoremen's Association. Pragmatically, the vast majority of individuals working the docks and wharves stood on the sidelines in the looming contest between employers and the International Longshoremen's Association, which lacked sufficient numbers and flexibility in thought and organization to be truly effective.

Private shipping companies and sawmills possessed a dominant position by controlling hiring, work conditions, and the terms of employment, and had no intention of conceding those prerogatives to the International Longshoremen's Association, or any other union claiming to represent longshoremen.

Conditions of Longshore Labour

Whether union or non-union, waterfront employment in New Westminster related to the lumber export trade, and shipping was subject to cyclical downturns and arbitrary measures at the mercy of employers. Wage rates and working conditions varied from company to company depending upon location. The Shipowners or Marine Association of British Columbia — subsequently renamed the Shipping Federation of British Columbia — was a voluntary employers' association encompassing the principal shipping and stevedoring companies in the Vancouver and Victoria areas.[25] Employers acting together introduced some degree of regularization — at worst collusion — in dictating terms.[26] Local longshoremen were convinced in ever-increasing numbers to join the rebounding International Longshoremen's Association. The preamble to the 1913 constitution of Vancouver's ILA Local 38-52 reflected the influences of the American movement as well as an emerging sense of worker identity and unionism on the waterfront:

> "Labor is prior to and independent of capital. Capital is only the Fruit of Labor, it could not have existed if Labor had not first existed, and inasmuch as most good things have been produced by Labor, it follows that they belong by right to the people who produce them." These words uttered by Abraham Lincoln, himself a member of the governing class, tend to show the workers that they are defrauded of their rights, and it is apparent that in the great struggle for existence their lot is

becoming ever more precarious. The wealth produced in the present is many times greater than that produced in the past, yet the workers do not benefit by this increase in production, but instead are forced to compete more bitterly for employment.

The Transport Industry is the artery of Commerce, yet the Longshoremen only receive a bare pittance in exchange for their labor. We realize that in order to assure better working conditions and secure our share of the good things of life, we must learn to cast aside racial prejudice, military traditions, and all ogres of a like nature, and in their place instill a spirit of unity and determination. This justifies the existence of our Association, and we unite determined to do all in our power to promote the welfare of labor in general, to improve our physical, mental, and social conditions and educate ourselves to understand the true needs of all Longshoremen.[26]

This statement, articulated more than one hundred years ago, echoes many of the principles that Local 502 and the wider ILWU steadfastly hold true up to the present day.

Vancouver's ILA Local 38-52 was the largest union local by numbers in the entire Pacific District, bigger than locals in Portland and Seattle. The International Longshoremen's Association's international president, Thomas O'Connor, district president, John Kean, and district secretary-treasurer, James Madsen, negotiated an agreement for union waterfront workers in Vancouver (*see page 47*) that lasted until the end of 1914.[27] Another separate agreement was negotiated for Victoria.

Generally known by his initials T.V., Thomas Ventry O'Connor was born in Toronto to Irish immigrant parents who moved to the United States when he was four years old. As a boy, he rowed passengers across the Niagara River from Buffalo, New York, to the Canadian side for ten cents a trip, and came to work on the waterfront at a young age.[28] During his tenure, the international union's headquarters was located in Buffalo, though during and after World War I, he spent much time in Washington D.C. serving on public boards and committees, including the United States Shipping Board. His leadership of longshore workers was characterized as middle-of-the-road and shunning radical action. Under O'Connor, the International Longshoremen's Association made inroads on the Pacific coast with new locals at Victoria and Vancouver, and agreements personally negotiated by him governing those locales. He made many trips to British Columbia to see conditions and union organization firsthand.[29]

The type of basic agreement negotiated by O'Connor and his officials, really one of the first for the International Longshoremen's Association in British Columbia, contains many features that any union believed necessary, though other parts can only be seen as arbitrary and archaic by today's standards of fair labour relations. Handling general cargo was paid at the rate of forty-five cents per hour for regular time and fifty-five cents for overtime; lumber was fifty cents and seventy-five cents respectively. Longshoremen in the rated positions of hatch tender, side runner, and winch driver received more. Non-union rates, though, were generally twenty or thirty percent lower, subject to the discretion of owners and foremen hiring day or casual labour. Several classes of labour existed on the New Westminster waterfront. George Heatherton, a general organizer sent by the American Federation of Labor to unionize workers in the city's lumber mills, decried the high cost of living in the vicinity.[30]

Making individual employers and the association that represented them actually live up to the terms in practice was oftentimes difficult. Pacific coast delegates from the International Longshoremen's Association met for the district annual convention at Vancouver in May 1914, where executive board member George Thomas reported:

> all the little incidents by which the employers have tried to irritate the Local [38-52] and force them to some act which would precipitate a fight, but Vancouver has so far steered clear of the breakers. That conditions are better than they were a year ago, cannot be denied, but unless those conditions can be maintained, I have no hesitancy in saying that the cost of obtaining them has been too great.[31]

Organizing of longshore workers in nearby ports like New Westminster was essential to keep momentum going forward.

A general economic depression and the detrimental effects of World War I on shipping patterns resulted in dramatic reductions in exports from the province and virtual collapse of lumber markets. Elaborate plans for harbour development in New Westminster announced in 1912 and a local harbour commission created in May the following year by act of Parliament were essentially postponed for the duration of the war.[32] The city council had engaged a well-known consulting civil engineer with specific expertise in ports, Archibald Powell, to draw up a master scheme for harbour improvement in New Westminster and along the Fraser River.

C.H. Stuart Wade, New Westminster's publicity commissioner, described the pre-war ambition:

> *The most important of these from a citizen's point of view, is the Westminster Harbour Plan, which provides for a frontage of seven miles, with 15 docks, each 600 feet long. Already $500,000 has been voted by the citizens to prepare for this work, which will make New Westminster the 'Pacific Liverpool' and the great maritime terminal of the world's shipping; for, at no other point in Western Canada is there to be found so many advantages for wharves, warehouses, factories, and deep water facilities; with the wholesale and retail stores practically adjoining the harbour, and railway trackage which enables the importer or exporter to load direct from the vessel or freight car and forward to any part of the continent of America.[33]*

The plan envisioned a shipping waterway with terminal docks and reclaimed land set aside for ancillary industries on Lulu Island, as well as docks eastward toward Sapperton, on government lands in the penitentiary reserve. With the funds approved by New Westminster rate-payers, the main waterfront below Front Street was to be completely transformed into a working port for international shipping.

John Lee, the city's main harbour advocate, died suddenly in June 1913, just when preparations were being made for building of the new docks.[34] He was an appointee designate for the new harbour commission and a new one had to be found. Arthur Wells Gray, the city's new youthful mayor elected on his earlier notoriety as a lacrosse player, made sure the work proceeded, and officiated at the opening ceremony.[35] He also became a keen harbour proponent, like Lee.

Once the war started, regular shipping coming up the Fraser River trickled. Longshoremen were thrown out of work. The numbers of the unemployed swelled, creating a large pool of men desperate for jobs and willing to earn less. The shape-up returned in full force since companies found little trouble engaging casual labour for longshore work. One shipping firm, the Harrison Line, unilaterally reduced pay to non-union levels for everyone. Other companies either followed suit or refused to entertain renewal of the previous expired agreement that had ended on 31 December 1914. In other words, the union was left without a collective agreement.

The union soon confronted the imposition of a general reduction in wages across the board. The International Longshoremen's Association's Pacific District president, John Kean, sanctioned a strike in Vancouver during March 1915, to hold the line.[36] Affected companies brought in replacement workers as strikebreakers. A telegram sent to Vancouver Centre Member of Parliament Henry Herbert Stevens reported, "Bad situation here over reduction of wages of longshoremen by employers without notice and in defiance of Lemieux act, followed by strike of employees equally illegal."[37] Longshoremen in district locals along the entire Pacific coast responded with an embargo on all cargo destined to or from Vancouver as 'unfair', in effect from 11 March. Thomas O'Connor and Rowland Mahaney, a conciliation commissioner with the US Department of Labor, arrived from Buffalo for discussions with local union officials in Seattle, and then travelled to Vancouver on 25 March. Once there, O'Connor met with several waterfront employers to effect a settlement.[38]

Due to the efforts of O'Connor and Mahaney, the unfair declaration on Vancouver shipping was lifted by 2 April 1915. Stevedoring and shipping companies in British Columbia still adamantly resisted any suggestion of adopting coast-wide wage scales and contract conditions. In June 1916, American longshoremen in San Francisco and other US ports collectively went on strike after abrogating the existing agreement. American longshoremen stayed out a month in San Francisco and longer elsewhere, resulting in modest wage gains and loosening of the union shop in favour of an open shop.[39] Afterwards, the general perception though was a loss for the union. New Westminster, notwithstanding no formal International Longshoremen's Association presence, was still involved because sympathetic longshoremen refused to handle ships and cargoes from ports under strike conditions. When entire gangs declined to work during the American strike, replacement workers travelled from Vancouver and Burnaby at the instigation of the stevedoring companies.

Notwithstanding a number of withdrawals from the Shipping Federation, new agreements negotiated between individual companies and the International Longshoremen's Association restored previous wage rates on the understanding that due notice would be given before future strike action to allow opportunity for discussion. Gordon Kelly, the energetic and capable Pacific District secretary-treasurer from Vancouver, negotiated longshoremen falling under provincial workmen's compensation legislation and represented ILA Local 38-52 at the annual convention in Tacoma during May 1917.

Kelly was a prodigious individual. Born in the English industrial city of Birmingham from a prominent family, with a level of education not common among longshoremen, he came to Vancouver in 1905 and worked his way up the ranks of the union, eventually to ILA Pacific District vice-president. Later in 1918, Gordon Kelly contracted influenza and died of hard work and pneumonia. He was unmarried and wholly committed to the cause of advancing trade unionism on the waterfront.[40] His body was brought back from Seattle on a steamship accompanied by the ILA Pacific District secretary-treasurer, Marshal Wright, made available for public visitation in the longshoremen's union hall on Pender Street, and taken by a long procession for burial in Mountain View Cemetery, on 13 November 1918. Friends and acquaintances from New Westminster were in attendance.

Faced with escalating costs of living, longshore workers demanded a significant wage increase and better working conditions. They held out for one general schedule applicable to longshore and dock work in all British Columbia ports, instead of separate agreements. Elimination of differentials between dock and shipside work also attracted particular attention. A referendum of the membership decided in favour of stopping work on behalf of all companies if increases were not acceded to by 30 July 1917. Five hundred general cargo and freight handlers started a strike at Canadian Pacific Railway, the one hold-out amongst employers in Vancouver, an action which other longshoremen felt obliged to support by staying away from work.[41]

The new wage structure was accepted, though other parts went to a board of arbitration with representations from the company and the union. The harbour in Vancouver gained a reputation amongst shippers for interruptions through work stoppages and militant union action. Victoria's Joseph Taylor and other delegates from British Columbia walked out in protest when Seattle's mayor addressed the ILA Pacific District convention after general and waterfront strikes in that city.[42] New Westminster, by contrast, continued to operate its shipping facilities and, in fact, might have benefitted from the rerouting of ships to load at ports untouched by International Longshoremen's Association influence. Non-union still outnumbered card-carrying union men on the Fraser River by a wide margin.

In the later war years, business at New Westminster's mills and wharves steadily picked up again. The city's primary wartime industries were not amenable to the skills possessed by most longshoremen left without steady work. Munitions production at Vulcan Iron Works and Schaake Machine Works favoured machinists and temporary female workers, while wooden shipbuilding on Poplar Island by the New Westminster Construction and Engineering Company employed shipwrights and house carpenters drawn from the building and construction trades. In Vancouver, waterfront men who left for the shipyards were asked to return, and faced expulsion from the longshore union.

During 1918, the Imperial Munitions Board, by special arrangement with the provincial government, began cutting spruce and Douglas fir trees for use in aircraft manufacturing. Felled logs were towed in booms from the Queen Charlotte Islands to New Westminster for milling into lumber. The Canadian Western Lumber Company, based at Fraser Mills outside New Westminster's city limits in Coquitlam, was the largest sawmill in the British Empire.[43] Longshoremen loaded the cut lumber onto barges for delivery at Port Mann to be transported by rail to points in eastern Canada and the United States.

Empire Stevedoring, a leading waterfront company in the province, was controlled by Colonel Walter Dockrill. Dockrill had gone to public school and apprenticed as a druggist dispenser in New Westminster before building his commercial enterprise from lumber loading at Chemainus.[44] In 1913, he had been the first president of the Marine Association of British Columbia, a forerunner to the Shipping Federation of British Columbia and the present British Columbia

Maritime Employers Association. Empire Stevedoring provided gangs of longshoremen at Fraser Mills and most other New Westminster locations. Residents of New Westminster were given preference as longshoremen by Empire Stevedoring, though workers were dispatched from Vancouver and the North Shore to handle lumber as needed and received travel money to do so.

After the armistice in November 1918, deep-sea ships began returning to the Fraser River in increasing numbers as international markets and shipping routes were restored. New Westminster's mills processed surplus logs into lumber, but the Imperial Munitions Board decided to abandon the rest in forests once prices dropped below a break-even basis.[45] American producers swamped the regional market with cheap lumber. Overseas, reconstruction in Europe and the United Kingdom created demand for lumber and foodstuffs such as canned salmon. The Panama Canal, opened at the start of the war, lived up to its billing for reducing travel time and saving money for shippers. Longshoremen in New Westminster, in comparison to other labour groups, benefitted from the general upswing in exports passing through the port and the resumption of normal business.

James Shaver (J.S.) Woodsworth, the social democrat leader of the reformist Cooperative Commonwealth Federation (CCF) Party, who worked on the Vancouver waterfront for a stint, described the hierarchy of men hoping for work:

> *They are waiting for a possible job. The Longshoremen proper have the preference. If there is a rush, the orders for men are turned over to the Auxiliary. In normal times, the members of the Auxiliary Union are able to handle the work. If several large boats come in at once they must secure outside help. The waterfront has been unusually active. So men laid off from the shipyards, or who have drifted in from the camps, have been picking up short jobs at good wages per hour. But for a week now, things have been quiet. The Longshoremen are working coast boats which when work is plentiful, they will not touch. The hall is full of men hungry for work — like wolves after an enforced fast. So the men on the outside stand waiting.*[46]

The availability of work ebbed and flowed with shipping coming up the river to the harbour — no ships, no work, no pay.

New Westminster, while not immune from the general labour unrest of 1918 and 1919, certainly was much more subdued in its overall reaction. The police killing of labour leader and war evader Albert 'Ginger' Goodwin, in the woods near Cumberland on Vancouver Island, compelled waterfront and other workers concerned with unionism to hold a twenty-four hour general strike in Vancouver, during which indignant returned soldiers besieged the longshoremen's hall.[47] A surge of strikes and violent upheavals amongst the unemployed swept across major cities in Western Canada. From Victoria, ILA Pacific District president Joseph Taylor called upon all union workers to support a general strike in Winnipeg.[48] Taylor's open support for 'One Big Union' embracing all Canadian and Washington State transportation workers including longshore, brought him in direct conflict with Thomas O'Connor and the ILA higher leadership.

Although really an outburst of accumulated frustration by labour and ordinary people, the extraordinary events happening in 1919 portended open class warfare and revolution, in the view of government and established business interests. Longshoremen were prominent in protests and demonstrations within Vancouver proper, where Ernest Winch and Jack Kavanagh of ILA Local 38-52 adopted a surprisingly radical stance, or at least they let members get swept up in the moment. Sympathy strikes in New Westminster, organized in support of the events in Winnipeg and elsewhere, mostly affected telephone exchanges and the city's railway shops, though these did not include any longshoremen, according to a return given to the Department of Labour.[49]

No waterfront union belonged to the New Westminster Trades and Labour Council, the main body in the city behind pushing labour's demands. The number of wartime workers in temporary industries such as shipbuilding was fewer in New Westminster than Vancouver and Victoria and, therefore, the readjustment to postwar conditions less abrupt. Longshoremen working in New Westminster, not counted amongst the ranks of the unemployed, appeared content to support labour's desire for a fair deal and wider recognition within society.

City officials and the New Westminster Board of Trade revisited plans for development of the harbour that wartime requirements had interrupted and delayed.[50] The docks and wharves represented the economic lifeblood of the city and a continued source of good employment.

Return to Normal Times

In the wake of major general and waterfront strikes in Seattle after World War I, the International Longshoremen's Association concluded a regional agreement with employer associations covering Oregon, Washington state, and British Columbia. The Shipping Federation and ILA Local 38-52 in Vancouver were signed parties to the agreement and observed its terms, which superseded the less generous local agreement renewed after December 1918: longshoremen on coastwise and deep-sea, ninety cents per hour regular time and one dollar thirty-five cents per hour overtime; truckers, eighty cents per hour regular time and one dollar twenty cents overtime; lumber handlers, ninety-five cents per hour regular time and one dollar forty cents overtime. Along with these rates, there was recognition of the principle of collective bargaining, union shop conditions, limits on strikes and work stoppages, and a binding grievance committee and arbitration process.[51] A short period of relative stability governed wage rates and relations with the private company employers like Empire Stevedoring.

A report into a dispute between the western branch of Canadian Pacific Railway and waterfront freight handlers in Vancouver, delivered to Minister of Labour Gideon Robertson by Justice Denis Murphy, Edwin James, and Joseph Taylor in July 1920, acknowledged "as in the case of the longshoremen, long hours of continuous work for a short period, and then long stretches of enforced idleness, during which there would be no work at all."[52]

Any work longer than ten hours in a day received higher pay. Joseph Taylor was most concerned about making sure all Canadian employers respected rates and wages paid in American ports on the Pacific coast, in keeping with the existing regional agreement. General non-unionized labourers received thirty-five to forty-five cents hourly or an even lesser amount if they were Asian, immigrant or openly identified with a visible minority.

For unionized labour on British Columbia's waterfronts, it was merely the calm before the storm. Company owners and managers of the Shipping Federation, interested in new schemes introduced by Pacific coast employer associations in the United States, looked to cut out the International Longshoremen's Association entirely from labour relations with longshoremen. The goal was a more compliant and less radical workforce on the waterfront, accepting of the wage rates given and inclined to follow employer direction without question. The open shop occupied the centrepiece of this movement.[53] Employers simply did not want to be beholden to any one union.

Shipping numbers grew during the next few years for New Westminster and its harbour (thirteen deep-sea ships in 1921, thirty-five in 1922, forty-eight in 1923). Economic conditions overall, however, cut prices and demand for commodities, putting a drag on the provincial and regional economies. Work on the waterfront remained good when available.

In New Westminster, collective association amongst longshoremen was distributed between the International Longshoremen's Association and competing local labour organizations. It is hard to determine when longshoremen in the city started joining unions in appreciable numbers. The New Westminster Longshoremen's Association, one of the first recognized independent waterfront unions in the city, boasted the largest number of workers employed at the city's wharves and docks by 1921, and was favoured by Empire Stevedoring and other companies. Its conservative-minded leadership accepted the principle of the open shop pushed by employers and avoided any actions disruptive to business.

The New Westminster Longshoremen's Association sought inclusion in the Canadian Longshoremen's Association, a moderate waterfront labour body dating from 1902, with locals in Victoria and Prince Rupert. The syndicalism of the Industrial Workers of the World — the so-called 'Wobblies', which tried to unite workers across resource industries in British Columbia behind the protest One Big Union movement — was also still around though waning in influence and reception.[54] The local and district organizing done by the Canadian Longshoremen's Association and International Longshoremen's Association proved more effective amongst longshoremen in signing up new members. Men finding regular work on the waterfront counted only several dozen, though the number of casuals fluctuated, either available for a shipside pick or to fill out vacancies in existing gangs.

Casuals provide a ready body of trained workers in times of strike and labour unrest for employers. Nimble waterfront unions should never allow numbers of casuals to grow too large, and certainly not equal to or outpacing regular members. As any good union member knows, someone is always ready and willing to take your job.

The Strike in 1923

The events behind the first major strike in 1923 deserve to be better known by every working longshoreman in ILWU Local 502. Anthony Chlopek, who replaced O'Connor as international president in 1921, travelled from Buffalo to New Westminster to discuss granting of a charter for a local. He was accompanied by George Soule from Seattle and William Pritchard from Vancouver, released from a year in jail after the Winnipeg general strike. Ten months of back-and-forth negotiations with the International Longshoremen's Association Pacific District representatives followed. In the end, the New Westminster Longshoremen's Association decided to join the Canadian Longshoremen's Association instead. Thereafter, seventy men — with considerable encouragement from Chlopek and his district organizers — left that union to establish an auxiliary local within the International Longshoremen's Association. It was separate from the established Vancouver ILA Local 38-52 but with limited autonomy to run its own affairs without a formal charter from the international union.[55]

At the time, it was still undecided whether Fraser River longshoremen should combine with Vancouver or hold out for a local of their own. The ILA Pacific District executive board was on record of supporting only one local in each port. The auxiliary neatly sidestepped the issue and gave men in New Westminster more time to find capable and experienced individuals to take up leadership positions of president, business agent, and secretary-treasurer.

The mass defection to the International Longshoremen's Association left the Canadian Longshoremen's Association in New Westminster weakened in terms of numbers and organization. Though

A freighter loading lumber at the main New Westminster docks in 1923
Longshoremen are on the deck working the equipment and sling loads. This
was the scene of the major longshore strike from October to December 1923.
*Source: City of Vancouver Archives, Extract from AM 54-S-4-e PAN N166B,
W.J. Moore, photographer*

formally Local 1, New Westminster was surpassed by the Canadian
Longshoremen's Association Local 2 in Prince Rupert, which grew and
represented roughly the same number of members. Prince Rupert was
a much smaller port than New Westminster, and longshoremen at that
northern location handled mostly coastwise shipping.[56] The influence
of the International Longshoremen's Association was outside and apart
from the New Westminster Longshoremen's Association, affiliated with
the Canadian Longshoremen's Association. In fact, they were really two
competing bodies of longshoremen holding very different views.

In March 1923, the International Longshoremen's Association
local auxiliary in New Westminster backed the Vancouver union in the
context of the Shipping Federation proposing a revised schedule which
made changes to the existing agreement set to expire on 6 October.
The International Longshoremen's Association opposed any attempt
to reduce or cut wages by employers.[57] Threatening to strike or
seek application to the government in Ottawa for conciliation, the
International Longshoremen's Association asked for wage advances and
five cents extra per hour for handling lumber.

The audacious move, though popular amongst the membership,
was badly mistimed and played directly into the hands of the

Shipping Federation. The employer's association told the provincial attorney general in Victoria that the longshoremen's requests were "a detriment to the shipping in British Columbia ports if this demand was granted, on account of putting the British Columbia ports on a non-competitive basis, as the wages asked for are higher than paid at any other Pacific coast port."[58] The assertion was simply untrue because rates in key American cities were still higher after the proposed cuts. It did not matter. The International Longshoremen's Association, not the Canadian Longshoremen's Association, lost almost all in the resulting showdown on the waterfront of New Westminster.

The stakes in the major strike started in 1923 were certainly the highest ever in British Columbia. On the evening of 8 October, twelve hundred International Longshoremen's Association-affiliated longshoremen in Vancouver and thirty-five loading lumber along the Fraser River refused work until employers acceded to the demands of paying ninety cents per hour base pay and one dollar thirty-five cents for overtime work, five cents premium for handling lumber, and making all checkers, another related waterfront occupation, belong to the union.[59] The Shipping Federation countered with the prevailing rate of eighty cents per hour and one dollar twenty-five cents for overtime, extra pay for handling bulk grain and sulphur instead of lumber, and continued employer control over checkers. Differences between the two sides appeared irreconcilable, particularly since the Shipping Federation declined to negotiate with any International Longshoremen's Association representatives whom they accused of being 'Reds' and rebuffed several offers of mediation by the government's Department of Labour.

Within days, shippers and waterfront employers were bringing in non-union men across picket lines as strikebreakers. These men were housed in bunkhouses onsite at Fraser Mills. The feeding and housing of workers as well as extra police protection during the strike cost the Shipping Federation $112,000 — collected from special cargo and payroll assessments against the shipping companies and put into a special emergency fund.[60] Strikers occasionally followed visiting wives of replacement workers back home as a form of gentle intimidation.

By the next month, sufficient numbers of men were available to load and unload ships without significant delay or interruption, in fact even a surplus came forward. Most strikebreakers were not as skilled or experienced as the men they replaced and more had to be used to complete the same work. On 20 November 1923, the Shipping Federation offered, through the intermediary of the Vancouver Trades and Labour Council, to take back any strikers on its own terms:

1. No further negotiations or agreements with International Longshoremen's Association.
2. On application, former employees to be given such work as is available, married men being given the preference, under the wages and conditions of work as contained in schedule dated 7 April 1923.
3. Former foremen who may desire to return to work to make application to the stevedoring contractors.
4. Checkers to be appointed as heretofore by the employers.
5. Coastal steamship lines which are not members of the Shipping Federation are not to be included in this arrangement.
6. Men at present employed on the waterfront to be retained as far as suitable.
7. Shipping Federation to agree to discuss with committee of their employees any grievances that may arise, or any change in conditions which the latter may desire to present.
8. Notice of work available to be given to the Powell Street office of the Employment Service of Canada and men to be sent from there to the ship's side or dock, where they will be placed.
9. It is understood that during the period of readjustment following the re-engagement of former employees a committee of the Trades and Labour Council will be available for consultation should any unforeseen difficulty arise in connection with the scheme of re-employment.

This list of employer dictates intentionally targeted the solidarity of longshoremen after weeks of walking the picket line with no pay and apparently little effect. The International Longshoremen's Association strike committee stayed defiant and, in a newsletter, reported that the vote from New Westminster members was solidly behind continuing on with the strike.[61] The true state of affairs was far different, as individuals put themselves before the union because the presented choice was so stark: unemployment or acceptance of the Shipping Federation's terms.

Employers Break the Union

Calling of the strike by the International Longshoremen's Association in the first place against such a formidable opponent bound and determined to fight further advances of unionism on the waterfront may have been ill-planned, but the membership gave broad support at the start. Thomas Nixon, ILA Local 38-52's president during the strike, came to regret the decision. The 1923 strike, especially in New Westminster, was characterized neither by violence nor visible confrontation between striking longshoremen and employers. Longshoremen, longing to get back to work, quietly conceded to employer demands by abandoning the International Longshoremen's Association.

Except for a committed few individuals who stayed true to the aims of the International Longshoremen's Association, the cause appeared lost. On 7 December 1923, a majority of striking longshoremen at a meeting in Vancouver voted to halt the strike and resume work by presenting themselves for registration. The Shipping Federation could pick and choose whom it wanted to employ from strikers and strikebreakers alike. Most striking members belonging to the International Longshoremen's Association auxiliary on the Fraser River were realistic, as Ottawa's local labour official in Vancouver, Frederick Harrison, reported, "At New Westminster and other points the men have gradually drifted back to work, and it is to be presumed by the end of this week conditions at those centres will be normal."[62] The Empire Stevedoring Company, a Shipping Federation member, was selective about persons brought back to employment. Those blacklisted or otherwise deemed objectionable for union and other activities were denied work.

The Shipping Federation meanwhile opened its own dispatch hall in Vancouver. The unilateral move, done without consultation, attracted the notice of the provincial Department of Labour: "Quite a number of the old employees have pointed out that the new policy is a distinct violation of the terms on which the recent strike was called off, and with this view we are, of course, compelled to agree, pointing out, however, that the matter is one over which we have no control."[63] A new organization, the Vancouver and District Waterfront Workers Association — not quite a 'yellow-dog' company union but a body comprised of returned workers, strikebreakers, and military veterans under the thumb of the Shipping Federation — received preference in dispatch and employment over former members from the International Longshoremen's Association. At this point in time, the Vancouver and District Waterfront Workers Association possessed no visible presence at New Westminster and on the Fraser River.

Some longshoremen instead rejoined Canadian Longshoremen's Association Local 1, the other union that had sat on the sidelines during the 1923 strike and observed the downfall of the International Longshoremen's Association. This moderate labourist, Canadian-focused organization was still very much in favour with Empire Stevedoring and other employers. The union's president, Thomas Douglas, and secretary, Leonard Bonwick, exhibited a cooperative approach in relations. They were also quick to take advantage of opportunity, though certain longshoremen questioned their motives.

Bonwick, an immigrant from England, had been a resident of New Westminster since 1917. He came to the Fraser River waterfront when work was scarce and every man competed for available jobs. Nonetheless, Leonard Bonwick was always devoted to any union to which he belonged, especially if he was running it behind the scenes. His eighteen-year working longshore career featured a variety of loyalties and functions.

Men belonging to the Canadian Longshoremen's Association congregated at the Hart block for fellowship and employment. The names of individual members for gangs to be dispatched appeared on a large chalkboard in the hall. The other option was to remain non-union, since the terms were essentially the same. When all unionized longshoremen were taken for jobs, non-unionized were selected on a casual basis. Unrepentant former strikers were the last in line.

As New Westminster entered into the next stage of major port expansion, the International Longshoremen's Association and those men identified with that union lingered in the background — effectively shut out. Local men like secretary Jack Adie tried to whip up interest and a little work once Anthony Chlopek and the international office in Buffalo granted New Westminster the long-awaited charter for ILA Local 38-71. Lack of consistent employment for its members, however, meant that ILA Local 38-71 did not last longer than two years. In the aftermath of the 1923 strike, no one labour group dominated the waterfront, which only played into the hands of the employers. With one union broken and the others tamed, the waterfront scene was fragmented amongst several competing groups of longshoremen.

	New Westminster	Vancouver	Victoria	Prince Rupert
1920	.90	.90	.90	.90
1921	.90	.90	.80	.90
1922	.80	.80	.80	.90
1923	.80	.80	.80	.80
1924	.80	.80	.80	.80
1925	.80	.80	.80	.80
1926	.80	.84	.84	.80
1927	.84	.84	.84	.80
1928	.84	.84	.84	.80
1929	.87	.87	.87	.80
1930	.87	.87	.87	.80

Prevailing hourly wage rates paid unionized longshore workers for general cargo work based on a typical nine-hour day. Note the differences from locale to locale in British Columbia and between southern and northern coasts.
Source: Department of Labour Canada, Wages and Hours of Labour in Canada 1920–1930 (Ottawa: F.A. Acland, 1931)

Divided and in Disarray

By 1924, New Westminster had emerged as a port with good prospects for increasing shipping volume, deep-sea in particular, and increasingly attractive to shore-side companies employing longshoremen catering to that business. The federal government's efforts at dredging a permanent channel and their improvements to navigation and public works allowed ships up to twenty-five feet in draught to pass up the river, day and night. The choice of New Westminster instead of shipping goods and commodities through Vancouver or Seattle received encouragements and incentives. Advertisements and promotional literature touted New Westminster as 'Canada's Liverpool', comparing it to the famous English commercial port, as well as the largest and fastest growing freshwater port in Western Canada. The Shipping Federation of British Columbia claimed no jurisdiction over the Fraser River, so employment and relations with longshoremen was left to individual companies.

Captain William Crawford, active in Vancouver shipping circles, was the new president of Empire Stevedoring, which handled most lumber loading at the Canadian Western Lumber Company's wharf and a sizeable share on the main city-owned docks. Walter Dockrill went into the shipping of lumber internationally as president of the Canadian Trading Company, with R. Drape Williams as manager. Empire Stevedoring moved its local office from Fraser Mills to Dock No. 1 on the main New Westminster waterfront. The Victoria and Vancouver Stevedoring Company and Canada Stevedoring Company, competitors to Empire Stevedoring, also worked ships as required by contracts with shipping lines.

The Consolidated Mining and Smelting Company, due to affiliation and convenience, chose to ship semi-processed concentrates from its smelter in Trail across the Canadian Pacific Railway's wharf at New Westminster. In 1919, just five years previous, Alfred Wilson, of the Department of Mines had proclaimed: "With respect to ores and metals, there does not appear to be any reason to anticipate the development in the future of any waterborne traffic of this kind over Fraser River water either inward or outward. Such traffic, if any, would be largely barge traffic."[64] Yet in May 1924, longshoremen loaded three thousand tons of metal concentrates onto the SS *Camilla Gilbert* from a dock leased by the City of New Westminster to the Fraser River Dock and Stevedoring Company. The prevailing wage paid was sixty cents an hour working in the railcars and ninety cents an hour on the dock, raking the loose concentrate onto conveyors into the ship. This type of work was very dirty.

The milestone event signified both the culmination of considerable effort over many years to create a nationally-important port open to diversified shipping and the beginning of locally-inspired private interests committed to building the facilities and hiring workforces to make that ambition possible.

August 1925	SS *City of Victoria*	$ 2,155.00
September 1925	SS *Dionyssios Stathatos*	$ 35.70
	SS *West Notus*	$ 13.00
October 1925	MS *Vinemoor*	$ 578.00
	SS *Berwindmoor*	$ 1,202.00
November 1925	SS *Torvanger*	$ 704.00
January 1926	SS *Grelbank*	$ 774.00
February 1926	SS *Maria Stathatos*	$ 684.00

**Canadian Stevedoring Company payrolls for ships
worked by longshoremen in New Westminster**

These ships commonly loaded a partial cargo of lumber in the city and then topped up in Burrard Inlet at Vancouver, Dollarton, or Barnet because of depth restrictions on parts of the Fraser River. The stevedoring company paid a 1% assessment to the Shipping Federation based on the wages paid to longshoremen. Ships loaded in Vancouver were also subject to a cargo assessment. The stevedoring companies, not the Shipping Federation, were technically the employers, as pointed out by the labour manager in wage negotiations with the unions. British Columbia-based Canadian Stevedoring is not to be confused with another private company of the same name in Montreal in the early 1920s. The two were not related corporately.

Source: City of Vancouver Archives, AM 279 Shipping Federation of BC 520-E-6 file 6

Fraser River Dock and Stevedoring was a company formed by local business interests with a registered office in New Westminster. It was a new arrival ready "to enter into contract with any stevedoring Union or body of Stevedores or individuals for the loading and unloading of ships and handling of lumber, timber, wood products, and other commodities to, from, and on the Company's dock."[65] A share of the metals-concentrate business passing through the port went to the local stevedoring company and it hoped to break into the lumber trade. In a short period of time, Fraser River Dock and Stevedoring established itself as a presence on the crowded New Westminster waterfront.

As part of its lease with the city, Fraser River Dock and Stevedoring agreed to employ residents of New Westminster in the first instance as longshoremen. This stipulation favoured the dockside labour organizations already in the city, namely the Canadian Longshoremen's Association, the Fraser River Longshoremen's Union — yet another break-away group from that other body, and the remnants of ILA Local 38-71. Separate halls controlled dispatching and provided gangs of men to work the docks and ships as required by the stevedoring companies.

FRASER RIVER DOCK AND STEVEDORING CO. LTD.

LUMBER ASSEMBLING

7 Acres Lumber Assembling Yard with 4,500 Feet Trackage
25-Ton Brown Hoist Locomotive Cranes Equipment

GENERAL WHARFAGE AND STORAGE

1,800 Feet Water Front, 3 Berths for Deep Water Vessels

Civic officials exercised vigilance in respect to Fraser River Dock and Stevedoring using longshoremen sent from Vancouver by making sure the terms of the lease were met in full. Claude Lambson, representing Fraser River Dock and Stevedoring, assured a committee appointed by city council that only New Westminster residents would be so employed, when available. Local longshoremen resented the practice of some shipping companies using gangs of First Nations men from the North Shore known as the 'Bows and Arrows', to load and unload ships at New Westminster.[66] They were experienced and good at working lumber, which meant other gangs were left without work on occasion. When Fraser River Dock and Stevedoring refused to employ former members of the International Longshoremen's Association from Vancouver, Arthur Bond, an alderman sitting on the committee, "thought that any resident of the City who was fit to work should have a chance to work there regardless of his former connection with a labour organization."[67] The blacklist maintained by Empire Stevedoring and other outside companies belonging to the Shipping Federation was fitfully enforced, depending on the inclinations of managers and supervisors who shared information amongst themselves. A Victoria man "trying to get onto the waterfront at New Westminster" known as a "trouble-maker of the first order" was warned off before he arrived.[68]

Captain Phillip Groves, Empire Stevedoring's assistant manager, and Captain John Macmillan, the company's representative at Fraser Mills, personally knew most working longshoremen on the New Westminster waterfront. Roland Cope affectionately remembered Macmillan ('Old Cap'), a Scot who lived on Imperial Street in Burnaby, as "one of the real fathers of the New Westminster Waterfront, and many of the improvements which we [the longshore workers] have today was due to his foresight, particularly in regard to Safety on the job."[69] Both bosses were loyal subordinates to William Crawford.

At the end of 1924, the groups of New Westminster men represented by the Canadian Longshoremen's Association and the International Longshoremen's Association combined to form one union local based out of Room 21 of the Hart block. It sought affiliation with the Canadian Federation of Labour in Toronto, as Canadian Longshoremen's Association Local 1, but soon after was expelled from that larger labour body for non-payment of mandatory monthly remittances.[70]

The splinter group of longshoremen that called themselves the Fraser River Longshoremen's Union asked the Shipping Federation informally to set up a dispatch hall in New Westminster. The Fraser River Longshoremen's Union possessed a large number of returned military veterans from World War I, representing a little less than half the total membership. It described itself as a Canadian union, at odds with the views and policies of the International Longshoremen's Association. The Shipping Federation considered the proposition, a special committee having recommended in favour of extending jurisdiction to the Fraser River and registering longshoremen working there, but it was eventually deferred and rejected.[71]

The Vancouver and District Waterfront Workers Association, in the meantime, set up its own New Westminster branch at 735 Columbia

Street. Grant Currie was listed as secretary and the business agents were Edwin Graham and H.F. Lumsden, the first two with South Vancouver addresses and last on West Twenty-Third Street. They were not New Westminster residents. The Vancouver-based group accepted memberships from interested persons "with a view to improving conditions for the men working there who were split into various little groups, none of whom were making a decent living, nor were they organized sufficiently to be in a position to give anything like efficient service to the Stevedoring Companies concerned."[72]

Numerous separate labour organizations solicited dockside work in the city, and each had its own hall known by the last name of the lead dispatcher or business agent — Scott's Hall, Shaw's Hall, Blake's Hall, and so on. Out of this competitive and fragmented situation, the New Westminster and District Longshoremen's Association gradually gained the advantage over its chief rivals.

New Westminster and District Longshoremen's Association

The New Westminster and District Longshoremen's Association, not to be confused with the similar-sounding Vancouver and District Waterfront Workers Association, was a distinct local entity that came to represent the majority of experienced longshoremen working the New Westminster docks. Ralph Butters was the independent union's president in 1925, and William Clitheroe secretary.[73] After the mishandled attempt at Canadian affiliation, remaining members in the labour organization renewed connections with the International Longshoremen's Association and sought advice on organizing. The forced marriage between the two groups had never been a happy one, and factional infighting resulted. John Doig, the New Westminster and District Longshoremen's Association's president for the next three years, added more divisiveness by his actions and personality. Those most dissatisfied with the situation and direction left and tried to re-form a Canadian Longshoremen's Association out of the Fraser River Longshoremen's Union. The provincial charter for use of the older name was still active.

In January 1926, the Fraser River Longshoremen's Union listed Llewellyn Vivian Joseph Griffin as president, John Berry as business agent, and John W. Thomas as secretary-treasurer. All three were military veterans from World War I. Griffin's attestation papers listed him as teamster in his pre-military occupation, married, and place of residence, Edmonds, Burnaby. By 1926, he lived in New Westminster, at 904 Third Avenue, up the hill from the docks between Eighth and Tenth Streets. John W. Thomas resided near Burnaby Lake, on Laurel Avenue.

John Berry, born in Wales in 1893, joined the Canadian army on 23 November 1914, in Victoria, where his brother William lived; his declared vocation at the time of enlistment was sailor. In January 1916, Berry won the Distinguished Conduct Medal after being wounded in the field fighting with the 7th Battalion, an award given for the bravery of non-commissioned officers and other ranks, and second only to the Victoria Cross.[74] He was a war hero. After recovering from influenza in 1919, and being discharged with the rank of sergeant, Berry moved to New Westminster and settled down on Royal Avenue. His military connections and previous sea background gained him a spot on the waterfront. These were the beginnings of one of the ILWU's international representatives representing longshoremen in British Columbia twenty years later.

	Rank/Service/Regiment	Place of Residence
L.V.J. Griffin	Regimental Sergeant Major	New Westminster
John Berry, D.C.M	Sergeant 7th Battalion	New Westminster
E. Williams	131st Battalion	New Westminster
R. Thompson	3rd Governor General Imperial	New Westminster
W. Bence	Railway Company	New Westminster
C.H. Cowan	Lance Corporal 47th Battalion	New Westminster
L.E. Barber	Royal Navy	New Westminster
N. Jackson	7th Battalion	New Westminster
W. Crawshaw	Royal Navy	New Westminster
T. Kipp	Royal Marines	New Westminster
F. Tracey	Royal Navy	New Westminster
G.R. Gutteridge	82nd Battalion	New Westminster
J. Countryman	104th Home Service	New Westminster
F. Tucker	131st Battalion	Burnaby
D.J. Mitchell	58th Battalion	New Westminster

	Rank/Service/Regiment	Place of Residence
J.M. McCormack	131st Battalion	New Westminster
J.W. Thomas	Canadian Engineers	Burnaby
R. McLean	179th Battalion	New Westminster
R.T. Stewart	49th Battalion	New Westminster
W. Scott	10th Battalion	Burnaby
F. Peplow	51st Battalion	New Westminster
L.J. Tellier	2nd Canadian Mounted Rifles	New Westminster
J. Green	11th Army Service Corps	New Westminster
E.A. Powys	Captain Royal Engineers Train Ferry	Burnaby
G.S. Robinson	Battalion Staff Sergeant S.A	New Westminster
T. Buckland	24th Battalion	New Westminster
W.L. Archibald	Royal Artillery	New Westminster
T.L. Curne	16th Battalion	New Westminster
E.H. Reid	63rd Battalion	New Westminster
C. Watts	Naval Patrol	Burnaby
L. Lynch	131st Battalion	New Westminster
H. Maidens	47th Battalion	New Westminster
B. Gunston	Royal Horse Artillery	New Westminster
G. Wilson	Royal Canadian Engineers	New Westminster
O. Gagnon	102nd Battalion	Coquitlam (Maillardville)

Returned soldiers and sailors from World War I in the Fraser River Longshoremen's Union

Some individuals had served together overseas in the same military units. This concentration and background influenced the character of the union and relations with other unions and employers, as well as the general approach to seeking a fair deal for its members.

Source: City of Vancouver Archives, AM 279 Shipping Federation of BC 520-G-5 file 7

The New Westminster and District Longshoremen's Association won out in the slow contest of numbers and reliability. The figures in the table provide a rare snapshot into who really owned work on the waterfront at this time. The Canadian Longshoremen's Association, with its smaller membership, was hard-pressed to put together more than four or five gangs at any one time.

John Berry, now secretary-treasurer of the Canadian Longshoremen's Association, and two other members from New Westminster, sought a meeting with the president and the labour manager of the Shipping Federation.[75] The thirty-five-year-old Berry was the hatch tender in Gang No. 1 and active on the union's executive.

	Ships	Gangs Canadian Longshoremen's Association	Gangs New Westminster and District Longshoremen's Association	Total Equivalent Working Days
January	15	4	54	62.5
February	10	2	37	52
March	9	2	35	47.5
April	17	12	48	64.5
May	19	6	68	46
June	29	16	59	56.5
July	9	2	34	27
August	22	19	63	63
September	20	2	59	57
October	9	5	27	25.5
November	15	16	41	53
December	11	3	40	38.5

Longshore gangs dispatched in New Westminster during the year 1926. Note the wide disparity in numbers between the two waterfront labour organizations.

A gang consisted of thirteen men: a hatch tender, two winch drivers, and two slingmen made up the 'topside', while below in the hatch, two groups of four worked on each side of the hatch, a siderunner in each. The hatch tender, customarily a rated person chosen on seniority, was the leader and relied on signals to communicate with the others.

Since the Shipping Federation declined to open a dispatch hall in the city, the Canadian Longshoremen's Association received little assistance in competing with the other dominant waterfront union in New Westminster gaining the upper hand. The New Westminster and District Longshoremen's Association provided the overwhelming number of men in formed gangs for the available ships.

Gang	No. 1	No. 2	No. 3	No. 4	No. 5
Hatch tender	J. Berry	F. Langdon	J. Morrison	G. Faulkner	J. Stewart
Dbl winch driver	R. Chapman	A. Ogden	J. Hall	W. Grant	A. Olsen
Winch driver	T. Cleghorn	A. Langille	J. Blakemore	J. Armstrong	W. Crawshaw
Side Runner	W. Scott	G. Arter	P. Newcomb	B. Bradford	J. Gonzales
Side Runner	J. Harry	J. Gillard	J. Nahu	G. Alexander	D. Jack
Hold	T. Bugge	W. Chalmers	L. Newcomb	A. Blaine	A. Gonzales
Hold	F. Gerow	F. Morgan	R. Sutherby	W. Heaton	T. Findlay
Hold	W. Kohn	J. Clarke	A. Phillips	W. Chasthon	A. Gonzales
Hold	J. Gordon	C. Clarke	E. Newcomb	G. Morgan	R. Matthes
Hold	J. Tribe	M. Zoblosky	J. McDade	F. Sutherby	B. Gorham
Hold	H. Cuthbertson	J. Scott	J. Doig	S. McIlwaine	C. O'Brien
Sling	L. Griffin	J. Lynch	D. Romero	F. Wright	J. Jerome
Sling	G. Harding	B. Lynch	J. Miller	T. Allen	P. Jerome

Individuals employed on numbered gangs with Canadian Longshoremen's Association Local No. 1, New Westminster

Many of these names featured in the later leadership and membership of the Royal City Waterfront Workers Association and ILWU Local 502, particularly from Gang No. 1, demonstrating the lineage.

Source: City of Vancouver Archives, AM 279, Shipping Federation of BC 520-E-5 file 20

In March 1927, John Doig and Wilbur Scott, from the New Westminster and District Longshoremen's Association complained to the mayor and city council that the Canadian Longshoremen's Association was bringing in longshoremen from Vancouver to make up deficiencies. An informal agreement brokered with local representatives from the two leading stevedoring companies divided the work proportionally, but it proved too cumbersome

Hatch tender hand, whistle, and arm signals:

Go Ahead — hand well out to side, palm towards operator, fingers closed and thumb pointing upwards (one blast or pull)

Stop — hand well out, palm towards operator and hand wide open (one blast or pull with emphasis)

Come Back — hand well out, palm downwards fingers extended (two blasts or pulls; for slow, three blasts or pulls)

Slow motion can be implied by the slower making of the signals, but this should be accompanied by a spoken word to this effect.

Principles underlying good signalling by hatch tenders:

1. All signals should be distinct. They are for the purpose of changing the motion of a load and not for carrying that motion through — i.e. the signal should be discontinued immediately the desired motion is commenced. Laziness in making signals is a fairly prevalent fault.

2. Hand signals should be easily seen. The motions should be bold and the hands clearly visible. Gloves should not be worn by signallers at night or at any time when the visibility is bad. Signallers should stand so that there is no possibility of confusion between their hands.

3. Hand signals should be made correctly. Finger tip signals are difficult to see when the visibility is bad and when the winchman is wearing gloves. When leaving adopt the standard way. Do it right.

4. Whistle signals, especially on adjacent jobs, should be avoided except where efficient hand signalling is impossible.

In 1926, the Shipping Federation standardized signals for hatch tenders in an attempt to promote greater safety and decrease accidents on the waterfront. Longshoremen injured or killed on the job could be compensated through the provincial Workers Compensation Board. A special assessment was collected on a regular basis for this purpose. Longshoremen, supercargoes, and checkers also had the option of taking legal action against ship owners directly for compensation instead. Under changes to the *Canada Shipping Act*, the federal government appointed inspectors of ship gear and tackle who oversaw adherence to safety regulations in the harbours of Vancouver and New Westminster.

Source: City of Vancouver Archives, AM 279 Shipping Federation of British Columbia 521-D-1 file 2

and unworkable in practical application.[76] Empire Stevedoring preferred men provided by another independent union established under the name New Westminster Waterfront Workers Union, with Arthur Lanoue from Maillardville as president and James Shaw, secretary. Its handful of gangs worked the main docks and Fraser Mills.

Roland Cope remembered:

[John Macmillan] was also enthused with a dozen or so men, men who occasionally worked for the Empire [Stevedoring] at Fraser Mills. He made a gang of them. They became known as #3 Gang, the French Gang. Len Bonwick was the Hatch Tender. The Empire Stevedoring was the big fish in stevedoring on the [Fraser] River. It made up six gangs.

In another building, a few blocks away, another group was formed. The key men were Wilbur Scott and [John] Jack Berry and a man named Mahout.

They catered to the V & V work and in time quite a few men like George Arter, Huntay, Shaw, Cock, Langdon, J. Gommell and Tango made up another six gangs.

As time went on, an agreement was made between the groups that if a ship came into Port and was an Empire job, there would be four gangs from Shaw's Empire Hall and one from Scott's V&V Hall… Friction, in a way, developed and as the Port was being used more and more by the year, talks started between the three Halls with the idea of forming one Hall in New Westminster.[77]

Otherwise, it was simply survival of the fittest as each hall competed with the others for any available work. Some employers simply preferred to keep it that way.

To meet demand, the larger labour groups also began bringing longshoremen from Vancouver to load and unload ships in New Westminster, supplemental to the members residing in the city. All the while, the Canadian Longshoremen's Association struggled to secure sufficient work for its members. The Fraser River Longshoremen's Union surrendered its charter and dissolved in late 1927.[78] Many men put aside their principles and joined the New Westminster and District Longshoremen's Association.

Claude Lambson, from Fraser River Dock and Stevedoring observed:

In 1923, there were but 13 to 26 men available for longshore work in New Westminster, while today we have over 200 men depending on the shipping for livelihood and the majority are married men with families with homes in the City or District.[79]

Whether they belonged to one hall or another, longshoremen desired steady employment and fair pay. In January 1928, longshoremen in New Westminster loaded eight hundred and forty tons of cargo into the SS *Corvus,* consisting of zinc, canned goods, and broomsticks, during sixteen working hours, a rate at least comparable to or better than the port in Vancouver.[80] The skill and organization needed to attain such efficiency was high. Likewise, the numbers for effective organizing were now there, but the absence of one strong union meant competing loyalties and rival labour groupings working at cross-purposes.

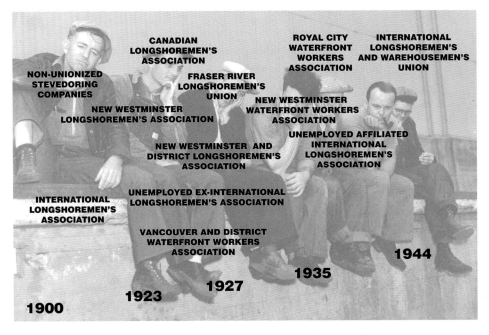

Evolution of Unionism on the Fraser River Waterfront
Source: Dean Johnson

The whole situation demonstrated the perils of division within labour ranks and the internal obstacles to uniting all longshoremen

**The waterfront cold storage plant at
Pacific Coast Terminals under construction in March 1929**
This type of specialized facility, subsidized in part by the federal and provincial
governments, increased the competitiveness of New Westminster as a port and
place of steady employment for longshoremen.
Source: Library and Archives Canada, RG 30 A-1 vol. 13039 file 1820-5 pt. 1

together in New Westminster. The need for solidarity became especially pressing with concentration of most dockside work into the hands of a select few private employers.

Local promoter Valentine Quinn secured government subsidies and private investment to build a cold storage plant and terminals on the main New Westminster waterfront. He persuaded Canadian National Railways' president, Henry Thornton, to sell the old Royal City Mills site in return for a $100,000 stake in a new company, first called Westminster Terminals Limited, then changed to Pacific Coast Terminals Limited, which Quinn incorporated under the new name using $10,000 of his own money.[81] Construction on the new facilities progressed through 1928 and into early 1929. The leases, held by Fraser River Dock and Stevedoring with the city, were transferred when that company was bought out and made a subsidiary.

Quinn accepted a salaried position of vice president and managing director after he sold all title and interest in Pacific Coast Terminals Limited in return for $69,800, a tidy sum indeed for his speculative work. The improvements and new company bode good employment for greater numbers of men choosing to work on the waterfront.

Still divided and unsure about which brand of unionism to choose, longshoremen on the Fraser River waterfront either backed or went against the New Westminster Waterfront Workers Association in the run up to the 1935 strike, inspired by an upsurge of militancy among the International Longshoremen's Association on the American side of the border and tied in sympathy to a standoff with the Shipping Federation in Vancouver.

Memorandum of Agreement

Memorandum of agreement made and entered into at Vancouver, B.C., this twenty-first day of May, 1913, by and between the Marine Association of British Columbia, through their duly authorized representatives, as parties of the first part, and the International Longshoremen's Association, on behalf of all Locals of Vancouver, as party of the second part.

Witnesseth: This agreement is made to cover general longshore work, which is to consist of loading and unloading vessels, sling to hold and hold to sling.

First. Party of the first part agrees to continue to employ members of the party of the second part in accordance with the conditions as they now exist in the several ports of British Columbia, and the purpose of this agreement is to fix the wages and conditions pertaining to longshore labor; and that nothing herein shall be construed as compelling the parties of the first part to employ exclusively members of the party of the second part, except as hereinafter provided.

Second. It is understood and agreed that the party of the second part shall furnish the party of the first part with men when called upon to do so, and when such men are available.

Rates of Wages for Handling Lumber

First. Nine hours constitute a day's work.

Second. Wages. Day work fifty cents (50c) per hour. Overtime seventy-five cents (75c) per hour. Side runners, hatch tenders, double winch and donkey drivers and boom men to be paid sixty cents (60c) per hour day work, ninety cents (90c) per hour overtime. Donkey drivers to be allowed one hour each day for getting up steam.

Third. Creosolted Lumber. Sixty cents per hour day work, ninety cents per hour overtime. Double winch and donkey drivers, slingers, boom men, side runners, hatch tenders, seventy cents per hour day work, one dollar and five cents overtime. Donkey drivers to be allowed one hour each day for getting up steam.

Wage Scale and Conditions for General Cargo

First. Nine hours constitutes a day's work.

Second. General cargo to be forty-five cents (45c) per hour for day work and fifty-five cents (55c) per hour for overtime. It is understood and agreed by the party of the first part that they will order all truckers and pilers required from the party of the second part; provided, however, that should the party of the second part be unable to furnish the necessary number of men, they will so advise the party of the first part, who will then engage such men as can be secured.

Third. Wheat, oats, barley, three in one (flour), cement, plaster, lime, sulphur, fertilizer, nitrate, creosote, coal, dynamite and explosives, fifty cents (50c) per hour day work, and seventy-five cents (75c) per hour overtime.

Fourth. Vessels in the coastwise trade shall pay only general cargo rates, i.e., forty-five cents (45c) and fifty-five cents (55c) for longshoremen, and forty cents (40c) and fifty cents (50c) for truckers and pilers, except where they may take full cargoes of any of the various commodities above mentioned, in which event they shall pay the rates above specified for such commodities, excepting that the rate of fifty cents (50c) straight time and seventy-five cents (75c) overtime for longshoremen, truckers and pilers shall apply on cement and plaster where the aggregate quantity on any ship amounts to over one hundred tons, or on the fertilizer, in any quantities. On lumber up to one hundred thousand (100,000) feet regular general cargo rates will apply.

Fifth. Meaning of overtime under this agreement is all work performed between the hours of six P.M. and eight A.M., Sundays, legal holidays, and the noon hour, except that in case it is more convenient on account of shifting or waiting cargo, for the vessel to knock off work at eleven A.M. and turn to at twelve noon, or to knock off work at one P.M. for the meal hour and turn to at two P.M., no overtime shall be paid between twelve noon and one P.M.

Sixth. There shall be no discrimination by the party of the first part against any member of the party of the second part, unless for just cause, nor shall the party of the second part discriminate against any member of the party of the first part, or their employees.

Seventh. Whenever any controversy arises between the party of the first part and the party of the second part, the men shall continue to work and the controversy shall be adjusted between representatives of the party of the second part. A standing committee of three representatives of both parties to this agreement shall be appointed, who shall jointly act on all questions of difference between them. If said controversy cannot be adjusted, then it shall be submitted to arbitration. Said arbitration board shall consist of one representative, selected by the party of the first part and one to be selected by the party of the second part, and the two so selected shall select a third man, who must be a disinterested person and the decision of any two shall be final and binding, and both parties shall abide thereby. Said arbitration board shall meet within three days after request has been made.

Eighth. Any member of the Local who violates any part of this agreement or agitates a stoppage of work under any circumstances, shall be discharged and will be given no future employment. All disputes, controversies and grievances must be taken up under Article Seven of this agreement.

Ninth. Stevedore firms and captains applying for men to go from one port to another to work on vessels, shall pay fare of men both ways, and allow time while travelling to and from such ports as follows: Port Mann two hours each way, and Departure Bay three hours each way, providing the men fulfill their contract. In case any man fails to fulfill his contract, such allowances shall not be made, and all advances for fares deducted.

Tenth. Men shall not be paid while standing by a ship when shifting from one dock to another, but at night time when men are kept standing by for the purpose of working at a third dock, then they shall be given the same pay as those who are kept continually employed on ship.

Eleventh. When men are ordered to work after seven P.M., and required to wait for vessel, they shall be paid from one hour after the time appointed up to eleven P.M. at the rate of one-half pay; after eleven P.M. they shall be paid full time.

Twelfth. All conditions not herein mentioned to remain as heretofore.

Thirteenth. This agreement entered into shall remain in full force from the first day of June 1913, to the thirty-first of December 1914.

Source: "Proceedings of the Sixth Annual Convention of the Pacific District of the International Longshoremen's Association held at Sailors Union Hall, San Pedro, California May 5 to 10, 1913", 101–104

Chapter Notes

1 Barry Mather and Margaret McDonald, *New Westminster: The Royal City* (Vancouver: J.M. Dent & Sons, 1958), 106.

2 New Westminster map drawn by Lance Corporal James Conroy, Royal Engineers, RG 2 H3/640 New Westminster 1861, Library and Archives Canada, Ottawa (hereafter LAC).

3 "Opinion of the Attorney General in re Water Frontage New Westminster 8th April 1872", RG 13 A-2 vol. 2138 file 1872–746, LAC.

4 Interview with Danny Amero by Joseph Breaks, 29 January 2013.

5 Andrew Parnaby, "'The best men that worked the lumber': Aboriginal Longshoremen on Burrard Inlet, British Columbia, 1863–1939", *Canadian Historical Review* vol. 87 no. 1 (2006), 61.

6 Allen Seager, "Workers, class, and industrial conflict in New Westminster, 1900–1930", in *Workers, Capital, and the State in British Columbia: Selected Papers*, edited by Rennie Warburton and David Coburn (Vancouver: University of British Columbia Press, 1988), 118–119.

7 PC 528 3/4, Order-in-council establishing separate pilotage authority in Yale and New Westminster electoral district, 15 April 1879, RG 2 vol. 173, LAC; Minutes of meeting Yale and New Westminster Pilotage Authority, 4 July 1879, AM 36 500-D-9 file 1, City of Vancouver Archives, Vancouver (hereafter CVA).

8 PC 124, Order-in-council proclaiming the port of New Westminster, 23 January 1880; PC 1360, Order-in-council establishing port limits on the Fraser River, 10 August 1880, RG 6 A-1 vol. 39 file 331, LAC; New Westminster shipping register 1880–1899, MF 652 (RG 12 A-1) vol. 364, Queen's University Archives, Kingston.

9 "Souvenir — New Westminster Bridge Official Opening, July 23rd, 1904", AM 1519 PAM 1904-3, CVA; Barrie Sanford, *Royal Metal: The People, Times and Trains of New Westminster Bridge* (Vancouver: National Railway Historical Society, British Columbia Chapter, 2004), 74.

10 Special meeting, 3 May 1906, AM 440, New Westminster Board of Trade, reel M 8-1, CVA; Assistant deputy minister marine and fisheries to deputy minister of justice, 18 June 1909, RG 13 A-2 vol. 156 file 1909-989, LAC.

11 Roy Smith, "Vancouver Longshoremen, Resilient Solidarity, and the 1935 Interruption: Company Unionism 1923–1945", MA thesis (Burnaby: Simon Fraser University, 2013), 14.

12 Ronald E. Magden, *A History of Seattle Waterfront Workers 1884–1934* (Seattle: International Longshore and Warehouse Union Local 19, 1991), 43–50.

13 *Labour Gazette* vol. 1 (1900–1901), 415.

14 "Proceedings of the Tenth Annual Convention of the International Longshoremen's Association, Toledo, Ohio, July 8th to 13th, inclusive, 1901", 26–27; "Longshoremen's Wages", *Daily Colonist* (7 March 1901).

15 *Labour Gazette* vol. 2 (1901–1902), 430.

16 "Proceedings of the Thirteenth Annual Convention of the International Longshoremen, Marine and Transport Workers' Association held in Milwaukee, Wisconsin, July 11th to 16th inclusive 1904", 115.

17 *Man Along the Shore! The Story of the Vancouver Waterfront as told by Longshoremen Themselves 1860's–1975* (Vancouver: ILWU Local 500 Pensioners, 1975), 33; freight handlers stood together against employers during a strike against wage reductions in New Westminster during April 1903.

18 George Bartley to W.L. Mackenzie King, 28 May 1907, RG 27 reel T-2684 vol. 294 file 2910, LAC; *Labour Gazette* vol. 7 (1906–1907), 1441.

19 George Bartley to F.A. Acland, 11 April 1909, RG 27 reel T-2685 vol. 296 file 3123, LAC.

20 "Longshoremen's Union of the Pacific, Proceedings of the Second Annual Convention held at Building Trades Temple 14th and Guerrero, San Francisco Sept. 13 to 17, 1909", 33–34; Maud Russell, *Men Along the Shore* (New York: Brussel and Brussel, 1966), 84.

21 "Victoria Stevedores Win", *BC Federationist* (5 April 1912).

22 Minutes regular meeting, 2 May 1912, AM 307 Vancouver Trades and Labour Council reel M 5-1, CVA.

23 Department of Labour Canada, *Report on Labour Organization in Canada 1913* (Ottawa: Government Printing Bureau, 1914), 33; The Halifax Longshoremen's Association, founded in 1907, received a charter from the International Longshoremen's Association as Local 269 in July 1913. Sandy MacDonald, *The Halifax Longshoremen's Association 1907–2007: Celebrating 100 Years* (Halifax: ILA Local 269, 2007), 12.

24 "The Fifth Annual Convention of the Pacific District of the International Longshoremen's Association held at Tacoma, Washington, May 6 to 11, 1912", 43–44.

25 Andrew Yarmie, "The Right to Manage: Vancouver Employers' Associations, 1900–1923", *BC Studies* no. 90 (Summer 1991), 45.

26 "Preamble to Constitution I.L.A. Vancouver, B.C.", 8 January 1913, ILWU-Canada file "General Material thru 1965", ILWU Ann Rand Research Library, San Francisco (hereafter ILWU Library).

27 "Proceedings of the Sixth Annual Convention of the Pacific District of the International Longshoremen's Association held at Sailors Union Hall, San Pedro, California May 5 to 10, 1913", 101–104; "Summary of agreement

in respect of wages and hours, June 1, 1913 to December 31, 1914. Parties — Marine Association of B.C., Vancouver Local — International Longshoremen's Association", RG 27 reel T-2691 vol. 303 file 5, LAC; "Longshoremen's Convention", *BC Federationist* (23 May 1913).

28 Biographical details, Mss. A75-49 Thomas V. O'Connor collection, Buffalo History Museum Research Library, Buffalo, New York.

29 Report on Marine and Dock Industrial Relations, prepared under direction of Commissioner T.V. O'Connor, U.S. Shipping Board covering Period June 1921 to February 1922 (1 March 1922).

30 "A.F. of L. Organizer Heatherton a Busy Man", *BC Federationist* (3 October 1913).

31 "Seventh Annual Convention, Pacific District [ILA], Vancouver, B.C., May 18–24, 1914", 38–39; "Pacific Coast District, No. 38, I.L.A.", *BC Federationist* (29 May 1914); Victoria had tried to host the 1912 ILA Pacific District convention, but had lost out narrowly to San Diego in the final tally of votes. "Victoria Close for Convention", *Daily Colonist* (14 May 1912).

32 *An Act to Incorporate the New Westminster Harbour Commissioners*, 3–4 George V (1913), chap. 158; Jacqueline Gresko and Richard Howard (eds), *Fraser Port: Freightway to the Pacific* (Victoria: Sono Nis Press, 1986), 46–50.

33 "[New] Westminster Welcomes Workers", *BC Federationist* (27 December 1912).

34 "Difficult to Fill the Gap", *British Columbian* (18 June 1913).

35 A. Wells Gray to secretary Department of Public Works, 17 April 1913, RG 11 B-3-a vol. 4339 file 3691-1-B, LAC.

36 "General Tie-up of All Shipping on Pacific", *BC Federationist* (12 March 1915).

37 James McVety to H.H. Stevens, 9 March 1915, MG 27 III B9 Henry Stevens vol. 177 file "Labour Council", LAC.

38 "Longshoremen's Pacific Coast Difficulties", *BC Federationist* (20 August 1915).

39 "The Longshoremen's Strike: A Brief Historical Sketch of the Strike inaugurated on June 1, 1916, in Pacific Coast Ports of the United States, compiled and published by the Waterfront Workers' Federation, San Francisco, California, August 23, 1916", International Longshoremen's Association, Local Pacific Coast District records, collection 412 box 8 file 7, Special Collections and University Archives, Knight Library, University of Oregon, Eugene; "Strike Will Tie Up Shipping", *Daily Colonist* (1 June 1916); "Longshoremen's Strike along Pacific Coast", *BC Federationist* (21 July 1916); Philip Taft, *Labor Politics American Style: The California State Federation of Labor* (Cambridge: Harvard University Press, 1968), 60–62.

40 "Gordon J. Kelly is Near Death", *Daily Colonist* (9 November 1918);

"Labor Leader Laid to Rest", *Vancouver Daily World* (13 November 1918).

41 Strike return, Canadian Pacific Railway Company and Empire Stevedoring Company, 9 August 1917, RG 27 reel T-2694 vol. 307 file 116, LAC; General officer commanding Military District No. 11 to Ottawa, 6 August 1917, RG 24 C-1-a vol. 6518 file HQ-363-24-5, LAC; "Waterfront Labor Makes Notable Progress", *BC Federationist* (10 August 1917); *ILA 38-52 Local Vancouver: constitution, bylaws, and rules of order — amended February 2, 1917*, SPAM 10957, SC/UBC.

42 "Proceedings of the Twelfth Annual Convention of the Pacific Coast District of the International Longshoremen's Association held in the Labor Temple, Seattle, Washington, May 5th to 10th, 1919", 7–8; "Longshoremen in Convention", *BC Federationist* (9 May 1919).

43 H.A.J. Monk and John Stewart, *History of Coquitlam and Fraser Mills, 1858–1958* (Coquitlam: District of Coquitlam-Fraser Mills Centennial Commission, 1958).

44 F.W. Howay and E.O.S. Scholefield, *British Columbia from the Earliest Times to the Present* vol. IV *Biographical* (Vancouver: S.J. Clarke Publishing Co., 1914), 146–149.

45 Joseph Flavelle to A.C. Taylor, 2 December 1918, MG 30 A16 Joseph Flavelle papers vol. 48 file "Taylor, Austin", LAC.

46 J.S. Woodsworth, *On the Waterfront* (Ottawa: Mutual Press, 1927), 13.

47 "Another Riot Almost Precipitated at Noon Today — Veterans Visit the Longshoremen's Hall — Ugly Situation Saved by Mayor", *Vancouver Daily World* (3 August 1918); Susan Mayse, *Ginger: The Life and Death of Albert Goodwin* (Madeira Park: Harbour Publishing, 1990).

48 "Mr. Taylor Talks of General Strike", *Daily Colonist* (25 May 1919).

49 Strike return, New Westminster, 14 August 1919, RG 27 reel T-2700 vol. 315 file 221, LAC; "Local Labour Takes a Stand", *British Columbian* (12 April 1919).

50 "New Plans to Improve Fraser", *British Columbian* (18 October 1919).

51 "Longshoremen Get Increase", *BC Federationist* (29 August 1919); *Labour Gazette* vol. 19 (1919), 839–840.

52 *Labour Gazette* vol. 20 (1920), 991.

53 Andrew Yarmie, "The State and Employers' Associations in British Columbia: 1900–1932", *Labour/Le travail* vol. 45 (Spring 2000), 85; Dana Frank, *Purchasing Power: Consumer Organizing, Gender and the Seattle Labor Movement, 1919–1929* (New York: Cambridge University, 1994), 165–166.

54 Mark Leier, *Where the Fraser River Flows: The Industrial Workers of the World in British Columbia* (Vancouver: New Star Books, 1990); Carlos A. Schwantes,

Radical Heritage: Labor, Socialism and Reform in Washington and British Columbia 1885–1917 (Seattle: University of Washington Press, 1979).

55 L.C. Mabbott to W.C.D. Crombie, 28 April 1927, AM 279 Shipping Federation of BC, 520-E-5 file 20, CVA.

56 W.B.M. Hick, *Canada's Pacific Gateways: Realizing the Vision* (Prince Rupert: Prince Rupert Port Authority, 2011), 74–76.

57 "Longshoremen to Join City Union", *Vancouver Daily World* (22 March 1923), RG 27 reel T-2714 vol. 332 file 95, LAC.

58 Chairman protection committee to A.M. Manson, 10 October 1923, AM 279 Shipping Federation of BC 520-E-1 file 3, CVA.

59 Strike return, Shipping Federation of British Columbia and International Longshoremen's Association Local 38-52, 15 October 1923, RG 27 reel T-2714 vol. 331 file 95, LAC; *Labour Gazette* vol. 23 (1923), 1232.

60 J. Stewart to R.E. Borchgrevink "Longshoremen's Strike at Vancouver, B.C.", 13 March 1924, AM 279 Shipping Federation of BC 520-D-7 file 5, CVA; "Shipping Federation Emergency Fund Cash Account — Commencement of Strike to 3rd March", 3 March 1924, AM 279 Shipping Federation of BC 520-E-1 file 5, CVA.

61 "A Review of the Strike", *Longshoremen's Strike Bulletin issued by the Strike Committee of Local No. 38-52 I.L.A.* no. 7 (29 November 1923), AM 279 Shipping Federation of BC, Oversize 1-K, CVA.

62 "Final Report Regarding the Strike of Longshoremen Employed on the Docks at Vancouver, Victoria and other points in the Province of British Columbia", F.E. Harrison to H.H. Ward, 11 December 1923, RG 27 reel T-2714 vol. 331 file 95, LAC; *Labour Gazette* vol. 24 (1924), 20.

63 James McVety to W.C.D. Crombie, 12 April 1924, AM 279 Shipping Federation of BC 521-A-6 file 4, CVA.

64 "Report of the Committee Appointed to Investigate Prospective Trade on the Fraser River, British Columbia" February 1921, RG 11 B-3-a vol. 2897 file 69-1-G, LAC.

65 "Memorandum of Association of Fraser River Dock & Stevedoring Co. Ltd.", 11 February 1924, IH981.27 Pacific Coast Terminals fonds box 1 file 125, New Westminster Museum and Archives (hereafter NWMA); Hick, *Canada's Pacific Gateways: Realizing the Vision*, 74.

66 Secretary to all stevedoring companies, "B & A Gangs — [New] Westminster", 13 August 1925, AM 279 Shipping Federation of BC 520-F-1 file 1, CVA.

67 City council meeting, 28 July 1925, New Westminster Public Library (hereafter NWPL).

68 R.M Angus to Captain Baird, 16 December 1926, AM 279 Shipping

Federation of BC 521-E-3 file 2, CVA.

69 "Captain John Macmillan", *Gang Plank* no. 41 (September 1961), ILWU–Canada file "Publications Local 502 — *Gang Plank*", ILWU Library; John Macmillan to Phillip Groves, [nd], AM 279 Shipping Federation of BC 520-G-4 file 5, CVA.

70 L.C. Mabbott to W.C.D. Crombie, 28 April 1927, AM 279 Shipping Federation of BC 520-E-5 file 20, CVA.

71 W.C.D. Crombie to R.G. Parkhurst "New Westminster", 28 July 1927, AM 279 Shipping Federation of BC 521-C-2 file 6, CVA.

72 Allan Walker to W.C.D. Crombie, 4 December 1928, AM 279 Shipping Federation of BC 517-G-5 file 4, CVA.

73 Department of Labour Canada, *Fifteenth Annual Report on Labour Organization in Canada (For the Calendar Year 1925)* (Ottawa: F.A. Acland, 1926), 132.

74 Service file, John Edward Berry regimental no. 77848, RG 150 acc. 1992–93/166 box 687 file 22, LAC.

75 J.C. Irons to W.C.D. Crombie, 11 February 1926, AM 279 Shipping Federation of BC 521-C-2 file 5, CVA.

76 City council meeting, 28 March 1927, NWPL.

77 *Man Along the Shore!*, 79.

78 Department of Labour Canada, *Seventeenth Annual Report of Labour Organization in Canada (For the Calendar Year 1927)* (Ottawa: F.A. Acland, 1928), 290.

79 Meeting board of trade council and members, 25 July 1927, AM 440 New Westminster Board of Trade reel M 8-7, CVA.

80 K.J. Burns to W.C.D. Crombie, 30 January 1928, AM 279 Shipping Federation of BC 521-E-2 file 12, CVA.

81 Agreement between Valentine Quinn and Pacific Coast Terminals Limited, 21 August 1928, IH981.27 Pacific Coast Terminals fonds box 4 file 88, NWMA.

Chapter 2
Toward One Union
1929–1945

Chris Madsen

The story of the ILWU and its rise on the Pacific coast gives prominence to the struggles of the 1930s and 1940s, both in the streets and around the negotiating table. Monument markers and special events memorialize the violent clashes with police during waterfront strikes and the resolve of longshoremen to stand up for the benefit of all members, under the leadership of Harry Bridges. San Francisco has 'Bloody Thursday', Seattle has 'The Battle of Smith Cove', and Vancouver, 'The Battle of Ballantyne Pier'. Myth becomes intertwined with the historical recounting.[1]

Lance Carlson says his grandfather was present during the march on Ballantyne Pier and spent time in jail, as did other strikers. Although ILWU members now share in the general narrative and sympathize with the goals, the chain of events in New Westminster on the Fraser River waterfront was unique and different. While a few individuals from New Westminster confronted police in Vancouver, the actions taken by the majority of longshoremen on the Fraser River are equally significant. They met with city officials, manned picket lines, and risked arrest for what they believed in. Considerable numbers of them also flocked to a city-backed replacement union for very practical reasons. Longshoremen wanted to work and had families to feed. The violence and bloodshed elsewhere bypassed New Westminster.

The present ILWU Local 502 traces its roots to the association or union that morally came to be on the opposite side in the big strike of 1935, the Royal City Waterfront Workers Association.

The 'Scabs of '35', Joe Breaks tells, were represented on the executive and those longshoremen accorded the most seniority from induction in 1936:

> ... there were lots of '35 strike scabs we called them, when they were still there, and so that would sometimes start something. 'Cause you would do something, and then the guy would say, 'You're nothing but a blankety-blankety-blank '35er.' Well, then that would start the pushing match. And sometimes they would get into it.[2]

The effect on the union of this divide was profound. Understanding why this was the case, and how the city's longshoremen were still a part of the larger union movement along the Pacific coast that asserted independence in demanding better working conditions and fairer compensation for all members working on the docks, deserves to be told. Tension between local autonomy and external association existed in the formation of ILWU Local 502.

A Busier Waterfront

Work on New Westminster's waterfront was directly related to the shipping that came up the Fraser River to take commodities abroad to international markets. The primary exports were lumber, metals in concentrate and bar forms, fertilizer, grain, and agricultural produce from the Fraser Valley and Okanagan. To attract this business, city officials and private companies on the waterfront invested significantly in the physical footprint with dedicated assets and the latest technological devices connecting to broader railway networks that brought railcars directly dockside.

Deep-sea ship arrivals held steady and increased marginally from year to year, in spite of the severe effects of economic depression.

	Ships	Exports (in tons)	Imports (in tons)	Value (CDN$)
1929	248	376,839	12,873	$11,632,897
1930	297	395,340	36,270	$13,396,184
1931	301	420,544	13,465	$16,498,615
1932	311	446,754	14,634	$12,369,686
1933	409	657,879	20,699	$16,193,840
1934	453	766,299	36,127	$23,497,021

Source: New Westminster Harbour Commissioners annual reports

Longshoremen on the Fraser River worked for good wages when other workers were unemployed. An exchange between Shipping Federation officials described the situation in late 1929:

> *Mr. Hart: [New] Westminster is busy at present time. I do not think a man could get enough work in [New] Westminster.*
>
> *Capt. Groves: There are about 13 gangs in [New] Westminster.*
>
> *Mr. Law: There are 180 in two outfits.*
>
> *Mr. Clendenning: It doesn't seem right that men should live over there and then ask for transportation back there again. With the number of men out of work in Vancouver, we should take care of Vancouver men.*
>
> *Capt. Baird: Are there any Vancouver men in [New] Westminster.*
>
> *Major Crombie: A lot of them.*
>
> *Capt. Baird: There is then a lot of lost energy.*[3]

An informal agreement allowed the interchange of gangs between Vancouver and New Westminster when either port ran short.

By 1930, the Westminster Waterfront Workers Association, whose hall was at 635 Clarkson Street, amalgamated the New Westminster and District Longshoremen's Association and parts of the independent New Westminster Waterfront Workers Union. This initiative came from discussions between the respective presidents, James Kelvin and Arthur Lanoue. Secretary and business agent James Shaw worked tirelessly in the background to make the merger happen.

The Vancouver and District Waterfront Workers Association operated from another hall at 735 Columbia Street. Stanley Blake was the business agent. Employers acting through the Shipping Federation reimbursed the expense of taking the tram or bus, and paid travelling time at set rates. The principal stevedoring companies, especially Empire Stevedoring, employed longshoremen dispatched from both cities.

Hamper No. 1 (family of 4)	Hamper No. 2 (family of 6)
six tins Pacific milk	eight tins Pacific milk
one sack Robin Hood rolled oats	one sack Robin Hood rolled oats
fifteen pounds potatoes	twenty-five pounds potatoes
half-pound Malkin's Best tea	half-pound Malkin's Best tea
one carton granulated sugar	one carton granulated sugar
one picnic ham	one picnic ham
one sack Windsor salt	one sack Windsor salt
one pound Fraser Valley butter	one pound Fraser Valley butter
one tin Malkin's Best baking powder	one tin Malkin's Best baking powder
one sack Robin Hood flour	one sack Royal Standard flour
one pound lard	one pound of lard
one tin plum jam	one tin plum jam
ten pounds small white beans	ten pounds small white beans
one bar soap	one bar soap

The onset of the Great Depression left many longshoremen with intermittent work and wages. In order to provide some relief, the Shipping Federation distributed, as an act of charity, relief packages of groceries, coal, and other necessities to needy union members and their families during the holiday season in 1930, paid in part by donations from the shipping and stevedoring companies to a Christmas Cheer Fund. The listed standard grocery hampers above were prepared and delivered by W.H. Malkin Company to New Westminster addresses for A. Thomson, George Bradford, and Dolga Dominic. One New Westminster recipient wrote back: "Please will you be so kind and change our order a little for once. And send us instead of tea some coffee. Rolled oats for some rice. And instead of beans send me some laundry soap. Instead of Baking Powder, Makroni [sic]. And send me 49 lb. of Bread Flour. Please."
Source: City of Vancouver Archives AM 279 Shipping Federation of BC 521-C-4 file 16

Fraser River Elevator No. 1
on the south river bank across from New Westminster
This grain elevator was built by the harbour commissioners and leased to private companies who employed longshoremen and men working as grain liners.
Source: Port Metro Vancouver

The nature of that work changed as the handling of cargo in increasing quantities became more skilled and specialized. Though still physically demanding, the job involved operating machinery and working in formed gangs suited to particular commodities. Apples, eggs, and nuts were kept in cold storage, metal bars carried by passenger liners to the United Kingdom largely replaced concentrates, and lumber was brought by barge from nearby mills to the main docks for loading. At a grain elevator built by the New Westminster Harbour Commissioners on the south side of the river, bushels of wheat increased from 61,417 in the first year of operation in 1931 to 315,700 when leased to the Searle Grain Company in August 1933.[4]

Shipping lines, some new to New Westminster, called on the Fraser River with increasing frequency. Pacific Coast Terminals Limited, the primary conveyer of goods and commodities dockside through its subsidiary, Fraser River Dock and Stevedoring, accounted for roughly ninety percent of all trade passing through the port of New Westminster.

Pacific Coast Terminals, judged by the scale of investment in waterfront facilities and backing from principal stakeholders, possessed a dominant position on the main waterfront that hid some really serious financial shortcomings. A cold storage plant had been built with federal and provincial subsidies, while the leases with the city on wharves held by Fraser River Dock and Stevedoring were taken over and improvements made. The constructed facilities were modern, state-of-the art, and first-class for the time. Connections between rail, dock, and ship were almost seamless. Mechanical lifters and motorized conveyances increased speed and productivity from traditional methods.

Dockside operations at Pacific Coast Terminals
The extent of mechanization in moving goods with tractors is shown. This view is taken from the second floor of the cold storage building.
Source: New Westminster Museum and Archives, IHP 1653

In 1931, Pacific Coast Terminals recorded a loss of $75,420.51 on balance sheets, which coupled with losses from the previous two years threatened corporate failure. Consolidated Mining and Smelting, one of the existing shareholders, put up $100,000 in return for a majority position of common shares and a controlling interest in the direction of the company. When Pacific Coast Terminals defaulted on paying interest to bondholders in February 1932 and missed several scheduled payments, the City of New Westminster was obligated to pay out interest on the company's debentures, according to an earlier guarantee. Various proposals put forth by the company's president, William Blackstock Lanigan, to revise or write down the existing financial obligations, achieved mixed results. Lanigan was formerly general freight traffic manager for Canadian Pacific Railway in Winnipeg and essentially represented that company.

In September 1933, the Montreal Trust Company, acting on behalf of bondholders owed outstanding interest, took possession of all assets and affairs by application to the Supreme Court of British Columbia. Pacific Coast Terminals Limited was placed into court-appointed trusteeship, with certain conditions attached for continued operation pending resolution of outstanding commitments or eventual sale. The company teetered on the brink of liquidation.

The fragile state of Pacific Coast Terminals on the financial side was hardly apparent to ordinary people working on the docks. Business appeared brisk as ships steamed to and from New Westminster and the Fraser River. Weekly lists of arrivals appeared in the shipping and industrial section of the *British Columbian* newspaper. Pacific Coast Terminals was the major employer on the city's waterfront, with a sizeable payroll. Labour costs in relation to revenue were acceptable, and certainly in line with competitors and other ports. The prevailing wage paid longshoremen was still seventy-five to eighty cents an hour. By comparison, Valentine Quinn, the company's operating manager, earned over $9,000 per month, nearly three times the next highest-paid employee, the assistant general manager. Quinn drove an expensive car to work and benefitted from company-paid trips to Eastern Canada, the United States, and Europe, as well as a private loan backed by the company to buy a New Westminster-area house. Longshoremen working the docks received none of these considerations. Collapse of markets for certain key commodities during the Depression was no doubt the underlying cause of the poor financial performance, but management of the company was also a contributing factor.

Pacific Coast Terminals, in fact, could draw upon a large pool of men looking for work during bad economic times, and thus kept overall wages lower. The modest growth in trade and business, while remarkable given the tough environment, was insufficient to cover all expenses. The company was highly leveraged, with far too much debt accumulated mostly from the initial construction and start-up costs. Put simply, it could not make the interest payments on the amounts owing with the available revenue coming in. Only the favoured treatment from the city and the interest of Consolidated Mining and Smelting kept operations going and longshoremen on the New Westminster docks employed.

Pacific Coast Terminals, in the midst of its deepest problems, faced other local competition for business and employment on the waterfront. A new company, the New Westminster Dock and Forwarding Company, leased land from the city beside the New Westminster railway bridge, and began construction of a deepwater wharf catering to lumber exports.[5] Fred Hume, an alderman and owner of a successful electrical contracting firm, became president. Harry Sullivan, a barrister and solicitor, was secretary-treasurer. Claude Lambson, previously of Fraser River Dock and Stevedoring before the sale to Pacific Coast Terminals, was managing director. Hume and Sullivan ran on a twin ticket in the January 1934 civic election, during which allegations were raised that their involvement with the freight company was an apparent conflict of interest for anyone seeking political office.[6] Voters were more forgiving. Fred Hume was elected mayor to replace Arthur Wells Gray, who entered the provincial legislature and premier's cabinet in the post of Minister of Lands and Municipal Affairs, while Harry Sullivan was elected alderman for a two-year term. Claude Lambson subsequently became the public face of New Westminster Dock and Forwarding, which, with its one wharf, challenged the position of neighbouring Pacific Coast Terminals.

To the credit of Hume and Sullivan, the city diligently paid out the outstanding interest guaranteed on the debentures of Pacific Coast Terminals, though certain tax exemptions at roughly the same value were ended. Valentine Quinn, on behalf of the trustee, promised to pay back all monies owing the city when the company turned profitable. If not for major repairs and equipment upgrades, the company might have shown profit for the period of trusteeship up to 31 December

1934, but the actual figure was a loss of $28,569.73.[7] It was no secret that dissatisfied bondholders wanted the trustee to find new owners and obtain the best price possible. Consolidated Mining and Smelting appeared a good prospect, but wanted a bargain and concessions from the city. Financially, Pacific Coast Terminals was probably the worst type of company for longshoremen to strike against because any dislocation would mean loss of business and quick bankruptcy. Strident demands from labour — better organized, militant, and willing to undertake collective action — would nearly tip the balance.

Demands from Longshoremen

Addressing longstanding inequalities marred relations between employers and longshoremen on waterfronts along the entire Pacific coast that touched directly and indirectly onto New Westminster. Unions and labour groups, erstwhile compliant and accommodating, came under more forceful leadership, with a clearer message about what they wanted by way of collective bargaining and treatment in the workplace. On Burrard Inlet, the Vancouver and District Waterfront Workers Association rejected the Shipping Federation's proposals for an agreement over differences about discrimination, equal wages, and the dispatch. The union came out on the losing end of a conciliation board, chaired by Justice Harold Robertson, which was stacked in the employer association's favour, and nearly voted to strike in May 1934.[8]

The same month, longshoremen in US Pacific ports represented by the International Longshoremen's Association, started a coast-wide strike after negotiations with employers and last-hour attempts at mediation and government intervention stalled. The Canadians stayed apart from the resulting major American longshore strike. The International Longshoremen Association's Pacific District, headed by William Lewis, stood defiant, backed by some seven to ten thousand striking US longshoremen.[9] Violence and deaths erupted on waterfronts when police clashed with strikers in San Francisco, Portland, and Seattle. A backroom agreement brokered during a whirlwind trip from New York in June 1934 by Joseph Ryan, the president of the International Longshoremen's Association, failed to gain acceptance when put to a vote by most rank-and-file west coast longshoremen facing police bullets on the picket lines.

Harry Bridges, the chair of the San Francisco local strike committee, emerged as a central figure, who rallied longshoremen and other maritime workers behind a united front, even raising the bogeyman of a general strike. Australian by birth and a working longshoreman himself, Bridges understood the concerns of the ordinary worker, and proved hard-nosed (interestingly, people joked about the size of his nose) and smart enough to stand up to the hard tactics used against organized labour.[10] In other words, he beat the maritime employers at their own game. Longshoremen in New Westminster, while still working as usual, declined to discharge any ship originating or diverting from American ports under strike by Bridges and the International Longshoremen's Association.[11] Front pages in the *British Columbian* carried sensational stories about the progress of the US maritime strike until its end in late July 1934.

When the matter went to arbitration, Harry Bridges and International Longshoremen's Association locals won key concessions from maritime employers, including union control over hiring and dispatch, which served to solidify a sense of independent local autonomy, being at times defiant of influence and direction from Joseph Ryan and the larger organization. A publicity pamphlet left no doubts about the efficacy of the new leadership and stakes involved for the union:

> The I.L.A. is fighting for its life as a *bona fide* labor organization, for the rights and welfare of thousands of waterfront workers and their families — men and women whose best interests are bound up with the best interests of the community as a whole.
>
> The I.L.A. and the maritime unions generally know the game the employers are playing. They intend to retain their unions, to retain the conditions won by the struggle and sacrifices of 1934 and to support as their officials the men who have proved in action that they can be trusted by *the workers*.[12]

The message appeared to be that collective action, when capably led and true to principles, could actually deliver results. For longshoremen in New Westminster, solidarity and militancy was a call to action.

West coast longshore leader Harry Bridges
He was a tough negotiator and shrewd advocate for locals and members in his union.
Source: Chris Madsen

Notwithstanding the dramatic and historical events of the 'Great 1934 Pacific Maritime Strike' in the United States, the path to a comparable major strike to afflict British Columbia ports during the following year was peculiarly Canadian, born from the dictates that longshoremen faced at the hands of the Shipping Federation and individual employers as well as decisions made to effect a change in relationships. The American example, while similar in purpose, hardly accounted for the unique conditions and divisions pertaining to the Canadian context. The welfare capitalism model espoused by the Shipping Federation and imposed on longshoremen if they wanted consistent work, ever since 1923, was weakening though still operable.[13]

In fact, employer representatives like William Crawford and William Crombie believed longshoremen should know their place and reasonably accept what was given them. A process of decasualization pushed longshoremen into formed gangs, a practice first started in Seattle and spread to British Columbia.[14] The Shipping Federation discontinued the shape-up or shipside pick of longshoremen in 1931. The Canadian Waterfront Workers Association, a new labour body, was formed under the *Societies Act* to promote fraternal association and "obtain work suitable for various members to make them self-supporting and to improve their standards of efficiency and productivity."[15] This union and others was a reaction, though a contrivance, to the focused resolve of the Vancouver and District Waterfront Workers Association, increasingly seen as militant and demanding.

The Shipping Federation used a detective service to collect information and infiltrate operatives into the internal workings of waterfront labour organizations deemed of interest. William Crombie, as the Shipping Federation's labour manager, was remarkably well-informed about the backgrounds and goings-on of progressive individuals occupying leadership positions, in particular Ivan Emery, soon to be head of the Longshore and Transport Workers of Canada, and those involved in the editorship and production of a waterfront-targeted broadsheet, *Heavy Lift*. The publishing of this labour periodical, distributed amongst longshoremen in Vancouver and New Westminster, was done in secret on a mimeograph machine moved from house to house ahead of repeated attempts by private detectives to discover its location.

A key feature of *Heavy Lift* was the rough drawings that caricatured Crombie, Crawford, and other figures on the employer's side. In August 1934, one of Crombie's operatives clandestinely attended a secretive meeting of thirty-four persons chaired by "a member of the Longshoremen's Union from New Westminster" until the unwelcome guest was recognized and "gently but firmly requested to leave the hall."[16] Such involvement suggests that certain individuals in the Westminster Waterfront Workers Association, soon renamed the New Westminster Waterfront Workers Association, were deeply engaged in organizing

and propaganda activities some time before the strike and shared in the overall goals of uniting maritime workers on the waterfront. Extension of union control over the dispatch, as existed in New Westminster, to Vancouver was a favourite topic in the pages of *Heavy Lift*.

Steamship lines	
Anglo Canadian Shipping Company	Matson Line
Blue Funnel Line	Nippon Yusen Kaisha Line
Blue Star Line	North German Lloyd
Klaveness Line	Oceanic & Oriental Navigation Company
Danish East Asiatic Line	Ocean Shipping Company
Donaldson Line	Pacific Argentine Brazil Line
Fred Olsen Line	Royal Mail Line
Fruit Express Line	Silver Java Pacific Line
Furness Pacific Line	Tacoma Oriental Steamship Company
Grace Line	Transatlantic Steamship Company Limited
Hamburg-America Line	United Ocean Transport Company
Holland-Amerika Line	Vancouver–St. Lawrence Line
Inter Ocean Line	Vancouver–West Indies Line
Isthmian Line	Yamashita Kisen Kaisha
Union Steamship Company of New Zealand Limited	Compagnie Generale Transatlantique Line

Steamship lines using the Port of New Westminster during 1934
A number of these shipping lines offered regular service to worldwide destinations, particularly the United Kingdom, Europe, and Asia. New Westminster longshoremen interacted with shipmasters and seamen from all parts of the globe. After the outbreak of World War II, the German and Japanese ships on the list obviously stopped coming to Canadian ports.
Source: Library and Archives Canada, RG 20 A-3 vol. 878 file 6-157

The existing process governing labour relations on the waterfront was increasingly seen to be unfair and entrenching the power of employers. A three-year agreement signed in October 1934 through conciliation left the longshoremen represented by the Vancouver and District Waterfront Workers Association unhappy and dissatisfied.[17] Base wage rates were eighty-five cents for ship work and eighty-one cents for dock work, work stoppages were prohibited, and the Shipping Federation ran dispatching through its own office. In the United States, the wages were ninety-five cents and eighty-five cents respectively, while the west coast side of the International Longshoremen's Association now controlled the dispatch. In February 1935, Vancouver longshoremen gave notice to the Shipping Federation that a Pacific coast scale of wages and union control over distribution of work were demanded by a deadline of 27 April.[18] Instead of conceding to this ultimatum, the employers readied for a showdown, backed by a tough-talking Vancouver mayor with no affection for "Reds and Communists".

In Powell River, affiliated casual longshoremen asking for wage increases were shut out and ships loaded lumber with non-union workers. In support, the Vancouver and District Waterfront Workers Association declared any ships from that port unfair and refused to handle them. With both sides itching for a fight, the issue was really a pretext. In May 1935, the Vancouver and District Waterfront Workers Association put the question of self-dispatch to a vote and gained a majority in favour of transfer to union control, knowing full well that it was unacceptable to the Shipping Federation. When longshoremen refused to work fifteen ships on 5 June 1935, the Shipping Federation nullified the existing agreement, a move the longshoremen's union claimed was a lockout.[19] The employers set up their own registration office to recruit new workers and no longer recognized delegates from the Vancouver and District Waterfront Workers Association. Communication abruptly stopped.

The Strike in 1935

With no specific grievances of their own against employers, longshoremen in New Westminster felt duty-bound to support striking longshoremen in Vancouver and Powell River for the sake of the greater good. In terms of affiliation, the New Westminster Waterfront Workers Association was Local 2 of the Longshore and Transport Workers of Canada, a central body encompassing unionized longshoremen in British Columbia ports. The idea was to act together through strength in numbers. New Westminster longshoremen voted two hundred and ninety to fifty-five in favour of a sympathy strike.[20] At the time, the total membership in the local union was three hundred and five regular members and fifty-nine casuals or spares. John McKinnie represented New Westminster on a delegation of affiliated unions which met with the Shipping Federation's board of directors on 13 June and again the following day. It was to no avail, as further dealings with the Vancouver union, Local 1 of the Longshoremen and Transport Workers of Canada, the delegates were told "were impossible and the agreement was at an end."[21] The central committee of the Longshoremen and Transport Workers of Canada called upon affiliated unions to stop work in their respective ports the next morning.

On 15 June 1935, the New Westminster docks were brought to a standstill when longshoremen refused work and put up information pickets. Only two ships were present on the river, the SS *King Lud* at Fraser Mills, ready to take on lumber for export to Australia, and the SS *Leeds City*, recently arrived at Pacific Coast Terminals for lumber and general cargo. Four other ships, MS *Trondanger*, SS *Daldorch*, SS *Lochkatrine*, and SS *Memphis City*, speedily left port before the strike began. The affected companies made no attempt to load either ship with the labour available. On the *Leeds City*, curious sailors milled about on the deck, watching the spectacle of empty docks on shore.

Mayor Fred Hume, initially supportive, conferred with the strike leaders and company managers to reach some sort of amicable understanding to keep the port open, and thus not interfere with business that might negatively impact local industries and employment. The longshoremen and the city stood to lose much for somebody else's fight, he declared. Hume, accompanied by Valentine Quinn and Alderman Alex Courtney, went to Victoria to huddle with New Westminster's sitting legislative member, Arthur Wells Gray, (on Pacific Coast Terminals' board of directors since his days as mayor) and the Deputy Minister of Labour, Adam Bell, about the situation and learn the stance of the provincial government.[22] New Westminster's elected representatives were prepared to facilitate mediation, but also wanted quick action. Arthur Wells Gray immediately phoned Frederick Harrison, the federal government's Western Fair Wage Officer, to do what he could to bring the various sides together.

Fred Hume, Adam Bell and a delegation of longshoremen met with Frederick Harrison at New Westminster City Hall the same day. The mayor and three members of the New Westminster Waterfront Workers Association, Arthur Lanoue, John McKinnie and Jack Adie, then went with Harrison for a day-and-a-half meeting at the Shipping Federation's head office.[23] The effort was completely unproductive. The

Vancouver maritime employers declined to budge from their firm stand of neither recognizing nor dealing with the Vancouver and District Waterfront Workers Association. Harrison explained the existing law governing conciliation and the lack of any real differences to mediate in the case of New Westminster. He suggested that the sympathetic longshoremen resume work, pending a settlement in Vancouver.

The violent clash between police and striking longshoremen in Vancouver popularly known as the 'Battle of Ballantyne Pier' happened the very same day Fred Hume and the New Westminster union representatives met with the Shipping Federation.

Captain Ed Taylor commented on the unfavourable position of the striking workers and what they stood to lose:

> On the Vancouver waterfront, my father was working at Ballantyne Pier. And the strike came on, everyone of course was laid off. And then the operators started recruiting people to take their place. They were called scabs in those days. Unfortunately, what happened, and I can tell you this from experience, my father never got back to work again. Scabs took over one hundred percent. And the original longshoremen never got back. One of our neighbours was the crane operator at Ballantyne Pier for about fifteen years. He got laid off and somebody took his place. He never did work again. That's what happened as far as the strike at the Vancouver waterfront was concerned.[24]

These were desperate times. On 18 June 1935, a procession of nearly one thousand striking longshoremen marched toward the Vancouver waterfront, only to be met by a line of city police, provincial police, and the Royal Canadian Mounted Police ready to use force. World War I veteran and Victoria Cross winner, Private James 'Mickey' O'Rourke, was at the forefront with the strikers. After being warned and told to disperse, they received the initial blow — "following the use of [tear] gas which stopped the rush, mounted men charged the crowd both, from the front and from the flank on Powell Street, where City and Provincial mounted men had been placed for such a contingency."[25] Longshoremen threw rocks and anything at hand, while the police beat with batons any men they caught in the open. The rumpus lasted more than three hours. The police pursued fleeing strikers into the adjoining commercial strip and nearby residential neighbourhoods. On that day, waterfront union leader Ivan Emery and twenty-five other strikers were arrested for assault, riotous behaviour, and carrying weapons. The situation meant emotions were running high and a great sense of indignation pertained on both sides.

As an event, the confrontation in Vancouver really had only passing relevance to longshoremen in New Westminster at the time. The police stopped and turned back longshoremen from New Westminster trying to reach the area and only a few arrived in time to participate actively in the fighting. The Battle of Ballantyne Pier instead influenced decision-making at a crucial time, that put the strikers into an untenable position. Above all, it hardened viewpoints. In a public statement released on 18 June, the New Westminster strike committee described in their own words who they felt was responsible in the days leading up to the clash between Vancouver longshoremen and police:

Resume of the Facts Pertaining to the Strike That Involves Men of the Port of New Westminster

The set-up brought about by the consolidation of all men engaged in the longshore industry is expressed in a national organization, known as the Longshore and Transport Workers of Canada. This national group embraces the various organizations along the British Columbia coast. The individual locals are represented by elected delegates to this national group, and they constitute the centralized expressions of all longshoremen up and down this coast.

Developments in the past two years, due to the activities of the national group being successful in bringing about the amalgamation of separate groups, which had been functioning heretofore in Vancouver and New Westminster, brought about the antagonism which finally forced a lock-out by the Shipping Federation of British Columbia of the men in Vancouver, organized as the Vancouver and District Waterfront Workers Association on June 4th.

On Friday, June 7, the central board of the Longshore and Transport Workers of Canada presented to all these affiliated groups, of which the men in New Westminster are one, the resolution asking if a decision on the question as to whether or not a vote should be taken on the question as to whether we would be prepared to back up the lock-out men in Vancouver, by taking action on their behalf, by a strike ballot.

A mass meeting of the men of the port of New Westminster was called the night of Friday, June 7 and an authorization ordering the men by secret ballot to express their opinion whether or not we would put ourselves in the hands of the central board and have them issue a call for us to strike if the prospects of early reconciliation between the lock-out men in Vancouver and the Shipping Federation could not be brought about.

By a vote of 290 to 55, the men decided to stand by for a strike call. During the following week every effort has been made to bring about negotiations between the men in Vancouver and Shipping Federation and to assist in this effort, the outlying ports elected a committee to intercede with the Shipping Federation on behalf of these lock-out men.

This latter committee was granted an interview with the Shipping Federation on Friday, June 14. The Shipping Federation was definitely opposed to any form of recognition of the V.D.W.W., pointing out to the committee that the only possible contact those men locked out could now make with their employers was to go back as individuals, forsake their organization, and take a membership in a new organization, alleged by the Shipping Federation now to be the only organized body with which they seek to deal, known as the Canadian Waterfront Workers Association.

Obviously this decision could not possibly be considered by the delegation or the men represented, because it denied them the right to determine for themselves to what kind of organization they desired to belong.

When this impasse was reached, the committee reported the results of their interview to the central board of the national group and the result was that the board came to the conclusion that the time had now arrived to exercise the power which was vested in them by virtue of the strike mandate given them by their affiliated groups to issue a general strike call in the industry.

This call was dispatched to all organizations on Friday, June 14, asking that the cessation of all work be brought about at 7 a.m. Saturday, June 15th. All work in New Westminster was stopped — picket lines organized and dispatched to the various points of contract along the whole river front this morning. There is nothing working. Today has been very quiet.

The situation thus presented puts the basis fairly up to the Shipping Federation, to agree to open up negotiations with the representatives of all the men involved.

This condition being acceded to, the road is immediately opened to end the strike in New Westminster.[26]

Longshoremen on the Fraser River would only return to work if negotiations convened with the striking Vancouver longshoremen, according to strike committee members Fred Jackson, Stanley Blake, and William Clitheroe. It was not the answer that Hume and his city council wanted to hear.

The decision of New Westminster longshoremen to continue on with the strike, in sympathy with the dispute between the Shipping Federation and the Vancouver and District Waterfront Workers Association, obliged Hume, as the city's top official protective of business and finances, to take decisive action. He was no longer objectively standing on the sidelines but became the main protagonist behind a concerted effort to get the port running again as quickly as possible, using whatever means were necessary. It was completely self-interest on the city's part. Pacific Coast Terminals, the largest of the waterfront employers, had been sold out of trusteeship to bondholders for $750,000, and was in no position to offer leadership — Valentine Quinn was merely the operating manager and appeared now to be taking direction and orders from Hume. The City of New Westminster was paying $10,500 interest every year on debenture guarantees and stood to lose even more money if Pacific Coast Terminals slipped into bankruptcy. It was imperative that a strike of longshoremen not be allowed to interfere with shipping traffic for any length of time.

To this end, Hume called a mass meeting at the Queen's Park Arena on 21 June 1935 to explain his perspective on the situation and gain consent from interested citizens for a definite plan of action. The

The Port of . . .  New Westminster

MASS
MEETING
OF CITIZENS
QUEEN'S PARK ARENA
TONIGHT
AT 8.00 P.M.

A Crisis having arisen with respect to our Shipping, threatening closing of our Mills and Other Industries, the Mayor and City Council, representing the Citizens, Owners of all our Waterfront, have called a General Meeting of the Citizens.

BUSINESS:

To review the local Strike situation and to consider what action would be in the best interests of the Port.

This is a most important Meeting. Every Citizen is directly interested. EVERYONE SHOULD ATTEND.

By Order,

F. J. HUME, Mayor

next morning, a longshore delegation consisting of Charles Wright, Henry Sabourin, Robert Chapman, John E. Brown, and Frank Neilson informed a special meeting of city council, the harbour commissioners, and shipping representatives, of the intention to stay out on the sympathy strike.[27] Hume requested once and then twice for the striking longshoremen to go back to work. They declined and left the room. If they had said yes, the New Westminster Waterfront Workers Association would have still remained the recognized union on the waterfront. Hume and the city council, however, entertained another option.

Royal City Waterfront Workers Association

In a closed meeting afterwards, John Shaw of Pacific Coast Terminals and Captain John Macmillan of Empire Stevedoring reported that another hiring hall had been opened by the Royal City Waterfront Workers Association. This newly-formed labour organization, through the leadership of Arthur Gore and Leonard Bonwick, was willing to provide men for longshore work and a signed agreement was in the offing. Ever the opportunist, Leonard Bonwick had been secretary of the New Westminster Waterfront Workers Union in the two years leading up to the strike and disagreed with the rash action taken by the majority of his fellow longshoremen. He represented the fifty men who had voted against striking in the first place and wanted to continue working. The parties agreed to the following conditions for three years:

> *There is to be one Hall in New Westminster.*
>
> *One Dispatcher hereinafter named [Leonard Bonwick], and his Assistant to be chosen by himself later.*
>
> *Working hours and conditions as per present Agreement now in operation on the Vancouver waterfront.*
>
> *For the purpose of determining whether or not wages shall be increased or decreased, the parties hereto agree they will take into consideration in the case of the longshoremen, conditions which directly concern the welfare and livelihood of the men, and in the case of the employer, conditions which directly affect the well-being and prosperity of the port and shipping and lumber generally.*[28]

Once private companies resumed operations, civic officials committed to providing protection to any persons entering or working on the docks. The mayor himself would be the arbitrator of any future dispute between longshoremen and the shipping companies.

A proclamation under Fred Hume's name on the newspaper's front page announced that the city, as owner of the waterfront lands, no longer recognized the striking union and announced the new arrangements:

> *All efforts of the city council to conclude a satisfactory agreement with the local Longshoremen's Union have resulted in failure. The council was this morning notified of the union's decision to remain on strike.*
>
> *Public notice is hereby given that [the New] Westminster Waterfront Workers Association will be no longer recognized by the City of New Westminster.*
>
> *The city council on behalf of the corporation has given official sanction to an association of waterfront workers which was this day organized with headquarters at Clarkson and McKenzie streets, and registration of men is being there proceeded with. The officials in charge will receive applications until the necessary number of men — preferably local residents — have been registered.*
>
> *The decision of the city council is officially supported by New Westminster Harbor Commissioners and the executive heads of shipping and river industries. We appeal for and expect the co-operation and endorsement of all fair-minded citizens.*[29]

Harry Sullivan personally went to Victoria to register and file the necessary documentation for the newly-formed waterfront association.

A large number of unemployed men were on the city's relief rolls and the Royal City Waterfront Workers Association's charter explicitly confined hiring to residents of New Westminster. Many longshoremen in the New Westminster Waterfront Workers Association resided outside city limits and thus were no longer eligible for employment, even if they wanted to join the new labour body. In that sense, the Royal City Waterfront Workers Association was more a city union rather than a company union. The New Westminster Board of Trade unequivocally supported "the Mayor and City Council in the endeavour to keep the Port of New Westminster open to shipping activities."[30] Hume and some trusted councillors were clearly calling the shots in response to the militant action by shut-out longshoremen.

By the last week of June 1935, the port was open again using longshoremen provided by Leonard Bonwick and the Royal City

Waterfront Workers Association. The first fifty were rushed into Pacific Coast Terminals on the morning of 25 June in police cars, taking picketing strikers by surprise.[31] The SS *Leeds City* immediately started loading and took on 250,000 feet of lumber over six hours before topping off for departure to the United Kingdom. New ships arrived in the port. A telegram sent to American authorities reported seven gangs working at New Westminster, with one hundred men including fifteen former employees of the New Westminster Waterfront Workers Association.[32] Clearly, solidarity with the striking union's cause was problematic for some longshoremen. City police, twenty-six in number, and sixty temporarily-enlisted provincial constables kept the pickets at a safe distance with regular patrols. A high-wire fence was installed around the entire perimeter of Pacific Coast Terminals.

The police repulsed at least one try by strikers to rush the entrance to the docks but, for the most part, affairs were kept quiet by minimizing contact between the strikers and replacement workers. Sleeping and eating accommodation were provided so, once escorted inside, working longshoremen did not have to cross picket lines to leave. The city delivered one hundred and ten cots, one hundred and thirty-five mattresses, and two hundred and ninety blankets for use by the strikebreakers and police.[33] A newspaper reporter grimly remarked that the place looked like a fortress. The names of known scab longshoremen were chalked onto sidewalks and fences by strikers manning the pickets. On 27 June, loading of lumber onto the SS *King Lud* resumed at Fraser Mills and the wharves there were soon back in operation. The Royal City Waterfront Workers Association advertised for another one hundred and fifty men to apply for membership and employment, in order to extend loading from No. 1 to No. 2, No. 3, and No. 4 docks, thereby returning Pacific Coast Terminals to full capacity. The uptake was well-subscribed amongst those hard on their luck and out of work.

Arrests and Legal Actions

Any attempt to interfere with access or intimidate replacement longshoremen invited a swift police reaction and, in some cases, arrests. Harry Sullivan, acting as prosecutor, represented the city in the assize courts. Individual strikers were criminalized by charges for assault, robbery, use of threatening language, damage to property, and trespass. Jacob Unger, a replacement 'scab' worker, was relieved of $30 during an altercation outside the Edison Theatre on Columbia Street. Harry Sullivan defended a charge laid by striker Arthur Martin against Arthur Gore, the Royal City Waterfront Workers Association's president, who pulled a gun to defend himself against a couple of threatening strikers, even though police determined that the gun was unloaded and unworkable.[34] One longshoreman claimed that he was never so well-off as during the strike. For him, scabs were just fair game.

In another case, Fred Perchie and his sons, Leonard and Willis, the first two striking longshoremen, went to trial for allegedly putting a burning cross on the lawn of a replacement worker's house during the night. The actual culprits were identified later as a couple teenagers playing a prank with no other intent.[35] William McKay, a former member of the New Westminster Waterfront Workers Association who had returned to work and joined the Royal City Waterfront Workers Association, awoke to find an oil-rag soaked 'X' cross, not a Christian one, on fire in front of his house. An investigation by the deputy fire marshal and a 'reliable' witness coming forward enabled the police and Harry Sullivan to frame the wrong persons for the crime. All, however, were not entirely innocent. Striking longshoremen, when possible, resorted to minor acts of retaliation: putting nails on the roadway to puncture tires, cornering replacement workers in tight spots in superior numbers, and placing anonymous phone calls to wives and families when male earners were working the docks. The tactics were more nuisance than effective.

The normal routine of picketing, day after day, had clearly not interrupted the New Westminster port enough to make a substantial difference. Captain Ed Taylor observed, "Unless they were involved in it personally, I don't think too much was said about it because the work continued regardless of whether the strike was on. They had enough strikebreakers to do all the work so there was no slowdown on the waterfront."[36]

The replacement longshoremen kept behind the lines were eventually allowed to go home and by August, the fortress-like fences and additional buildings were dismantled. The private companies reimbursed the city the full $8,000 for the extraordinary strike expenses through a special levy on inward and outward cargo.[37] The police cordon was withdrawn and the contingent of special constables disbanded, with only a handful of provincial police left inside at Pacific Coast Terminals.

The strike in New Westminster never reached the violent dimensions seen in Vancouver or US ports, though periodic shoving and shouting matches broke out between picketing strikers and longshoremen attempting to enter or leave, mostly in the next two months when the strike dragged on and frustration mounted. Alderman Harry Sullivan petitioned in a mean-spirited way that the strikers and their families should be denied relief payments from the city because they were able but unwilling to work.

Police Intervene

Pressure mounted toward the major event that eventually brought an end to picketing on the New Westminster waterfront through deliberate police involvement. On 21 August 1935, a group of strikers shouted 'Scabs' to a truck driving into No. 4 dock at Pacific Coast Terminals and a person nicknamed 'Frenchy' jumped off and started to chase and punch one of the individuals. A general fight ensued between the strikers and working longshoremen. The police were called, though Frenchy and the situation had calmed down before they arrived on the scene. Nonetheless, New Westminster's Chief Constable, Peter Bruce, decided to put strict restrictions on picketing and issued a standing 'move along' order on all strikers, whom he blamed for the ongoing disturbances.[38] A collection of rough-plank shacks and abandoned vehicles used by the strikers for shelter were removed on Bruce's instructions. The strikers resorted to using tents.

By the end of the month, those longing for a settlement to the waterfront dispute expressed the opinion, "The strike has settled down to an endurance test — a test between the ability of longshoremen to endure being on relief and the ability of the shipping interests to continue carrying the heavy financial burden involved in working cargo with the personnel at their disposal."[39]

At the start, the striking union counted three hundred and five regular members and ninety-five casuals. At least sixty of those men had returned to work with the Royal City Waterfront Workers Association and with each passing week, a few more went back. With numbers dwindling, the union had to provide enough men for pickets at two or more locations: Fraser Mills, the long main waterfront in front of Pacific Coast Terminals, and the new wharf operated by New Westminster Dock and Forwarding Company on the eastern end near the New Westminster railway bridge. Summer was coming to a close and the autumn rains and cooler temperatures were around the corner. An outright winner was still unclear since neither side appeared willing to concede.

Arrival	Ship	Destination	Agent
20 Aug	SS *Atlanta City*	London, Liverpool, Avonmouth	B.W. Greer & Son Ltd.
20 Aug	SS *Askre*	United Kingdom	Canadian Shipping Co.
20 Aug	SS *Anglo-Indian*	Australia	Canadian Transport Co.
20 Aug	SS *Romulus*	Australia	Canadian Trading Co
21 Aug	MS *Parrakoola*	Brisbane, Sydney, Newcastle, Adelaide, Melbourne	Empire Shipping Co.
22 Aug	SS *Gracia*	London, Liverpool, Glasgow	Balfour, Guthrie & Co.
24 Aug	SS *Olympus*	United Kingdom	Anglo Canadian Shipping Co.
25 Aug	SS *Welch City*	London, Liverpool	Reardon Smith Line (Canada) Ltd.
27 Aug	SS *Fukuyo Maru*	Australia	Yamashita Shipping Co.
27 Aug	SS *Zurich Moor*	United Kingdom	Canadian Transport Co.
27 Aug	SS *Themoni*	US Atlantic coast	Empire Shipping Co.
27 Aug	SS *Phaex*	Hull, Grangemouth	Anglo Canadian Shipping Co.
27 Aug	SS *Tacoma Star* *	Liverpool, Glasgow, London, Southampton, Rotterdam, Newcastle	American Mail Line
27 Aug	SS *Helmspey*	Australia	Yamashita Shipping Co.
28 Aug	SS *Dionyssios Strathos*	Shanghai, Hankow	Ocean Shipping Co.

Arrival	Ship	Destination	Agent
30 Aug	MS *Pacific Enterprise*	London, Liverpool, Glasgow, Manchester	Furness Pacific Line Ltd.
31 Aug	SS *Laurits Swenson*	Liverpool, London, Hull, Oslo	Anglo Canadian Shipping Co.
1 Sep	SS *Ravnaas*	India	Canadian Transport Co.
3 Sep	SS *Great City*	Immingham, Hull	Reardon Smith Line (Canada) Ltd
3 Sep	SS *Janeta*	Australia	Canadian Transport Co.
3 Sep	MS *Drechtdyk*	Liverpool, Glasgow, Southampton, London, Rotterdam	Royal Mail Lines Ltd.
3 Sep	MS *Titanian*	Sydney	Anglo Canadian Shipping Co.
4 Sep	MS *San Diego*	Havre, Dunkirk, Antwerp, Rotterdam, Bordeaux	Empire Shipping Co.
4 Sep	SS *Olympus*	Liverpool, Manchester	Anglo Canadian Shipping Co.
4 Sep	SS *Meiwu Maru*	Yokohama, Kobe, Osaka	Yamashita Shipping Co.
4 Sep	SS *King Stephen*	Australia	Canadian Transport Co.
5 Sep	SS *Bradglen*	United Kingdom	Anglo Canadian Shipping Co.
10 Sep	SS *Lochgoll*	Liverpool, Southampton, London, Rotterdam	Royal Mail Lines Ltd.
10 Sep	SS *Hakushika Maru*	Yokohama, Kobe, Osaka	Yamashita Shipping Co.
12 Sep	SS *Induna*	Sydney	Anglo Canadian Shipping Co.
13 Sep	SS *Houston City*	London, Liverpool	Reardon Smith Line (Canada) Ltd.
15 Sep	SS *Nansenville*	Liverpool, London, Hull, Oslo	Anglo Canadian Shipping Co.

Arrival	Ship	Destination	Agent
17 Sep	MS *Pacific Trader*	London, Liverpool, Glasgow, Manchester	Furness Pacific Line Ltd.
17 Sep	SS *Tuscaloosa City*	London, Liverpool, Avonmouth, Swansea	B.W. Greer & Son Ltd.
18 Sep	SS *A Steamer*	United Kingdom	B.W. Greer & Son Ltd.
18 Sep	SS *Minerva*	Australia	Anglo-Canadian Shipping Co.
19 Sep	MS *Hikawa Maru*	Yokohama, Kobe, Osaka	B.W. Greer & Son Ltd.
19 Sep	SS *Ango-Peruvian*	United Kingdom	Canadian Transport Co.
19 Sep	SS *Sinnington Court*	Shanghai	Ocean Shipping Co.
19 Sep	SS *Delcroy*	Montreal	Canadian Transport Co.
23 Sep	SS *Forthbridge*	Shanghai, Dairen	Ocean Shipping Co.
23 Sep	MS *Damsterdyk*	Liverpool, Glasgow, Southampton, London, Rotterdam	Royal Mail Lines Ltd.
23 Sep	SS *Gothic Star*	United Kingdom	American Mail Line Ltd.
24 Sep	MS *Boren*	Australia	Empire Shipping Co.
25 Sep	SS *Atlanticos*	Atlantic coast	Empire Shipping Co.
25 Sep	SS *Oregon Maru*	Yokohama, Kobe, Osaka	Yamashita Shipping Co.

Steamships and motor ships present at Pacific Coast Terminals during the climatic finale for picketing by striking longshoremen in the five weeks between 20 August and 26 September 1935

The SS *Tacoma Star* was the first ship at the New Westminster Dock and Forwarding Company's new wharf near the New Westminster railway bridge, and began loading apples from the Okanagan on 23 September after the New Westminster police intervention on the main waterfront. As shown, the docks remained active and busy with shipping, using men from the Royal City Waterfront Workers Association to load and unload throughout this time, notwithstanding the longshore strike.

Source: Pacific Coast Terminals sailing lists no. 33 (20 August 1935), no. 34 (27 August 1935), no. 35 (3 September 1935), no. 36 (10 September 1935), no. 37 (17 September 1935), no. 38 (23 September 1935)

Mayor Fred Hume, coincidentally, happened to be chair of the New Westminster Police Commissioners. At city hall, he decided to force the issue and called in the chief constable for a solution. Alderman Harry Sullivan was also present.

Peter Bruce emerged from that informal meeting with renewed determination to stop the picketing. He may have even been given explicit instructions. His small police force had been taxed to the utmost during the months of the strike, responding to reports of crime and disturbances around the docks and throughout the city. New Westminster police cars were not even equipped with two-way radios, for which $2,345 had been requested in the new budget, and the police department's trials with a borrowed central transmitter of limited range only started a few months before.[40] Wherever the police responded, striking longshoremen were usually involved in some way, hassling scabs or intimidating those believed to be supporting them. With the docks so close to the downtown core in New Westminster, such behaviour was disruptive to commerce and citizens going about everyday business. Restoration of law and order was a high priority, both for the police and civic officials. The striking New Westminster Waterfront Workers Association naturally became the target as patience ran out.

The date of chosen action on the part of the city and its police force was 3 September 1935. Although defying the description of full-fledged battle akin to what happened three-and-a-half months earlier at Ballantyne Pier in Vancouver, the 'showdown' at Pacific Coast Terminals was the most significant event during the strike in terms of confrontation between striking longshoremen and the forces arrayed against them. Most strikers present that day probably knew something was brewing. It was not exactly a secret. Chief Constable Peter Bruce, no doubt with Fred Hume's quiet encouragement, told the press, "We have done everything but pray to them, and they will not stop congregating. So from now on every picket will be arrested and charged."[41] On the union side, word went out that extra support was needed. Longshoremen living in parts of Vancouver, Burnaby, and elsewhere travelled by streetcar to New Westminster on that day.

Bolstered by these reinforcements, a large crowd of nearly one hundred and fifty persons assembled in front of the entrances to the various docks at Pacific Coast Terminals during the morning of

3 September 1935. Headlights were reportedly broken on at least one vehicle, and stones picked up and thrown by some strikers — just the pretext that the police needed.

Longshoremen congregate around the strike captain's 'office' outside Pacific Coast Terminals during the six-month-long 1935 strike on the New Westminster waterfront

On the far left is Daniel 'Tango' Barrow, on the roof is Arthur Phillips, on the far right is George Zablosky, and the two men inside the vehicle are thought to be George and Luke Phelan. George Phelan subsequently became vice president of the Royal City Waterfront Workers Association, working alongside president Arthur Gore and business agent Leonard Bonwick. Later, he became a foreman. This photograph was taken before 3 September 1935, when Barrow, Phillips, and Zablosky were arrested during police raids against pickets on the instructions of Chief Constable Peter Bruce. Soon after, the city hired a junk dealer to haul away for scrap the abandoned vehicles used by the strikers near the docks.
Source: Lena West

Like at Ballantyne Pier, Peter Bruce and the New Westminster police force were prepared and waiting. Verbal instructions were given to the strikers to disperse and keep moving. The police were legally required to do so before acting with applied force. The strikers defiantly stood their ground. Unlike Colonel William Wasbrough Foster's paramilitary

Vancouver Police, New Westminster police were not trained in the use of tear gas, and mounted horse units were never employed. Fred Hume also preferred to keep a low-profile during the crack-down. An astute politician, Hume still considered himself a friend of working men and cultivated that image. Some longshoremen and their wives had even voted for him in the previous civic election.

A flying squad of police led by Sergeant Eric Edwin Anderson worked its way around the crowd and swooped in to seize individuals shouting and pushing the most forcefully at entrances to docks No. 1 and No. 4 during several raids. It was not random and the police had been watching beforehand to identify those persons directing or inciting others in the crowd. Forty-nine-year-old Daniel 'Tango' Barrow, with his big frame and loud voice, was easy to spot. He was a hatch tender, so the men looked toward him for leadership. Barrow and his compatriot, George Zablosky, were immediately picked out in the first sortie. A second launch into the crowd netted some older men from Vancouver and the younger Elof Per Lars Blixt. Blixt, one month away from his thirtieth birthday, was born in Surrey to Swedish parents and was active in the union as someone not shy about expressing his opinions. He was later a well-known figure on the ILWU Local 502 executive and as the local's president.

Sergeant Eric Anderson, a veteran policeman, had been chosen for his experience and steadiness. Born in Langley to a Swedish father and mother from Ontario, he had been with the New Westminster police force since 1915. With his catch in hand, Anderson and his squad assumed defensive positions. Formed in a square, the police then began prodding and tapping angry strikers on the head with batons to move back and not interfere with the arrested men. Spectators dockside rushed to see. Four provincial police constables still onsite and other police on hand restrained large numbers of working scab longshoremen inside Pacific Coast Terminals from entering the fray, some of whom declared loudly an intent to 'clean up' the crowd outside. Obviously, there were some scores to settle from previous encounters. The two sides were kept apart. The crowd of striking longshoremen, described by Sergeant Anderson after the event as 'ugly' at times, gradually broke down into smaller and smaller groups and dissipated over the next hour or two. Obscenities were hurled at the police as individuals left.

Injuries were relatively minor, while everyone's ego was just a little bruised. The police had several of their friends under arrest and striking longshoremen were powerless to influence the situation.

For ILWU Local 502 members, 3 September 1935 is a date worthy of commemoration and remembrance for the union and New Westminster. Some might even dare to call it the 'Showdown at Pacific Coast Terminals' or maybe slyly 'Confused Tuesday'. In reality, the event was a police intervention orchestrated by the mayor and police chief on a large group of unwitting strikers. Though the contest was unequal, the city's longshoremen stood up for the right to choose which union represented them on the waterfront and maintained solidarity with strikers in nearby Vancouver — the reason they had walked off the docks in the first place.

The real stories from ordinary longshoremen on that day manning the pickets and inside the docks, which would add colour and the human perspective, are largely gone. Retiree Norm Andresen remarked, "You know, it is too bad that this [oral history project] was not started thirty years ago. You had all the old guys from the '30s and '40s."[42] The old-timers would have recounted great exploits, some of which might or might not have been true.

On 3 September 1935, the strikers never held the initiative. The whole operation was instigated in a very staged manner by the police with one purpose in mind: to put a final end to picketing. The confrontation outside the docks represented the first tactical move to achieve this strategic aim. The courts would do the rest.

In all, twenty-one striking longshoremen entered police custody on 3 September 1935. After being photographed and fingerprinted, they were charged with 'watching and besetting' others not to work, which fell under the broader offence of intimidation. After a very cold and uncomfortable night crowded in jail cells, the accused were brought in front of police court and released on promises to appear again a week later before police magistrate Harry G. Johnston.[43] Gordon Wismer, a lawyer and provincial politician, offered to defend them free of charge.

The striking longshoremen raised several hundred dollars during a sanctioned tag day and received additional monies from external donors. A union or labour body could apply to the city for an officially-sanctioned day set aside for public fundraising, especially during times of strikes. People giving donations received a tag or badge showing their support for the cause. The money raised was usually set aside for legal expenses or distributed to needy families for buying basic essentials. In fact, the permission granted by Fred Hume was for the

Name	Place of Residence
Harry Harding	Burnaby
George Zablosky	New Westminster (Queensborough)
E. Clark	South Westminster
Daniel Barrow	New Westminster
Arthur Phillips	New Westminster
Alex Cameron	Vancouver
George Arter	Vancouver
Clayton Clark	New Westminster
Peter Winstall	New Westminster
Walter Quissy	Vancouver
Jack Matthews	Vancouver
Elof Blixt	South Westminster
James Stoddart	New Westminster
John Alaric	New Westminster
Robert Archibald	New Westminster
John Lynch	New Westminster
Ian Thorburn	New Westminster
Leslie Stead	New Westminster
Del Halladay	New Westminster
Winfred Tillotson	New Westminster
Thomas Cleghorn	Surrey

Names and places of residence for the twenty-one striking longshoremen arrested by the New Westminster Police Department during the 'great grab' at Pacific Coast Terminals on 3 September 1935
Whether or not the action was sanctioned by Mayor Fred Hume, their arrest and appearance before a magistrate in police court represented indirect intimidation of the union. Ironically, they were the ones being charged with intimidation.
Source: British Columbian (4 September 1935), "21 Strikers Facing Charge of Besetting"

striking longshoremen to hold a tag day on Saturday, 7 September 1935, "assisting them to outfit their children for school."[44] The recent arrests added a greater impetus for donations.

Parleys behind the scenes led to withdrawal of the charges against the remanded strikers in return for a halt to picketing. Representatives from the New Westminster Waterfront Workers Association had come to realize the futility of this course of action anyway. In spite of repeated confident pronouncements in the central strike committee's newsletter *Ship and Dock*, the likelihood of the strike being won on the picket line was increasingly remote. Hume and the private companies possessed enough longshoremen dispatched by the Royal City Waterfront Workers Association to keep cargo moving across the docks. The last remaining chance was political intervention to effect a final settlement allowing the striking longshoremen to return to work.

The hoped-for attention from the government in Ottawa came in the form of a judicial inquiry by a Supreme Court of Canada judge, Henry Hague Davis. Davis had only been sitting on the highest bench since his appointment in January 1935, though he had two decades of legal experience in Toronto and came from the Ontario Court of Appeal. Justice Davis arrived in Vancouver on 16 September 1935, ready to hear from the opposing sides.[45] Public hearings took place at Moose Hall in Vancouver over a three-week period. Witnesses recounted the causes and events of the strike and their particular perspectives on matters. Stanley Blake, from the New Westminster Waterfront Workers Association, testified on 21 September. He objected to longshoremen gangs being sent to Vancouver to work ships and, when asked why longshoremen in New Westminster were on strike, replied they were in sympathy with the striking Vancouver longshoremen.

In the final sessions, Ivan Emery, the vocal president of the Longshoremen and Transport Workers of Canada, squared off against the Shipping Federation's chief counsel, John Wallace de Beque Farris, who would be later appointed to the Canadian senate, when the latter asserted that the union's leadership and members had acted irresponsibly. Emery himself had been arrested during the conflagration at Ballantyne Pier for inciting a riot and leading an unlawful assembly, receiving from a police court the sentence of three months in prison.

A private hearing with Davis was unable to settle the differences, which were now firmly entrenched. In his final report, Justice Davis concluded, "A careful review of the evidence has satisfied me that the stage was so set by the leaders of the men, and the men so much under their influence, that what otherwise might seem harsh and abrupt action by the Shipping Federation was under all circumstances necessary for the assertion of their rights and the preservation of their interests."[46] For all intents and purposes, the striking longshoremen were blamed for their own situation and the Shipping Federation vindicated. Whether Davis was correct or biased in reaching that judgment is less important than the sobering effect that the judicial findings had on the will of the shut-out longshoremen to continue on with the strike. Capitulation, not victory, was the viable choice before them.

The end to the longshoremen's strike in New Westminster came sooner than in Vancouver and elsewhere. Informal discussions between company officials and the strike committee carried on which, at least in public, were not acknowledged. In the interval, small numbers of longshoremen made the personal choice to 'jump the gun' and go back to work by joining the Royal City Waterfront Workers Association, if the management would have them.[47] William Clitheroe admitted to at least fifty-eight returning. This figure was coincidentally near the number of casuals registered with the union before the strike. There was now a surplus of longshoremen for the three to four hundred available jobs.

The decision of the New Westminster Waterfront Workers Association to end the sympathy strike was first learned on 27 November 1935 in police court. Harry Sullivan, representing the city, applied to have charges of obstruction and use of insulting language withdrawn against two striking longshoremen, Edward Quinn and William Saul.[48] The Vancouver and District Waterfront Workers Association called off its strike against the Shipping Federation on 7 December 1935, and sympathetic unions affiliated with the Longshoremen and Water Transport Workers of Canada formally returned two days later.[49] City residents, private employers, and scores of longshoremen in New Westminster were relieved that the long strike, lasting almost six months, was finally over. Normal, however, could not describe the situation now pertaining on the waterfront.

Work Resumes After the Strike

The strike's legacy clouded relations between New Westminster longshoremen, those with constant work and those left without. In February 1936, the city sold a plot of land on Tenth Street for the Royal City Waterfront Workers Association to erect a purpose-built hiring and dispatch hall, at an estimated cost of $6,000.[50] Applications for membership were vetted and the residency requirement of the charter rigorously enforced; any longshoremen hired had to live in New Westminster. After the strike, the practice of interchanging gangs between Vancouver and New Westminster stopped due to opposition from the city council.[51] The experience of returning must have been humbling for once-defiant and combative men forced to beg for jobs from the same men they had so maligned and threatened during the strike. Seniority dated from the time of joining the Royal City Waterfront Workers Association. This ranking favoured the original strikebreakers and scabs. For longshoremen, seniority, job classification, and type of cargo determined the respective wage rates paid over and above the standard rate.

	Regular Time	Overtime	Non Meal Hours	Other Meals Hours
General Cargo				
general labour on ship	0.90	1.35	1.35	2.02
hatch tender	1.00	1.45	1.45	2.12
double winch driver	1.00	1.45	1.45	2.12
dock labour	0.86	1.29	1.29	1.94
Special Commodities				
hatch tender	1.00	1.45	1.45	2.12
single winch driver	1.00	1.45	1.45	2.12
hold and sling men	1.00	1.45	1.45	2.12
double winch driver	1.10	1.55	1.55	2.22
loader and piler	0.86	1.39	1.39	2.04
dock trucker	0.86	1.29	1.29	1.94
Creosoted Products				
hatch tender	1.10	1.55	1.55	2.22

	Regular Time	Overtime	Non Meal Hours	Other Meals Hours
double winch driver	1.10	1.55	1.55	2.22
side runner	1.10	1.55	1.55	2.22
single winch driver	1.00	1.45	1.45	2.12
sling and hold men	1.00	1.45	1.45	2.12
loader and oiler	0.96	1.39	1.39	2.04
dock trucker	0.86	1.29	1.29	1.94
Lumber, Logs, and Pile Products				
hatch tender	1.10	1.55	1.55	2.22
double winch driver	1.10	1.55	155	2.22
side runner	1.10	1.55	1.55	2.22
single winch driver	1.00	1.45	1.45	2.12
sling and hold men	1.00	1.45	1.45	2.12
loader and oiler	0.96	1.39	1.39	2.04
dock trucker	0.86	1.29	1.29	1.94
High Explosives and Damaged Cargo				
hatch tender	1.45	2.12		
double winch driver	1.45	2.12		
all other ship labour	1.35	2.02		
all other dock labour	1.29	1.94		

Schedule of hourly wage rates for deep-sea longshoremen working in Vancouver and New Westminster, as put into effect in 1936
All figures in Canadian dollars
Special commodities included sacked caustic soda, cement, fertilizer, rawhides, single-sacked lime, nitrates, salmon, eggs, bulk salt, and scrap iron in bulk or bales. Bulk cargo included ballast cement, cement-clinker, coal, coke, grain, raw ore, sulfur, and commodities in sacks weighing one hundred and twenty-five pounds or more.
Source: Labour Gazette vol. 36 (1936)

The working longshoremen refused to enroll certain individuals, even though Pacific Terminals and other private employers were ready to have them back. Arthur Gore issued a statement, enshrined in the Royal City Waterfront Workers Association charter, to the press reflecting the prejudice of the independent union toward former strikers:

> Since the formation of this association in June 1935, not one outside gang has ever been brought in, from Vancouver, or anywhere else.
>
> The situation on the waterfront is that members of Royal City Waterfront Workers Association have worked and will continue to work all vessels at the port of New Westminster. As additional men are needed, the association will add to its membership by taking in local residents with the qualifications required by its charter. One of the articles of the charter requires members to be 'submissive to the constituted authority of Canada.' Another article prohibits any form of demonstration, parades, radical methods or affiliation with any radical movement.
>
> Certain unemployed longshoremen have registered for work with the stevedoring companies but cannot or will not subscribe to the principles of our charter above mentioned. Their leaders would like to again dominate our waterfront by formation of an organization opposed to our union. This explains the circulation of false rumours and stories such as that of imported gangs. It is hoped the public will get the facts and not be misled by false rumours or unworthy appeals for sympathy.[52]

There was no love lost between the two groups. In all, one hundred and fifty former longshoremen could not secure work, even when the port was busy with ships and shortages of waterfront labour remained. In many cases, unemployed longshoremen refusing the terms of the new union were classed troublemakers and blacklisted. The Royal City Waterfront Workers Association, still relatively immature, exhibited many features of an accommodating union, much like the Canadian Waterfront Workers Association, subservient to the welfare-capitalism agenda put forth by employers aimed at keeping American-style industrial unionism away.[53]

New Westminster longshoremen and Mayor Fred Hume were invited to the Shipping Federation-sponsored annual picnic outings on Newcastle and Hornby islands, as reward for good and loyal service. A delegation of former strikers left a meeting called by Fred Hume with the government's Western Fair Wage Officer, Frederick Harrison, attending, claiming that the Royal City Waterfront Workers Association was no better than a company union, which never held meetings and lacked any real voice in labour relations with employers.[54] In truth, it was their union that no longer had any place on the working New Westminster waterfront.

More militant longshoremen, in the shunned New Westminster Waterfront Workers Association, who found themselves unemployable banded together. They desperately solicited outside assistance wherever possible.[55] Harry Bridges, during the 1935 strike and after becoming the International Longshoremen's Association Pacific District president, believed that longshoremen in British Columbia were deserving of support. The Longshoremen and Water Transport Workers of Canada formally dissolved, the last issue of its newsletter *Ship and Dock* published in March 1936.[56] Former strikers were left with no organization and little employment.

The much-delayed trial of George Goodwin, a Burnaby longshoreman accused of violently assaulting a man from Surrey on Scott Road, held before crown counsel Harry Sullivan, sparked a little interest and memories of the events from the previous year. William Ney, a replacement worker with the Royal City Waterfront Workers Association, had been badly beaten and robbed of $2.15 by three assailants. Witnesses identified George Goodwin and Harry Oliver, two striking longshoremen. Police magistrate Henry Edmonds had already convicted Harry Oliver in the case and gave him the choice between paying a fifty-dollar fine or two months hard labour. The penniless Oliver took the prison term. George Goodwin was released on $1,000 bail pending trial.

Harry Sullivan was elected alderman again in New Westminster's civic election. Though his role in prosecuting striking longshoremen in the assize courts and setting up a 'scab union' was criticized during a candidates' meeting in Sapperton,[57] Fred Hume, himself returned by acclamation as mayor in 1936, praised his old friend Sullivan publically for his service and was pleased to have him on city council. Neither civic politician paid a significant political price for personal involvement in the waterfront strike. The unemployed longshoremen likely held different views on the matter and choice words for Harry Sullivan's blatant anti-labour crusade. He and the likes of Arthur Gore and Leonard Bonwick in the Royal City Waterfront Workers

Association were the villains of the 1935 waterfront strike in New Westminster, in their perspective.

Stanley Blake, a fraternal delegate attending the International Longshoremen's Association convention in San Pedro during May 1936, outlined the state of affairs on the Fraser River:

> *In Vancouver alone there are no less than five organizations of longshoremen, namely, the Vancouver and District Waterfront Workers Association who were on strike, the coastwise longshoremen and Freight Handlers Association, who also were on strike and are now back on the job, and three scab groups that came into existence during the strike. In each of the other ports such as Victoria and New Westminster, there is in existence two groups: the union men who were on strike and the fink group. There has only been one west coast American ship in the port of New Westminster since the strike was terminated. This was the M.S. Carriso that arrived on April 23rd to load 500 tons of cargo for Stockton, California. It was intended by the employers to work this cargo with five gangs, hoping that it would be quickly loaded before the crew could determine who were the union men.*
>
> *However, we made contact with the ship delegates as soon as she docked and the steam was shut off after about 200 tons had been loaded. We offered to complete loading the ship with Union men, but the offer was turned down and she sailed leaving the balance of the cargo on the dock. The coastwise shipping into this port is practically the same as that in Vancouver. And through the cooperation of Local 38-12, Seattle, we have been able to have our members hired from the hall to work on some of these ships, and if the same cooperation can be extended by other ports, we would have no difficulty in controlling the whole of the work.*
>
> *We are at this time making application for affiliation with the I.L.A. and sincerely believe this to be the logical time for an I.L.A. charter to be issued to this port. Notice should be taken of the fact that the employers are working in conjunction with officials of the All Canadian Congress of Labour in an effort to have this body issue charters to the fink groups. This body, the All Canadian Congress of Labour, is nothing more than a group of legalized scab*

herders who are at this time trying to have legislation passed to the effect that it will be unlawful to place pickets on any job during a strike when members of the All Canadian Congress of Labour have taken the place of the strikers.[58]

The Royal City Waterfront Workers Association was counted among the Canadian scab unions running a fink hall decried by Blake and other unemployed longshoremen. Based on certain resolutions passed at the San Pedro convention, officials of the International Longshoremen's Association promised support for any group of longshoremen seeking application for a charter and a coordinated drive to 'invade British Columbia'.[59] American organizers, including Andy Larson, went north.

The longshoremen in New Westminster outside the Royal City Waterfront Workers Association, in due course, became Local 38-127 in the International Longshoremen's Association. Initially, not enough working longshoremen came forward to meet the minimum number required for a formal application, only four ready to join when at least ten were required.[60] Denied work, affiliated longshoremen stayed unemployed, and many feared they would be discriminated against if their ILA association was known. A meeting held by the Seafarer's Industrial Union included longshoremen from New Westminster to discuss "the local waterfront situation as it affects the men still unemployed, and ways and means of helping the men South of the Line."[61]

WORK, WAGES
and
SELF-RESPECT

JOIN IN THE
BENEFITS
OF THE I.L.A.

LONGSHOREMEN!
The I.L.A. Has Come To New Westminster

Do you know that there is an I.L.A. Charter in New Westminster? Yes, there is! Charter Number 38 127 was issued to this port only a short time ago, but in that short time many of your members have joined up. How many? Well, many more than you think,—so many more that the time has just about come to close our offer to you. The organization of Vancouver and the Island ports is going ahead by leaps and bounds. Don't be left out in the cold!

Remember, the entire Maritime Federation of the Pacific, 40,000 strong, is behind you. The I.L.A. district, both in communications and in their own Northwest Strike Bulletins have assured us that any settlement will include every local in District 38, INCLUDING B.C. LOCALS.

The slogan of the Maritime Federation, "An injury to one is an injury to all," has always been lived up to.

TO THE MEN ON THE JOB:

. . . Do You Want To Be Branded as a "Fink" All Your Life?

Under your company-controlled set-up you have no protection on the job. All you get is speed-up, favoritism, discrimination.

The I.L.A. offers you protection against speed-up, favoritism, and discrimination. It guarantees safe working conditions, equal distribution of work, coast wages ar l conditions, and SELF-RESPECT.

And remember this: the card of a legitimate union is an introduction to any other legitimate union into which you may want to go. Where can you go with your "Fink" card?

This is your chance to be a UNION man, and join in the benefits of the I.L.A.

Opportunity knocks but once
Grasp it while you can:
Join the I.L.A. and
Be a UNION MAN!

Send in the attached form. All information will be kept strictly confidential by the organizer.

STEVEDORING COMPANIES:

The establishment of the I.L.A. is to your benefit. It will put a stop to the chiseling of the ship-owners. It will establish conditions that will allow for better relations between you and the longshoremen. It stands to reason that a strong I.L.A. will mean stabilized contractual relations in B.C. ports.

Company Union Officials:

If you have the welfare of your members at heart, why is it that you have never held a meeting since your union was formed more than six months ago? Are you afraid they may decide to go into the I.L.A. en bloc? It is contended by the promoters of company unionism that this form of organization is not intimidation. If this is so, why have you not called your men together to discuss their position towards the I.L.A.?

TO THE PUBLIC:

A Unionized New Westminster Will Mean a Fuller Life for All!

The unionization of the New Westminster waterfront will be a boon to this port. The six-hour day, and the equal distribution of longshore work will almost double the number of men employed. With the application of these conditions on the U.S. Pacific Coast, San Francisco Local I.L.A. increased its membership from 2500 in 1934 to 4500, with the same comparative increase in all ports. Think what this will mean to the business men and the public generally of New Westminster. The business men of the U.S. Pacific Coast testify to the benefits of the I.L.A. They are solidly behind the strikers. We ask your assistance to carry on our strike. Do not wait for your club or union to talk action. Give your individual assistance. Your donation, large or small, is needed and needed urgently.

Never before have you had a better chance to help organized labor, and incidentally better the welfare of your city.

APPLICATION FORM
(This will be kept strictly confidential)

I,

Address

hereby apply for membership in Local 38 127, I.L.A., New Westminster.

Cut Out and Send to M RYAN 233 MAIN STREET, VANCOUVER, B C

DONATION FORM

M. Ryan,
233 Main St., Vancouver, B.C.

Enclosed please find   Dollars, a donation to Local 38 127, I.L.A., New Westminster.

Address

Name

International Longshoremen's Association organizing literature after the 1936 Pacific Coast District convention

Only a small number of men signed up. Most working longshoremen remained in the Royal City Waterfront Workers Association, which was an independent and unaffiliated union connected to the city.

Source: Library and Archives Canada, RG 27 reel T-2988 vol. 379 file 175

The New Westminster longshoremen applied for an International Longshoremen's Association charter on 8 December 1936 and received 38-127 by the end of that same month. An organizing broadsheet promised to "put a stop to the chiselling of the ship-owners" since "never before have you had a better chance to help organized labour, and incidentally better the welfare of your city."[62] But, even the cachet of the International Longshoremen's Association could not supplant the privileged standing of the Royal City Waterfront Workers Association accorded by the private companies and city officials.

Signed members increased from twenty-two in January 1937 to a mere sixty, four months later. New Westminster delegate A.G. Beer presented an organizational plan for ILA Local 38-127 at the Pacific Coast District convention in Seattle on 11 May 1937:

1. Steady organizational work among the company men on the waterfront.
2. Build up allied unions, warehousemen, checkers, truck drivers, etc.
3. Maintain steady line of propaganda through all available channels, especially the Joint Waterfront Paper.
4. Open an ILA office when funds and organizational progress warrants.
5. All unemployed members at present in the ILA who are not active in organizational work and are not willing to cooperate along these lines, to be dropped from membership.
6. A Joint Organizational Committee consisting of two members from the ILA, two from the New Westminster and District Waterfront Workers Association, and two from the Warehousemen's Union to be set up, to plan and carry out organizational work. Those appointed to this committee should be in a position to give a maximum of time to organizational work.[63]

These wilderness days tested the resolve of the most militant and radical because resentment naturally built up. Joe Labinsky, a working longshoreman from Surrey, alerted the police to the presence of two sticks of dynamite and a length of fuse put under the outside of the

Royal City Waterfront Workers Association hall on Tenth Street, though the culprit was never indentified.[64] Co-existence mingled with animosity.

New Westminster's port recovered from the dislocations and ill feelings of the longshore unrest and attained new heights of cargo handling and business for the city. Consolidated Mining and Smelting purchased Pacific Coast Terminals from bondholders and incorporated under a new name, Pacific Coast Terminals Company Limited.[65] The reorganized company cancelled all outstanding debts and issued common shares capitalized at $600,000. Assessments to the Shipping Federation on metals handled by the company and its employed longshoremen started to be paid.[66] Waterfront work picked up. According to Valentine Quinn, labour relations were governed by the agreement in place since the strike:

> Our Longshoremen's Association, The Royal City Waterfront Workers Association have no outside affiliations whatever, and have a three-year contract with the City of New Westminster, B.C., the several Stevedoring Companies operating in the Port, the Consolidated Mining & Smelting Co. of Canada Ltd., who ship about 300,000 tons of cargo a year over our Docks, and also with this Company.
>
> This contract which has still about two years to run has been conscientiously observed by all parties thereto and there appears to be every present reason to anticipate that the obligations of the several parties to this agreement will continue to be discharged for the balance of the contract term.[67]

Civic officials were still actively involved despite the change in management and ownership at Pacific Coast Terminals. Another poor financial year in 1936 marked by high operating costs and 'extravagances', led to a parting of ways with the services of Valentine Quinn, who received a golden handshake of $10,000 for one year.[68] Given that the average longshoreman made less than a dollar an hour, this payout was very generous indeed. William Blackstock Lanigan took over operating management of the company directly as president. He also probably questioned why Doug Quinn, Valentine Quinn's son, was the assistant general manager.

Pacific Coast Terminals, under new staff and leadership, turned a profit of $80,011.04 exclusive of taxes by the end of 1937, the first since the company started operations. A steady export trade for commodities shipped from the Fraser River made the financial turnaround possible:

	Ships	Exports (in tons)	Imports (in tons)	Value (CDN$)
1935	434	710,939	29,264	$22,706,441
1936	525	977,163	30,856	$34,767,000
1937	450	868,026	25,442	$39,739,443
1938	493	865,127	22,182	$27,493,550
1939	509	1,051,207	20,465	(unavailable)

Source: New Westminster Harbour Commissioners annual report

Strikes by American longshoremen in several Pacific coast ports diverted shipping to New Westminster because the Fraser River was unaffected by labour unrest. The Shipping Federation reassured one concerned banker, "Contractual relations are in effect at all of the principal ports in British Columbia, between ship operators and properly organized Canadian unions, to handle all longshore work. These undertakings are being carried out and the unions concerned state that they will continue to work all cargo offered regardless of its origin or destination." [69]

As an independent union, the Royal City Waterfront Workers Association was unaffiliated. The problem was that the Americans were not sending ships to British Columbia for fear they would not be loaded by longshoremen supporting the strike in the United States. In March 1937, the Maritime Federation of the Pacific Coast and the International Longshoremen's Association executive in San Francisco declared the port at New Westminster 'open and fair'.[70] That designation meant American ships could come to the Fraser River without interference owing to labour unrest. Shipment of apples doubled, while lead and zinc bar metals showed healthy gains. Derricks and ship slings were used to load straight from railcars.

The private employers engaged the Royal City Waterfront Workers Association to provide gangs for working the ships and paid overtime in rush and congested periods. In 1937, the prevailing wage rate rose

Longshoremen loading boxed apples
from railcars to ship by sling loads during the 1930s
Agricultural produce came from the Okanagan and Fraser Valley, then
mostly went to the United Kingdom through the port of New Westminster.
Source: Port Metro Vancouver

five cents to ninety-five cents per hour, to match similar increases given by the Shipping Federation in Vancouver, and the agreement with stevedoring and dock companies was extended another three years.[71] During busy times, anywhere from three hundred and fifty to four hundred and fifty longshoremen, all on the union's list, were employed. The influence of the International Longshoremen's Association was held at bay in the opinion of employers and union officials, who, when asked, "did not think there could possibly be more than five or six men actually working belonging to the Association."[72]

The unemployed longshoremen wooed by the International Longshoremen's Association were not sitting idle. Stanley Blake, secretary for the former New Westminster Waterfront Workers Association, was nominated to run for the CCF party, representing the city in the June 1937 provincial election.[73] His campaign was low-keyed compared to the juggernaut of newspaper advertisements and high-profile visitors endorsing the incumbent, former mayor and cabinet minister, Arthur Wells Gray. Stanley Blake placed third out of five candidates, fielding thirteen hundred votes to Wells Gray's four thousand.[74] Strongest in worker communities like Sapperton and Queensborough, unions and persons involved in them were the basis of labour politics in New Westminster.

A group of warehousemen at the New Westminster plant of Brackman-Ker Milling Company received a charter for ILA Local 38-147 in late April 1937, another first for the union in British Columbia. International Secretary-Treasurer Matt Meehan told delegates at the first ILWU convention in Aberdeen, Washington during April 1938, "In New Westminster, we have an excellent organization among the Warehousemen. The local is small, but very progressive, and recently was able to force the employers to re-employ one of our members who had been unjustly discharged."[75]

New Westminster residents apparently voted the right way since the city was rewarded. A high-level highway toll bridge opened at New Westminster in November 1937, named after the province's premier, Duff Pattullo, which improved access to the other side of the Fraser River and clearance enough for deep-sea ships to pass safely to the Fraser Mills wharf and other points. In December 1938, Mayor Fred Hume won a resounding re-election victory with his 'Why Change Course' political campaign.[76] Trade and industrial development were key planks in his vision for New Westminster and its port. The waterfront labour provided by longshoremen, day in and day out, made the whole public-private partnership achievable.

A New West Coast Union

The vesting of the Royal City Waterfront Workers Association in local initiatives proved inconvenient for the emerging movement in the United States wanting to organize all longshoremen along the Pacific coast into one union. After falling out with the International Longshoremen's Association old guard, Harry Bridges took most of the independent Pacific District locals by forming a new labour body, the International Longshoremen's and Warehousemen's Union.[77] Allegiance was switched from the American Federation of Labor to the Congress of Industrial Organizations (CIO), for whom Bridges became the Pacific Coast Director as well as head of his international union. New Westminster longshoremen and warehousemen belonging to the International Longshoremen's Association voted overwhelmingly to affiliate with the CIO: Local 38-127, twenty-eight to zero, and Local 38-147, twenty-one to one.[78] Harry Bridges, denounced as a Communist by some people, still enjoyed the affection and loyalty of the longshoremen who provided his power base. They revelled in their militant and radical tradition of standing up to maritime employers for a fairer deal.

On 13 October 1937, the first ILWU charter granted in British Columbia was issued to 'general longshore workers' in New Westminster as Local 58 in ILWU District 1. The document was signed by Harry Bridges personally as international president.[79] Many of the unemployed ex-strikers and others joined. Leo Labinsky, an individual who helped to get this charter, carried an ILWU union card in his wallet but kept it secret so he could keep his standing in the Royal City Waterfront Workers Association and stay employed. The majority of working longshoremen in New Westminster, Labinsky's friends and fellow gang members, were on the wrong side of the last big strike and lacked the perceived ideological commitment.

Increasingly, competing factions were putting aside differences and acting cooperatively through the auspices of the Royal City

Waterfront Workers Association. Harry Bridges and the ILWU executive board considered that body little better than a company-friendly union. Even like-minded longshoremen, in order to secure employment, were joining the city-backed union. George Phelan, for one, made that choice. New Westminster ILWU locals sent no delegates to the international conventions in San Francisco during April 1939 and North Bend, Oregon during April 1940. The underemployed longshoremen could not afford to travel and fell behind in payment of mandatory dues and assessments.

New Westminster was absent from delegates attending ILWU conventions held in 1939 and 1940
The local charters granted three years earlier were soon after declared null and void by the international executive board.
Source: Chris Madsen

International officials felt increasingly misled about actual membership numbers given by the New Westminster representatives. ILWU Local 1-58 had been inactive since October 1938 (though some monthly per-capita

President	
Arthur Gore	1935–1937, 1939–1942
Adrian Davis	1938
Peter Lavery	1943–1945
William Lawrence	1946
Vice President	
George Phelan	1940–1942, 1944
G. Elder	1943
William Oakes	1944–1946
Business Agent	
Leonard Bonwick	1935–1942
Charles Peter Latham	1943–1945
Wilbur Scott	1946
Secretary-Treasurer	
Harry Hopkins	1935
William Fyfe Herd	1936–1941
Leonard Bonwick	1942
Charles Peter Latham	1943–1946

Royal City Waterfront Workers Association leadership, 1935–1946
The Royal City Waterfront Workers Association was an amalgam of strikebreakers and former strikers working together for the benefit of member longshoremen. The organization allowed a surprisingly effective transition into ILWU Local 502, though divisions between the two groups still lingered for years to come. Members frequently disagreed with each other, but usually worked toward a common purpose.
Source: Department of Labour Canada, Annual Report on Labour Organization in Canada

dues were paid until at least July 1939), and the charter was eventually revoked by international officials.[80] The organized ILWU warehousemen presence in Local 1-65 also quietly disappeared in New Westminster when the remaining members were enticed into another Canadian union. By 1940, the ILWU national organizing committee decided to shift limited organizing resources elsewhere than British Columbia because "it would be impossible at this time to place organizers in the field due to the war situation."[81] This higher decision left the city's longshoremen with few options. The Royal City Waterfront Workers Association, despite its shortcomings, was the only organized labour body representing most longshoremen working on the New Westminster waterfront. Sooner or later, the ILWU would have to form a new local to challenge the Royal City Waterfront Workers Association's ascendancy or work from within to change the outlook of the organization and its members. Either way, the task was that much harder in a period of retrenchment and declines in shipping brought on by wartime.

The outbreak of global conflict in September 1939 impacted negatively on trade and waterfront employment along the Fraser River. War is never good for shipping. International trade routes were interrupted and merchant ships diverted elsewhere or taken up for naval auxiliary service. Large parts of Europe and Asia, former shipping destinations, fell under Axis occupation, and sea lines of communication to the United Kingdom, where much of New Westminster's lumber, metals, and agricultural products were sent, came under attack by German submarines and auxiliary cruisers.

The number of ship arrivals and quantity of cargo moving through the port's docks and the grain elevator experienced dramatic declines in the war years.

	Ships	Exports (in tons)	Imports (in tons)
1940	333	871,487	24,766
1941	156	336,969	11,407
1942	109	315,668	4,292
1943	86	443,446	none
1944	114	331,069	5,493
1945	176	615,962	6,823

Source: New Westminster Harbour Commissioners 1945 annual report

The largest drops in exports were lumber and grain, though nearly all commodities suffered. Pacific Coast Terminals submitted claims for discharging, storing, and diverting seized or suspended cargo.[82] In practical terms, fewer longshoremen were needed to work the ships and docks and not enough employment was available for everyone compared to previously high years before the war. When multiple ships came into port at the same time, shortages of topside men qualified to operate winches occurred.[83] The number of working gangs was reduced from twenty-eight down to nine in short order.

Remaining gangs were reorganized, as men stayed away or found other temporary employment for better wages and more consistent hours in the city's war industries. Some longshoremen went to work at Heaps Engineering, a local manufacturer of ship components and machinery in Queensborough, and wartime shipyards in nearby Vancouver and North Vancouver, as well as far away as Victoria, Seattle, and California.[84] The federal government instituted National Selective Service, which imposed greater controls and restrictions on recruitment and movement of workers from industry to industry.

During negotiations between the Shipping Federation and the British Columbia Council of Longshoremen (which included the Royal City Waterfront Workers Association though they negotiated separately), the New Westminster union was asked to accept the interchange of gangs with Vancouver during peak periods, despite the continued opposition of New Westminster's civic officials to the employment of non-city residents on the waterfront.[85] Since the Shipping Federation had no jurisdiction over New Westminster, the matter was left in the hands of the private employers party to a separate agreement with the Royal City Waterfront Workers Association.

This collective agreement was up for renewal. The association's president, Arthur Gore and secretary-treasurer, William Fyfe Herd consulted with employer representatives and asked for a little bit more. In June 1940, the membership of the union voted to extend the existing agreement and accept a five-cent hourly increase for the duration of the war and six months afterwards.[86] In practical terms, it was no better than a wage freeze in the expensive Lower Mainland under the effects of wartime prices and inflation. Men falling behind or not paying the monthly dues of $2 were not called for work and thrown out of the association. At the end of 1942, one hundred and fifty-five unionized longshoremen were registered in New Westminster.[87] Available work, however, was inconsistent. Association dues included a sick benefit should a paid-up member fall ill longer than a period of three weeks, payable after the first week and not longer than six weeks in a given year.

The Royal City Waterfront Workers Association held general meetings on Wednesdays after executive meetings the first Monday of every month. Any member missing a general meeting without good excuse was assessed $1, approximating one hour of paid work. Grumbling about the wages paid, New Westminster longshoremen petitioned "that owing to the uncertainty of the amount of work that we may get, we think it is unfair to freeze waterfront labour unless we could get a guaranteed wage of $40.00 per week."[88] The employers, Consolidated Mining and Smelting, Pacific Coast Terminals, Empire Stevedoring, Canadian Stevedoring, and Victoria and Vancouver Stevedoring were unmoved. They held fast to rates set by the Shipping Federation in Vancouver.

Instead, wartime cost-of-living bonuses were granted first in August 1942, then revised in November 1943. A ruling by the National War Labour Board gave longshoremen an additional ten-cents per hour of regular time and overtime, which was subsequently rolled into the basic wage rates; not the thirteen cents asked for in a joint employer and union application.[89] Nationally, longshoremen in the ports of Montreal and Halifax received the same ten cent per hour cost-of-living bonus. War conditions were tough for those able to secure work on the gangs and tougher for casuals listed as spares and auxiliaries, the latter only given a chance when all the other regular union members had been dispatched. The situation convinced the Royal City Waterfront Workers Association to reassess its status as an independent, unattached union and entertain for the first time affiliation.

Local 502 Gets a Charter

The courting of the Royal City Waterfront Workers Association into the open arms of the ILWU was not a straightforward process involving targeted organizing, infiltration of leadership roles, or any particular deep commitment to class struggle. In point of fact, it was a rather pragmatic choice among many that was democratic in nature rather than Communist, militant, or radical. The Royal City Waterfront Workers Association initially affiliated with the British Columbia

Council of Longshoremen, strongest on Vancouver Island and led by James Lackie. Lackie adamantly opposed the inroads made by American industrial unions, represented by the likes of Harry Bridges and the ILWU, by "keeping the party machine out or under control."[90] He wanted to take all the council's affiliated locals, including New Westminster, into the American Federation of Labor.

The Royal City Waterfront Workers Association, however, was still undecided and noncommittal. Vancouver longshoremen also voiced reservations. Sensing an opportunity, Rosco Craycraft, the ILWU's International First Vice President in Seattle, visited British Columbia and laid out the merits of joining his organization. In October 1943, he sent copies of ILWU's newsletter *The Dispatcher* to New Westminster, and invited Peter Lavery, the Royal City Waterfront Workers Association's president, to attend a caucus meeting in Portland during the third week of March 1944, with all expenses paid by the international, "You [Lavery] are in daily contact with the men and this will give you an opportunity to meet the local officers of the entire Pacific coast and to gather, at first-hand, a background on the various personalities with whom you will be in communication. Also to observe the working conditions and functions of the locals in the [United] States."[91] The singled-minded dedication to higher pay, improved working conditions, and union control over the dispatch system clearly resonated with Lavery and New Westminster longshoremen.

Rosco Craycraft received equal time with a representative from the International Longshoremen's Association and another from the Vancouver and New Westminster Trades and Labour Council to give the respective sales pitches during a general meeting. Peter Lavery, re-elected president in May 1944, believed there was only one clear choice. On 12 June 1944, members of the Royal City Waterfront Workers Association voted one hundred and five in favour and eleven against affiliating with the International Longshoremen's and Warehousemen's Union, with five spoiled ballots for a total of one hundred and twenty-one cast.[92] The result went back to the ILWU international office and Harry Bridges in San Francisco for action and approval. Rejection was highly unlikely. The invitation from New Westminster longshoremen provided another entry point for the American west coast union to break into Canada and British Columbia. Vancouver was the first to

"Where's Your Union Button?"

After disappointing results from earlier 1936–38 organizing drives in British Columbia, the International Longshoremen's and Warehousemen's Union had basically, by 1940, given up on Canada, in favour of other priorities. Seattle-based International First Vice President Rosco Craycraft, however, made organizing north of the international border a personal effort and sent a capable organizer from ILWU Local 10 named Steve Glumaz, a Mexican citizen with a Canadian wife, as international representative to make the connections. Craycraft, along with fellow executive board members, Robert Robertson and Louis Goldblatt, were instrumental in bringing the ILWU to New Westminster. Later, Steve Glumaz was not allowed back in the United States and eventually settled with his family on East Keith Road in North Vancouver.

Source: The Dispatcher vol. 2 no. 8 (7 April 1944), ILWU Anne Rand Library, San Francisco

join the International Longshoremen's and Warehousemen's Union and New Westminster was soon second in 1944.

Any misgivings about the Royal City Waterfront Workers Association and its pedigree as a curious assortment of former strikebreakers and shunned ILA malcontents were gone. Building the future was more important than dwelling on the past. Rosco Craycraft returned to New Westminster on 5 July to present a charter to Peter Lavery before presenting it to the general members. This event was attended by Louis Goldblatt, the ILWU secretary-treasurer from San Francisco, international representative Steve Glumaz, as well as Austin Smith, the secretary-treasurer, and Harry Chawner, the business agent from Vancouver ILWU Local 501.[93] The ceremony was simple and meaningful. As described in the ILWU's official newsletter, Craycraft "outlined to the membership what the relationship between the local and the international would be in the future. He also pointed out what the responsibilities of the members and the local were today in this free peoples' struggle towards a speedy Allied victory over fascism and in the building of a just and enduring peace with security for all in the postwar era. He further stressed the need for workers' participation in the political life of Canada."[94] Harry Chawner reinforced that his Vancouver local intended to honour the no-strike pledge given by the ILWU for the duration of the war if Local 502 would do the same.

Later that month, Peter Lavery was New Westminster's first formal delegate to a caucus meeting in San Francisco. The ILWU's new locals in Vancouver and New Westminster sought affiliation with the Canadian Congress of Labour (CCL) and were welcome because "on the whole they seem to be a fairly clean group of workers" though "there may be some difficulty with [Harry] Bridges' organization."[95] The autonomy and moderation of the Royal City Waterfront Workers Association helped in this regard: the union was still locally-based and Canadian in perspective and character. The official Local 502 charter signed by Harry Bridges is dated 3 October 1944.[96] Each longshoreman in the Royal City Waterfront Workers Association was required to take an oath of membership in ILWU Local 502. A constitution and bylaws governing the affairs of the local were drawn up and put before members early the next year.[97] The decision to join the ILWU was a weighty one.

Standing Together

Notwithstanding the absence of a thrilling storyline, the joining of the ILWU and New Westminster longshoremen proved mutually beneficial. There were no significant wartime strikes or walkouts on the New Westminster waterfront, either before or immediately after affiliation with the ILWU. In relations with employers, organized labour in Canada was subject to the mandatory framework imposed by government to prevent strikes and gain consent for broader lasting agreements, behind a new-found industrial legalism.[98] ILWU and CCL affiliations opened up opportunities for advice, strategy, and advantage to work within that system.

Although initiative still came from the local level, the Royal City Waterfront Workers Association as ILWU Local 502 no longer acted alone. Upon application, the National Wartime Labour Relations Board certified Local 502 and its representatives as the bargaining agent for all longshoremen in New Westminster, excluding foremen at Empire Stevedoring, Consolidated Mining and Smelting, and Canadian Stevedoring.[99] Victoria and Vancouver Stevedoring was only left out because the company was not operating regularly in New Westminster and had no longshoremen employed. The existing agreement was in force for the duration of the war and six months after. Certification ensured that the change to the ILWU was recognized by the principal stevedoring companies when they requested longshoremen from the union hall for dispatch as required.

Employers were not allowed to open up another hall or use competing unions to perform waterfront work at the signed companies. In effect, ILWU Local 502 was the sole source for employment of unionized longshoremen in New Westminster.

Membership, though nowhere near prewar levels, was recovering. In regards to New Westminster, international representative Steve Glumaz reported, "This local has been steadily expanding in gang strength. Their present working force has expanded within the past six months from about 150 to 240 men. Here little or nothing is being done about organizing other waterfront terminal workers into the union."[100] Numbers of reported dues-paying members reflected fluctuations from month to month as well as the gradual rising trend observed by Glumaz, as shown in the following monthly numbers.

	1944	1945
January		196
February		134
March		178
April		153
May		244
June		208
July		193
August		217
September	125	223
October	183	219
November	160	268
December	124	220

Number of reported dues-paying regular union members in Royal City Waterfront Workers Association ILWU Local 502, not including casuals
Source: Library and Archives Canada, MG 28 I103 Canadian Congress of Labour vol. 30 file 13

The Local 502 executive screened large numbers of new member applications for acceptance at general meetings. The stated policy was "that any member belonging to the armed forces on his return be given a job on the waterfront, and at the first opportunity, be given work the same as his former job."[101] Intakes kept pace with the availability of work, as shipping returned to the Fraser River and exports of commodities from New Westminster exploded after 1946. The ILWU locals, including New Westminster, entered a new round of negotiations for an agreement with the Shipping Federation, wider in scope and better in terms. Closely-guarded autonomy and genuine concern for members prepared ILWU Local 502 to meet the big changes coming.

Chapter Notes

1 Harvey Schwartz, *Solidarity Stories: An Oral History of the ILWU* (Seattle: University of Washington Press, 2009).

2 Interview with Joe Breaks by Andrea Walisser, 9 July 2013.

3 Transcript of proceedings, negotiating committee, 13 November 1929, AM 279 Shipping Federation of BC 520-F-4 file 12, CVA.

4 New Westminster Harbour Commissioners annual reports 1931 and 1932.

5 "Annual Report on Navigation to the New Westminster Board of Trade for the Year ending February 28th, 1934", AM 440 New Westminster Board of Trade reel M 8-7, CVA.

6 "Fred Hume and Harry Sullivan Answer Anonymous Letter Writers", *British Columbian* (10 January 1934).

7 "Pacific Coast Terminals Limited, and its Wholly Owned Subsidiary Fraser River Dock and Stevedoring Co. Ltd. in possession of the Trustee for the Bondholders Profit and Loss Account for the Period from September 15, 1933 to December 31, 1934", RG 30 A-1-c vol. 13039 file 1820-5 pt. 2, LAC.

8 "Majority Award and Minority Award In the Matter of the Industrial Disputes Investigation Act, Chapter 112, of the Revised States of Canada, 1927, and in the Matter of a Dispute between the Vancouver and District Waterfront Workers Association and the Shipping Federation of British Columbia, Limited", 30 June 1934, AM 279 Shipping Federation of BC 521-F-3 file 3, CVA; "Longshoremen's Vote Insufficient to Authorize Strike", *British Columbian* (14 May 1934).

9 Paul Eiliel, *The Waterfront and the General Strikes San Francisco, 1934* (San Francisco: Hooper Printing, 1934), 13.

10 Victor Anthony Walsh, "The International Longshoremen's Association: Rebirth of a Union", MA thesis (San Francisco: San Francisco State College, 1972), 186–187, San Francisco Public Library History Center, San Francisco.

11 "U.S. Strike is Not Affecting City Shipping", *British Columbian* (17 May 1934).

12 *The Truth About the Waterfront: The I.L.A. States its Case to the Public* (San Francisco: International Longshoremen's Association Local 38-79, 1935), 16, Oakland Public Library History Room, Oakland, California.

13 Andrew Parnaby, *Citizen Docker: Making a New Deal on the Vancouver Waterfront 1919–1939* (Toronto: University of Toronto Press, 2008), 126–127.

14 Marvel Keller, "Decasualization of Longshore Work in San Francisco", Report No. L-2 Works Progress Administration, National Research

Project, April 1939; James Clinton Harris, Jr., "A Study of the Pacific Coast Longshore Industry with Special Reference to Collective Bargaining and its Influence on the Stabilisation and Equalization of Longshoremen's Income", MA thesis (Eugene: University of Oregon, 1942), 87, Knight Library, University of Oregon, Eugene; John Bellamy Foster, "On the Waterfront: Longshoring in Canada", in Craig Heron and Robert Storey (eds), *On the Job: Confronting the Labour Process in Canada* (Montreal and Kingston: McGill-Queen's University Press, 1986), 283–285.

15 Declaration — Canadian Waterfront Workers' Association constitution and bylaws, 23 July 1934, AM 332 ILWU Local 501 541-D-7 file 5, CVA.

16 Report by Operator No. 3, 28 August 1934, AM 279 Shipping Federation of BC 521-C-2 file 2, CVA.

17 "The Agreement, Working Conditions, Wage Schedule and Despatching Regulations as agreed to by The Vancouver and District Waterfront Workers Association and the Shipping Federation of British Columbia, Limited", 10 October 1934, AM 279 Shipping Federation of BC 517-G-6 file 3, CVA.

18 "Longshoremen Seeking Higher Scale of Pay", *British Columbian* (13 February 1935).

19 R.C. McCandless, "Vancouver's 'Red Menace' of 1935: The Waterfront Situation", *BC Studies* no. 22 (Summer 1974), 64.

20 "Dock Workers in City Ready to Join Strike", *British Columbian* (10 June 1935).

21 "Minutes of the One Hundred and Fourteenth Meeting of the Board of Directors of the Shipping Federation of British Columbia, Limited, held at the Head Office of the Company, Thursday, 13th June 1935 at 9 a.m.", AM 279 Shipping Federation of BC 73-F-8 reel M 17-2, CVA.

22 City council meeting, 17 June 1935, NWPL; "Government Aid to Settle Dock Strike Sought", *British Columbian* (17 June 1935).

23 F.E. Harrison to W.M. Dickson, 22 June 1935, RG 27 reel T-2979 vol. 369 file 87A, LAC; "Minutes of the One Hundred and Eighteenth Meeting of the Board of Directors of the Shipping Federation of British Columbia, Limited, held at the Head Office of the Company, Vancouver, B.C., on Tuesday, the 18th June, 1935 at 9 a.m.", AM 279 Shipping Federation of BC 73-F-8 reel M 17-2, CVA.

24 Interview with Ed Taylor by Mark Mackenzie, 16 December 2012.

25 Colonel W.W. Foster to G.G. McGeer "Situation on the Waterfront", 19 June 1933, Vancouver Police Department S199-5 75-F-2 file 4, CVA.

26 Statement is Issued by City Dock Workers", *British Columbian* (18 June 1935).

27 City council special meeting, 22 June 1935, NWPL.

28 Agreement between Leonard Bonwick and stevedoring companies, 21 June 1935, RG 145 vol. 28 file 751:256:45, LAC.

29 "Proclamation Issued by Mayor in City Dock Strike", *British Columbian* (22 June 1935).

30 Special meeting board of trade council, 29 June 1935, AM 440 New Westminster Board of Trade reel M 8-7, CVA.

31 "Police Guarding Workers", *Montreal Gazette* (25 June 1935).

32 H.S. Cove to W.M. Minor, 25 June 1935, AM 279 Shipping Federation of BC 521-C-2 file 1, CVA.

33 "Another Ship Loading at City Docks", *British Columbian* (25 June 1935).

34 "Longshoremen Charged with Carrying Gun", *British Columbian* (3 August 1935).

35 "Youths Admit Burning Fiery Cross", *British Columbian* (23 October 1935).

36 Interview with Ed Taylor by Mark Mackenzie, 16 December 2012.

37 F.H. Clendenning to members Shipping Federation, 29 June 1935, AM 279 Shipping Federation of BC 520-F-1 file 2, CVA; "Strike Outlay at Royal City Fully Repaid", *Vancouver News-Herald* (12 August 1935).

38 "Police Ban Pickets at City Docks", *British Columbian* (22 August 1935).

39 "Agreement Near in Waterfront Strike?" *British Columbian* (28 August 1935).

40 *New Westminster Police Department Annual Report*, 1935–1936, NWPL.

41 "14 Pickets Arrested at City Docks", *British Columbian* (3 September 1935).

42 Interview with Norm Andresen by Joe Breaks, 23 January 2013.

43 "Dock Pickets Case Delayed Till Tuesday", *British Columbian* (11 September 1935).

44 City council regular meeting, 5 September 1935, NWPL.

45 "Dock Strike Inquiry Opens in Vancouver", *British Columbian* (17 September 1935).

46 "Findings and Report of the Commissioner The Hon. Mr. Justice H.H. Davis re Industrial Dispute on the Vancouver Waterfront Involving the Shipping Federation of British Columbia, Limited and the Longshore Workers at that Port", October 1935, 29, AM 279 Shipping Federation of BC 517-G-3 file 3, CVA; "Davis Blames Longshoremen: Complete Text of Davis Report on Waterfront Probe", *Vancouver Sun* (28 October 1935); "Longshoremen Lose in Judge's Report", *British Columbian* (28 October 1935).

47 *Man Along the Shore!*, 123.

48 "Strike of City Dock Workers Believed Ended", *British Columbian* (27 November 1935).

49 R.L. Mason to directors, "Labour Department", 6 December 1935, AM 279 Shipping Federation of BC 520-F-3 file 12, CVA; *Labour Gazette*

vol. 36 (1936), 28

50 "Longshoremen Buy Property for New Hall", *British Columbian* (5 February 1936).

51 D.C. Cameron to P.V.O. Evans, "Interchange of Gangs Vancouver/New Westminster", 2 December 1948, AM 279 Shipping Federation of BC 520-F-6 file 5, CVA.

52 "No Longshore Gangs Brought to Work Here", *British Columbian* (9 March 1936).

53 "Labour Situation: Memorandum of a Joint Meeting held in Hotel Georgia, Wednesday, June 2nd 1937", AM 279 Shipping Federation of BC 521-B-1 file 2, CVA.

54 "Hume Seeking Settlement in Dock Impasse", *British Columbian* (9 April 1936).

55 C. Lynn Fox to J.E. Hall, 28 May 1936, AM 279 Shipping Federation of BC 521-D-2 file 5, CVA

56 "L.&W.T.W. of C is Dissolved", *Ship and Dock* vol. 1 no. 21 (11 March 1936), ILWU — Canada file "Publications pre-ILWU period", ILWU Library.

57 "Ald. Sullivan Questioned in Dock Strike", *British Columbian* (16 January 1936).

58 "Proceedings of the 29th Annual Convention of the Pacific Coast District International Longshoremen's Association Held in the Carpenters' Hall, San Pedro, California, May 4–19, 1936", International Longshoremen's Association, Local Pacific District records, collection 412 box 5 file 15, Special Collections and University Archives, Knight Library, University of Oregon, Eugene.

59 Executive assistant to G.G. McGeer, 15 June 1936, AM 279 Shipping Federation of BC 520-F-2 file 3, CVA.

60 "Excerpts from Minutes of the Meetings of the Executive Board I.L.A. — District 38, Seattle, July 10–15, 1936", AM 279 Shipping Federation of BC 521-A-1 file 5, CVA; ILA executive board minutes, 13 July 1936, International Longshoremen's Association, Local Pacific District records, collection 412 box 4 file 16, Special Collections and University Archives, Knight Library, University of Oregon, Eugene.

61 Meeting agenda, 5 November 1936, AM 279 Shipping Federation of BC 521-D-3 file 10, CVA.

62 Flyer "Longshoremen! The I.L.A. Has Come to New Westminster", RG 27 reel T-2988 vol. 379 file 175, LAC; Executive assistant to Captain W.M. Crawford, 3 June 1936, AM 279 Shipping Federation of BC 520-G-3 file 3, CVA; Percy R. Bengough to longshoremen, 18 February 1936, AM 279 Shipping Federation of BC 521-E-2 file 21, CVA.

63 "30th Annual Convention Pacific Coast District I.L.A., Tuesday, May 11, Labor Temple, Seattle", International Longshoremen's Association, Local Pacific Coast District records, collection 412 box 1 file 7, Special Collections and University Archives, Knight Library, University of Oregon, Eugene.

64 "Dynamite is Found under Dockers' Hall", *British Columbian* (14 December 1936).

65 Council meeting, 20 December 1935, AM 440 New Westminster Board of Trade reel M 8-1, CVA; "The Port of New Westminster", *Canadian Merchant Marine Yearbook* (1936), 15.

66 C.W. Train, "Assessments at Outports", 29 July 1936, AM 279 Shipping Federation of BC 520-D-7 file 5, CVA.

67 Waterfront Employers of Portland news circular, 17 December 1936, AM 279 Shipping Federation of BC 521-D-4 file 1, CVA.

68 "Minutes of Meeting of the Directors of Pacific Coast Terminals Co. Ltd. held at the Company's offices at New Westminster, B.C. on Thursday, the 4th day of March, 1937, at 11:45 AM", RG 30 A-1-c vol. 1303 file 1820-5 pt. 3, LAC; "No Reduction In Rentals for City's Docks", *British Columbian* (12 March 1937); The city also took a hard line in relations with the demanding company, which had to be repaired by Lanigan.

69 Executive assistant to manager, Bank of Nova Scotia, Vancouver, 16 November 1936, AM 279 Shipping Federation of BC 520-E1-file 10, CVA; "Westminster on Fair List", *The Province* (5 March 1937); Jeffrey J. Safford, "The Pacific Coast Maritime Strike of 1936: Another View", *Pacific Historical Review* vol. 77 no. 4 (2008), 585–615.

70 "U.S. Marine Unions Lift Ban From New Westminster: Port Now Open to American Ships", *British Columbian* (5 March 1937).

71 "Agreement between Dock & Stevedoring Cos. operating in the Port of New Westminster B.C. & the Royal City Waterfront Workers Association", 1 October 1937, RG 145 vol. 28 file 751:256:45, LAC; "Increased Pay Announced for Longshoremen", *British Columbian* (8 April 1937).

72 A.E. McMaster to J.E. Hall, 11 March 1937, AM 279 Shipping Federation of BC 521-A-1 file 5, CVA.

73 "Blake Named as Candidate by City C.C.F.", *British Columbian* (26 April 1937).

74 Elections British Columbia, *Electoral History of British Columbia 1871–1986* (Victoria: Queen's Printer for British Columbia, 1988), 187.

75 Proceedings first annual ILWU Convention, Aberdeen, Washington, 4–17 April 1938, 108, ILWU — Conventions, ILWU Library.

76 "Mayor Hume Wins Sweeping Endorsement in City Voting; Retiring Aldermen Re-elected", *British Columbian* (16 December 1938).

77 Andrew Bonthius, "Origins of the International Longshoremen's and Warehousemen's Union", *Southern California Quarterly* vol. 59 no. 4 (Winter 1977), 418–419; Bruce Nelson, *Workers on the Waterfront: Seamen, Longshoremen, and Unionism in the 1930s* (Urbana and Chicago: University of Illinois Press, 1990), 238.

78 "Results of Balloting by Locals — Pacific Coast District ILA", collection 412 box 8 file 19, International Longshoremen's Association, Local Pacific Coast District records, Special Collections and Archives, Knight Library, University of Oregon, Eugene.

79 *ILWU Canada Waterfront News* Centennial Edition (November 1971), PAM 1971-101, CVA.

80 W. Dallamore to Matt Meehan, 5 August 1940, ILWU — Organizing, box 4 file "Correspondence and reports — general 1935–38", ILWU Library; "Minutes ILWU Executive Board Meeting, Sunday, July 30, 1939, San Francisco, Eagles Hall", ILWU — Executive Board, file "1939 San Francisco July 29–30", ILWU Library.

81 "Meeting of the ILWU National Organizing Committee, July 19, 1940, Portland, Oregon", ILWU — Executive Board, file "1940 Portland July 17–18", ILWU Library.

82 Edgar Read to Pacific Coast Terminals Co. Ltd., 3 June 1942, RG 117 A-3 vol. 2693 file 20238 pt. 2, LAC.

83 "All City Docks Occupied as Ten Freighters Load Cargo", *British Columbian* (9 January 1940).

84 D.M. Cameron to F.J. Pickett, 17 January 1942, AM 279 Shipping Federation of BC 521-C-3 file 4, CVA.

85 "Minutes of a Joint Meeting Between the Directors of Shipping Federation of British Columbia, and the B.C. Council of Longshoremen, held in the Hotel Vancouver, Vancouver, B.C., Wednesday, 1st May, 1940, at 8:00 p.m.", AM 279 Shipping Federation of BC 520-E-7 file 5, CVA

86 A. Gore to J.H. Mitchell, 27 June 1940, RG 145 vol. 28 file 751:256:45, LAC.

87 D.M. Cameron, "Shipping Federation of British Columbia President's Report — Year 1942", AM 279 SFBC 521-C-3 file 5, CVA.

88 General meeting, 13 October 1943, ILWU Local 502 minute book.

89 W.C.D. Crombie to members, "Cost of Living Bonus", 10 November 1943, AM 279 Shipping Federation of BC 521-F-5 file 8, CVA.

90 D. O'Brien to P. Conroy, 21 February 1944, MG 28 I103 CCL vol. 222 file 25, LAC.

91 Rosco Craycraft to Peter Lavery, 4 March 1944, ILWU — Officials — Correspondence, file "Craycraft, Rosco Vice President — British Columbia Locals", ILWU Library.

92 General meeting, 8 June 1944, ILWU Local 502 minute book; Royal City Waterfront Workers Association to Rosco Craycraft, June 1944, ILWU — Organizing — Canada, box 4 file "Correspondence and Reports Local 502 New Westminster", ILWU Library.

93 General meeting, 5 July 1944, ILWU Local 502 minute book; Interview with Joe Breaks by Andrea Walisser, 9 July 2013; Interview with Louis Goldblatt by Lucille Kendall, 7 November 1979, MS 3538, California Historical Society, San Francisco.

94 "New Westminster Record Meeting to Receive Charter", *The Dispatcher* vol. 2 no. 16 (28 July 1944), 3; Steve Glumaz, "Installation at New Westminster, B.C.", ILWU — Canada, file "Local 502 New Westminster (longshore) — general", ILWU Library.

95 Memorandum P. Conroy to A.R. Mosher, 5 August 1944, MG 28 I103 CCL vol. 30 file 13, LAC; Michael Torigian, "National Unity on the Waterfront: Communist Politics and the ILWU during the Second World War", *Labor History* vol. 30 no. 3 (July 1989), 422–423.

96 International Longshoremen's and Warehousemen's Union Charter Local 502, 3 October 1944, AM 332 ILWU Local 501 559-D, CVA.

97 *Constitution and By-Laws of Local 502 International Longshoremen's and Warehousemen's Union, as amended 3 September 1947*, ILWU — Canada, file "Local 502 New Westminster (longshore) — general", ILWU Library.

98 Jeremy Webber, "The Malaise of Compulsory Conciliation: Strike Prevention in Canada during World War II", *Labour/Le travail* vol. 15 (Spring 1985), 87–88; Peter S. McInnis, *Harnessing Labour Confrontation: Shaping the Postwar Settlement in Canada, 1943–1950* (Toronto: University of Toronto Press, 2002).

99 Release from Wartime Labour Relations Board (National), 22 June 1945, RG 145 vol. 27 file 751:255:45, LAC; "Weekly Report: Austin Smith: June 4th to June 9th, 1945", ILWU — Organizing — Canada, box 4 file "Smith, Austin 1945–46", ILWU Library; C.P. Latham to M.M. Maclean, 25 June 1945, RG 145 vol. 26 file 751:234:45, LAC.

100 Steve Glumaz to Rosco Craycraft, "Canada", 25 June 1945, ILWU — Officials — Correspondence, file "Glumaz, Steve International Representative" (2), ILWU Library.

101 General meeting, 16 March 1944, ILWU Local 502 minute book.

Chapter 3
Benefits of Membership
1946–1959

Chris Madsen

The decade and a half after World War II featured growth and stability in industry as well as trade along the Fraser River waterfront, underpinning steady employment conditions for longshoremen and their union. Markets for the main export commodities of lumber, metals, and agricultural produce returned to strong levels. The City of New Westminster, at perhaps its economic apex, was a prosperous and thriving community open for business. The stretch of Columbia Street popularly known as 'The Golden Mile' enjoyed some of the highest retail sales in the province during that era.

Work on the nearby docks across the railway tracks co-existed with this economic prosperity. Longshoremen could spend lunch breaks in local cafés and restaurants or frequent hotel bars and cinemas before going home, either inside or outside the city limits. Many owned cars and parking and congestion became a problem sometimes. These good times, when job security was assured and the main complaint was rising prices for real estate and a variety of household and luxury items, were not by accident, but instead the rewards of sound management decisions and farsightedness that created a civic and business environment conducive to integrating industrial, retail, and residential activities together in a relatively small municipal space.

The benefactors were longshoremen and the leadership of ILWU Local 502. The latter interacted with the employers in relations and ran the union's affairs on a participatory basis. Many advantages now taken for granted on the working waterfront were gained through persistent struggle and hard bargaining at this time: unemployment insurance, enforcement of safety regulations, paid holidays, group insurance benefits, pensions, extended union recognition, and control over the dispatch, as well as autonomous association within the ILWU construct. Belonging to a strong union local able to stand up for itself brought tangible individual and collective benefits.

Beginning of Good Times

The recovery in maritime trade, on which New Westminster's prosperity and employment numbers depended, was cheerfully quick. During 1946, the amount of lumber, grain, and other commodities moving across the city's docks doubled from the same months the year previous and neared prewar levels. Berths were often full with ships, and shortages of longshoremen and gangs occurred until men returning from other industries and overseas military service could be reintegrated, and new hires given spots on the spare board. A New Westminster Board of Trade committee observed that "the New Westminster Harbour was more or less governed in a dual capacity by the Harbour Commissioners and the City Council."[1] Mayor William Mott, soon to represent New Westminster in Ottawa as an elected Member of Parliament, and the harbour commissioners focused efforts on making improvements to existing facilities in New Westminster proper for handling higher volumes.

The timing seemed opportune. The year 1947 set new highs for the number of deep-sea ship arrivals and volume of exports. Subsequent years were marginally lower in regard to exports, though imports underwent truly astounding growth and shipped lumber accounted for an ever greater share. Ships calling at New Westminster also increased in size and capacity, including many wartime-built standard 10,000-gross-ton cargo freighters. Due to the existing system of Commonwealth preference, the outward destinations were mostly the United Kingdom via the Panama Canal and Australia across the Pacific. Zinc and lead bar metals replaced concentrates while lumber remained predominant.

	Ships	Net Tonnage Ships	Exports (in tons)	Imports (in tons)	Lumber (in board feet)
1946	287	1,112,751	804,282	2,507	300,035,000
1947	358	1,517,917	1,052,447	6,054	410,413,000
1948	280	1,179,123	769,650	24,194	362,541,000
1949	338	1,382,141	836,586	47,278	391,980,000
1950	342	1,393,731	723,101	77,974	476,074,000

Source: New Westminster Harbour Commissioners annual reports

For members of ILWU Local 502, the centre of work life and employment was the union hall at 71 Tenth Street, in the city's west end. It was here that longshoremen congregated for assignment to specific jobs and social company. In July 1946, the Royal City Waterfront Workers Association was formally dissolved by surrender of its certificate of incorporation, and the hall and property transferred to a holding society, with the assistance of lawyer John Stanton.[2]

At this time, the dispatch occurred three times per day — morning, afternoon, and evening. Gangs, known by the name of the hatch tender leader, were dispatched together as a unit. A gang was still comprised of thirteen men: a hatch tender with more years of seniority than the others, two winch drivers, two slingmen topside, and eight men below in the hold, four on each side.[3] Since dispatch was customarily by gang rather than individual, experience levels and personalities in the group were all-important and each gang became known by its own strengths and weaknesses. The dispatcher, Alva Currie, might assign one type of job to a particular gang or hold off jobs from others.

During this time, the ILWU Local 502 hall maintained twenty-three formed gangs under named hatch tenders as well as spare and auxiliary boards, which listed casual workers. First-call casuals (7,000 series board, referred to as 'preferred casual') and second-call casuals (4,000 series board) were used when numbers of available regular union members were exhausted. Each of these boards required registration.

Over a period of time, casuals might be able to move up to preferred casual and eventually be asked to join the union formally.

Bruce Briggs recounted:

When you went back to the hall for another dispatch, you felt good and you just showed respect to all the fellow members at that time, even though you were a casual. Them members treated their casuals back then with respect also. Not like it is happening on the waterfront these days. It seems like the membership is bitter at the casuals these days on the waterfront. And 'til they smarten up, our union is going to start getting weaker and weaker because there is no respect amongst the fellow men . . . anymore.[4]

Members of the union had to be in good standing and show up for work when dispatched. The Shipping Federation abolished the Preferred Casual category in 1952, but the union continued to use the term informally to cover the sons of existing members, even though it had no official basis after 1952.

	Union		Preferred Casual		Casual	
	No.	Earnings	No.	Earnings	No.	Earnings
1949	250	$50.00	125	$30.17	72	$36.76
1950	241	$57.44	136	$35.50	58	$41.14
1951	271	$61.20	125	$33.48	37	$43.16
1952	324	$68.04			125	$24.79

Average monthly earnings for the three classes of longshoremen in New Westminster, with average number of longshoremen employed over the respective year

Casuals, smaller in total numbers, typically earned more on average than preferred casuals on a monthly basis. Average earnings dropped significantly when the preferred casual category was discontinued in 1952 and all individuals were lumped in with casual. However, average monthly earnings consistently rose for regular union members in ILWU Local 502.

Source: City of Vancouver Archives, Yearly statistical surveys 1949–1952, AM 279 Shipping Federation of BC

ILWU Local 502 handled its own affairs from inside the hall. Executive, general, and special meetings were held there, unless the number of attendees justified the use of bigger venues. There was no night work after 5 pm on scheduled union meeting days. The number of dues-paying members in ILWU Local 502 fluctuated from month to month but never exceeded four hundred during these years. Not all members showed up on any given night for meetings and turnout was sometimes disappointing. Repeated attempts to ban gambling and drinking of alcohol in the hall also indicates some longshoremen found other ways to pass time between dispatches, or simply hung out with friends. One letter, signed anonymously "a longshoreman's wife", begged to have card-playing prohibited in the hall because her husband was losing money to the detriment of his family.[5] The hiring and dispatch hall represented among the most important connections between the individual longshoremen and the union, besides the collective agreement with the employers.

	1946	1947	1948
January	294	343	366
February	234	301	320
March	316	345	321
April	263	302	327
May	266	303	333
June	209	301	282
July	304	279	293
August	267	320	273
September	267	301	292
October	268	335	312
November	252	311	327
December	252	291	282

**Reported dues-paying regular union members
in ILWU Local 502, not including casuals**
Source: Library and Archives Canada, MG 28 I103 Canadian Congress of Labour vol. 30 files 11–13

A New Collective Agreement

ILWU Local 502 negotiated on behalf of its members the terms of employment and scale of remuneration for work performed by longshoremen on the New Westminster waterfront. Collective agreements, typically in effect for a year or two, governed pay and work conditions. In keeping with past practice, Local 502 initially concluded and renewed agreements with each private company employing members from the ILWU. In mid-December 1945, the ILWU formed a BC District Council for negotiations toward a master agreement to cover affiliated locals in Port Alberni, New Westminster, Vancouver, and Prince Rupert, similar to one in existence along the Pacific coast on the American side.[6] ILWU Local 502 chose delegates to attend the council meetings and serve on negotiating committees.

As part of this process, longshoremen in New Westminster requested $1.35 per hour regular time, $2.25 per hour for overtime, and a forty-hour workweek.[7] The necessary unity, however, was lacking. Vancouver longshoremen withdrew from the BC District Council and concluded a separate agreement with the Shipping Federation. This action, international representative Edward Wennerlow felt, lost "the golden opportunity of making Local 501 a local with a full-union dispatch, the same as the rest of the locals here."[8]

Brian Ringrose commented on the different stance of the two locals toward negotiations:

> *I knew a lot of guys from Vancouver. They were a good port. They were a big port. I mean, I can honestly tell you right today I used to bug them quite a bit in negotiations that they couldn't seem to get their crap together, I would call it. And we were small and tight. And we could as a caucus be tight and unified. Then I learned, when later on we got bigger, what they were going through. So I have actually apologized to a couple guys. I said, "Now, I know what you guys went through." When you get bigger, you get bigger problems . . .*
>
> *We were lucky in our local, we were a very tight local in those days. I think today we're not quite as tight because you have more people. The more people you have, the more diversity, the more opinions you're going to have. But we stuck together pretty good.*

When we went in as a caucus, we were solid. There was six of us, that's the way it was. One spokesman but six guys on the same track. That's how we were always tight. [It was a strong bargaining position] from our point of view. A lot of guys said no . . . you know, because you weren't speaking as a unit. We let everyone speak, but we all spoke the same way. We knew what we wanted, and our local stayed together with it so. We stuck with a decision. Sure, you would always have to change during negotiations. But you started with a game plan and stuck to it until you had to change. Whereas others would have had problems getting their plan together. We were lucky to be a small local and a tight local.[9]

The ILWU Local 502 negotiating committee presented an agreement to employers at New Westminster that included a proviso ceasing work at noon on Saturdays, which was passed by a secret ballot one hundred and seven to twenty-six at a special meeting. The local's president, William Lawrence, informed the general membership that several stevedoring companies found the terms acceptable and had signed.

When the negotiating committee resumed talks for the next year's agreement, they found themselves talking to officials from the Shipping Federation instead of the individual companies. The Shipping Federation wanted ILWU Local 502 to make concessions less favourable to the union and more like the situation in Vancouver, though at a closed-door meeting of the Shipping Federation's directors, Colonel R. Drape Williams from Empire Steverdoring acknowledged "that New Westminster, who had Union dispatching intended to keep it."[10] The end result was that ILWU Local 502 was allowed to preserve its more favourable employment conditions and union prerogatives once brought under the Shipping Federation's jurisdiction. A collective agreement dated 15 November 1947 was concluded, ratified by a vote of one hundred and nineteen to three at a general meeting, and duly signed in January 1948 by Duncan Cameron, the Shipping Federation's general manager.[11]

Stevedoring companies belonging to the Shipping Federation were subject to the agreement's pay rates and terms of employment, including the union dispatch in New Westminster, no work after midnight, and a day and a half off on weekends. The Shipping Federation agreed to contribute $350 monthly towards half the salary of the dispatcher and the assistant dispatcher, as well as pay for a telephone line in the hall. John Berry, the international representative still on the ILWU executive board, reported on the significance of the change, "We now have a complete turnover here in B.C. as regards the relationship between the Unions and the Employers. The bargaining rights, in so far as the Stevedoring Companies are concerned, have been taken over by the Shipping Federation so that we now have, through agreement, agreed to accept that position with certain conditions set out on behalf of the Longshore Unions."[12] Pacific Coast Terminals, still a major employer on the Fraser River waterfront, was not a Shipping Federation member and thus remained outside any agreement.

Since the new collective agreement with the Shipping Federation was binding, ILWU Local 502 generally avoided major disruptions to the work routine and shipping. Longshoremen continued working when the woodworkers union went on strike in area sawmills, though a great deal of sympathy existed for the cause and demands being made. New Westminster was reliant on the production and export of lumber, so even a temporary halt rippled throughout business and the community. Woodworkers on strike meant no work for longshoremen. Shipping activity at the docks slowed, and then Mother Nature intervened. High water levels and major flooding on the Fraser River during late spring 1948 closed the port completely in New Westminster "for some time and much work was lost both there and in Vancouver due to the interruption of communications on land."[13] Some longshoremen, left with no work, volunteered to help badly-stricken areas up the Fraser Valley at Agassiz and Chilliwack. Just as business resumed, a large-scale longshore strike tied up US ports along the west coast in September 1948, lasting for over three months.[14] This event threatened to interrupt or interfere with shipping coming to New Westminster.

Canadian west coast longshoremen followed affairs in the United States very closely without getting directly involved. The Waterfront Employers Association in San Francisco, emboldened by changes to federal labour legislation and anti-Communist sentiment, launched a full-scale assault on Harry Bridges and the ILWU over wages and union control over the dispatch hall. ILWU Local 502, like other British

Columbia locals, stayed on the job because the collective agreement with the Shipping Federation explicitly disallowed strikes and stoppages of work for reasons other than safety. New Westminster longshoremen instead declined to handle ships declared 'unfair' by virtue of port of origin or cargo. John Berry, the international representative, met with Duncan Cameron and Shipping Federation officials every morning for the strike's duration to determine which ships were on the fair list and thus could be worked. Tacoma, south of Seattle in Puget Sound, was considered an 'open' port outside of ILWU jurisdiction; an interpretation mutually agreed upon by both parties on the Canadian side.[15]

Local 502 supported American ILWU members in the union's core demands, though avoided making the strike Canadian as well. Jim Kearney, a visiting union official from San Francisco, "after investigating and seeing for himself, congratulated Berry and B.C. members for the job we are doing up here and when he goes back to Frisco, somebody was going to apologize for the false rumour circulating regarding British Columbia Ports."[16] Relations with the Shipping Federation under the existing agreement were, on the whole, satisfactory. New Westminster longshoremen were asked to contribute $5 each for a Bridges-Robertson-Schmidt legal defence fund when the US government went after the ILWU's top officials. As well, ILWU Local 502 appealed directly to President Harry Truman in writing to stop attempts to strip Harry Bridges of his citizenship and expel him from the United States. The events in the United States became a backdrop to coming negotiations in British Columbia, in which the Shipping Federation pursued its own agenda.

The Shipping Federation adopted a decidedly tougher and more aggressive stance to seize the initiative away from Canadian ILWU locals like Local 502. It had decided to offer a ten-cent increase in wages as "consideration was given to the situation arising out of the U.S. Pacific coast longshore strike, and the consensus of opinion was not to consider the strike as a factor in the wage negotiations."[17] The reasoning aimed to get ahead of the union before firm demands were made (thus not repeating the US situation) and shape the final settlement on favourable terms to the employer.

ILWU Local 502 was negotiating together with all other BC-area ILWU locals for the first time. The union turned down ten cents and countered with a twenty-cent increase, down from the initial twenty-five cents sought by John Berry at the outset of negotiations.[18] Eventually, ILWU Local 502's membership voted one hundred and thirty-two to eight, with two spoiled ballots, accepting a fifteen-cent increase in the collective agreement for 1949.[19] After the agreement was signed, the Shipping Federation came back, asking New Westminster for changes in dispatch hours and more flexibility in working Saturday afternoons and Sunday when the port was busy. ILWU Local 502, given a strong mandate from a membership vote, firmly replied 'no'.

The next year, a joint negotiating committee sought another fifteen-cent increase and better allowances. The Shipping Federation, having been rebuffed by ILWU Local 502 previously, was not feeling particularly generous. Fred Jackson, the local's firebrand president, asserted, "while he expressed himself as disappointed with the results of the negotiations, under the set-up, he thought the only thing left was for us to accept wages and conditions for the coming year."[20] The majority of members present reluctantly agreed with him, eighty-five to fourteen. The 1950 collective agreement, in that sense, represented a watershed moment for relations between the ILWU longshoremen and the employers.

John Berry told Robert Robertson in San Francisco, "It was evident to the negotiating committee that the Shipping Federation was prepared to go all the way in a demand for a reduction of fifteen cents per hour. That, in itself, caused the men to accept the same wage rate as we were using that merely as a means to obtain the Shipping Federation's commitment towards a Pension Plan."[21] The days of easy gains were over, as union negotiators from the locals faced a determination on the part of George McKee, who replaced Duncan Cameron as the Shipping Federation's labour manager, and the member waterfront employers to dominate relations with its workforce. Concessions and improvements to employment obtained by longshoremen on the New Westminster waterfront were hard-won, often in the face of opposition from the Shipping Federation.

Unemployment Insurance

The first differences of opinion involved extending unemployment insurance coverage to longshoremen. The federal *Unemployment*

Insurance Act, introduced in 1940, created a contributory plan mandated by industry that required employees to work a minimum of one hundred and eighty days to be eligible for benefits. The government, through an Unemployment Insurance Commission responsible for benefits, desired to encompass wider numbers from the Canadian labour force, including longshoremen and waterfront workers on federally-controlled harbour lands. Because unemployment was low in these years, more workers contributing to unemployment insurance meant potentially larger financial resources for pooling and less likelihood of government having to cover shortfalls. New Westminster was on a list of designated Canadian ports falling under a proposed government plan.[22] Most of the plan's administration, however, was borne by private employers required to register workers within industries and keep detailed employment records down to the number of days and hours worked.

The Shipping Federation outright opposed unemployment insurance for west coast longshoremen under its jurisdiction, citing reasons of cost and practicality. The actual figure was a mere $58,000 for all unionized longshoremen in Vancouver, New Westminster, and on Vancouver Island — $33,000 contributed by waterfront workers themselves and $25,000 to be paid by employers.[23] Moreover, strikes and unauthorized work stoppages made workers ineligible for collecting unemployment insurance, which should have been a great incentive for a disciplined waterfront workforce. Employers and officials in the Shipping Federation objected to the added record-keeping from existing practices, while ILWU Local 501 was not eager to add another payroll deduction to its Vancouver members.

The very nature of longshore employment was perhaps the greatest challenge. Longshoremen were not technically employees of any private company because gangs were dispatched to jobs on the docks and ships as required from the hall, in the case of New Westminster a union hall. Regular union members and casuals were registered with serial numbers from 2000 to 2999 for payroll, vacation calculation, and income tax reporting purposes.[24]

Annually, the Shipping Federation prepared federal T4 tax slips for distribution through the union local. The detailed returns and documentation given to the unemployment insurance commission necessitated further exchange of human resources information between employers and the union. For ILWU Local 502, problems with dispatching convinced the executive to question acceptance of longshoremen previously registered for unemployment insurance from other industries, particularly wartime ones.[25] With the Shipping Federation opposed and the ILWU locals unsure, action by the federal government was necessary to clarify the whole situation. An order-in-council made employing stevedoring companies and longshore workers subject to the *Unemployment Insurance Act*, effective 1 April 1948, with longshoremen in New Westminster registered on 15 March of that year.[26] It may not have been specifically sought, or even welcomed, but unemployment insurance was a benefit available to registered longshoremen in ILWU Local 502 from that date onwards.

Nick Feld, a longshoreman of Dutch descent, who started on the New Westminster waterfront in 1958, recalled the sporadic nature of work during his early employment period and before the safety-net of unemployment insurance:

> *That was a miserable year because of course I had no income you know except trying to get longshoring. I used to go down to the longshore hall for a seven o'clock dispatch and, if I didn't make a job, I went back home and worked around the house because I was still in the process of building it. And then at noon, I would go down there again hoping that someone got hurt or got sick and then they would be calling for spares. But I was not the only one. There were five or six of us, you know, for the one o'clock dispatch. Then I went back home and at four o'clock for the four o'clock dispatch, I was there again hoping, you know. That first year, I worked very, very little. At one time, I figured out how much I had worked that first year. I averaged a day and a half per week for my first year. So I was just living between you know a little bit of longshoring and unemployment insurance. That was how I drifted along, you know. And a day and a half that was all I got on average.*
>
> *But I stuck it out. Gradually, I got an extra day or, you know, especially on a rainy day because then guys would book off because they did not want to get wet or whatever it was, or on a snowy day,*

they did not want to work on the scows, you know, on the lumber, because the scows had loads of lumber on them, you know. That lumber, you had to shovel the snow off so the guys could work on the scows. So I got a few more days work later on. And as the years went by, I got more and more work, which was still very little. You know it took me many years — it took me five years before I finally got a number . . . Well, I had a number, but we were on a list. We were on a list just all the day guys that worked.

Once and awhile, some of them would come in and some of them would not come back anymore. It took me years before I finally got the odd day more. So I thought, I am going to stick it out because I am going to get in there. At that time, we had a little commotion going on because we were on a list and, all of a sudden, we found out that another list had been made up without us knowing and these were guys who had started after us, but they were the sons of longshoremen and they were getting preference. Oh, we were mad. But no matter what we did, how much we hollered, they stayed ahead of us, you know, and they became members ahead of us too. It took me years, it took me five years I think, before I finally became a member. It took me five years. And from then on you know, there was work, a little more work to make a fairly good living.[27]

Adherence to Safety Codes

Safety practices in the workplace and for the handling of cargo were another concern impacting ILWU Local 502 and its members. The presence of heavy machinery, large loads, and lofty heights made longshore work dangerous if certain established rules and procedures were not followed. Serious injury or even death could result from lax attention to safety matters on the waterfront. Bruce Briggs remembered:

Safety was a big concern. Those old longshoremen, they would not let those foremen tell you it was safe when it was unsafe. They just would not go to work. And then, of course, you would have to get a BA [Business Agent] out, and then after that, it would be the DOT [Department of Transport]. And then after, the DOT had passed it or failed it. And you always hoped that they would fail it at the time because you knew you might get an extra shift of work out of it. And then after, when everything was settled, you would put your head down and arsehole up.[28]

Technically, either the Shipping Federation's safety engineer or ILWU Local 502's business agent could order work to cease for safety reasons. Major accidents and mishaps had to be reported to the provincial Workmen's Compensation Board.

Work on the New Westminster waterfront fell under a patchwork of provincial and federal regulations. On 21 January 1948, longshoremen refused to unload nitraprills, a nitrate-based fertilizer considered a dangerous cargo prone to explosion, from SS *Riverside* at the Consolidated Mining and Smelting dock due to violations of harbour and federal safety regulations: no pressure in firehoses, blocked escape hatches, and insufficient ladder accommodation.[29] The federal Department of Transport subsequently declared nitraprills a dangerous cargo that required special handling, so the longshoremen knew what they were talking about. The port labour relations committee, consisting of W.A. Johnson, Captain John Macmillan, and members of the ILWU Local 502 executive, felt the action warranted workers who walked off the job should be paid two hours wages. The findings of an inquiry into the March 1945 explosion of the freighter *Greenhill Park* in Vancouver harbour along with another dangerous cargo that killed six ILWU longshoremen trapped below decks and other nitrates-related explosions on ships in the US state of Texas suggested the need of greater precautions. At the very least, ILWU Local 502 demanded extra ladders for longshoremen to make a quick escape in the event of fire. New Westminster longshoremen eventually agreed to accept an additional thirty-five cents per hour offered by the Shipping Federation and made part of the collective agreement as a commodity rate for handling nitraprills and other fertilizers.[30] The premium, however, still involved a very dangerous cargo in certain unsafe situations.

Gerry White recalled his duties as business agent in respect to safety:

When you are dealing across the table or even talking to the employer's representatives on main issues that you can do something with, they're usually smart people too and you can have a pretty good argument going, and come to some conclusion. But if you are arguing with some guy who is half-drunk when he showed up for work and he got fired, there is no good argument. And it is really hard to make an argument on his behalf. But I did. A lot of times I made the deal with, especially in New Westminster, the superintendents and walking bosses as we called them. We all knew each other fairly well. A lot of times, they would just call me — or the other business agent, just not me — and say, 'Come and take him away.' No repercussions, just come and take him away. He would go home and straighten up, and come back to work the next day or a day or so later. There were some pretty good arguments sometimes . . .

If we couldn't settle a dispute, then maybe a BCMEA rep would come out, but that, you know, that was at the moment, had the argument and it was over and on to the next thing. I never held a grudge or anything. I would always get even, though. Well, the advantage that we had is the job always has to go on, regardless of the argument whether it is safety or manning or that sort of thing. So you just say, listen, here's what we do. Let's get it done. And I'll get the guy out of here or get it fixed. Get the Ministry of Transport (MOT), down to do the inspection on the gear. A lot of times, the ship would be shut down for faulty gear and would have to be fixed. Shipyards would have to come in and do all kinds of repairs on some of the ships that had not been looked after before. So that was the main thing. The guys showing up drunk usually or half-drunk after a long night did happen, but not that much.

Mostly, it was safety concerns over ships that needed a lot of repair. Apparently, and this comes from some of the ships' captains and crews, that if a ship could work in New Westminster, it could work anywhere in the world — the gear and equipment, the booms, all the running wires, all the equipment you needed for loading the cargo was always in good shape. In New Westminster, if it wasn't, you didn't work until it got fixed.[31]

An updated safety code, issued under the Shipping Federation's authority, prohibited smoking in the presence of combustible cargo and set out other rules governing conduct and responsibilities. Rule 202 explicitly stated employees were disallowed from working "IF UNDER THE INFLUENCE OF LIQUOR."[32] Longshoremen discovered to be intoxicated or drinking on the job were subject to summary dismissal by foremen and stevedoring companies.

Brian Ringrose remarked on how the union confronted the issue:

Alcohol was a big problem on the waterfront — lots of drinking. And from the top down. Just an opportunity, it just was there. You could find it on the ship, buy it on the ship, or bring it on the ship. We could buy it way cheaper than from a liquor store. It was usually consumed [on the job]. Not too much would go home, unfortunately. Actually, it was a big problem. When I got to be a union official in 1976, we started to find out then that we were having a lot of problems. And a few years later, we worked hard as a union and as union officials to get a handle on it. 'Cause it was just ruining families, dangerous, and a whole gamut of things were involved in it. So we worked very hard to clean it up. I thought at the time we were pretty successful in doing a lot of that. But we self-discipline in our local. We did a lot of self-discipline. We have a grievance procedure, where if I have a problem or I get charged by the union official or union brother, it would go to a grievance and the grievance would deem a penalty. We do that still today.

But the employer will also discipline us. But we try to keep it away from the employer because, for a couple reasons. I mean, once you get in trouble with the employer, eventually you might lose your job. Whereas if we can discipline you, we can give you time off and still keep your job. And we work even with the employer. "Look, we know so and so has done wrong, we're giving him a two-week suspension or whatever." And they said, "Okay, that's good. We understand." And away we go. So it worked well. I think it is still working today on the waterfront for us. We were fortunate we could do it that way. We did help a lot of people. It did take a lot of time though.[33]

Theft and pilferage of goods from cargo were other grounds for dismissal. Violations were reported to the ILWU Local 502 leadership, which then imposed its own disciplinary measures. Offending members sometimes came before the grievance and credential committee to explain their actions. One New Westminster longshoremen, from Gang No. 23, who was caught by customs guards with goods stolen from a ship's cargo, received a six-month suspension from working for the shipping company, which the ILWU Local 502 executive felt served "as a warning to the Union membership as a whole."[34] Typically, a first offence invited a monetary fine, a second offence a work suspension

**Loading sacks of flour at Pacific Coast Terminals berth 1A
on the New Westminster waterfront**

The hatch tender, likely George Lavery, Sr., is peering into the hold, while the winch driver has rigged it so he can operate two winches at the same time. That meant the other winch driver was probably off somewhere for a break or getting coffee. The use of wooden pallets, stacked along the wall, became common in the 1950s. *Source: Port Metro Vancouver*

for a set period of time, and a third offence could affect your standing in the union. Japanese oranges and liquor were the items pilfered most often by longshoremen on the waterfront.

From this time, the union local assumed an active part in the enforcement of safety regulations and behaviour conducive to a safe work environment for members. Longshoremen considered lax in safety standards, inefficient, and abusing trust relationships were given opportunity to change or face further sanctions affecting their employability. Safety was a necessity, not discretionary. All members benefitted from a safer workplace made possible by a clear understanding of the rules bolstered by efforts at self-regulation. The Shipping Federation was content to leave exceptional cases of violations to ILWU Local 502, as long as the majority of longshoremen remained safety-conscious, sober, and responsible in fulfilment of their functions.

Paid Holidays

The idea of holidays with pay was still relatively new in the Canadian workplace, especially on the waterfront. A wartime innovation to cut down on absenteeism in the shipbuilding industry, the paid holiday was gradually extended to other wage-earning sectors of the economy in the following decade. Longshore work was variable by nature. Dispatch depended on the number of ships in port and availability of work. Paid holidays were the manifestation of regular employment, since longshoremen were idle and unpaid when the stevedoring companies could offer no work. Under the collective agreement with ILWU Local 502, the Shipping Federation replaced the existing practice of paying three additional cents per hour with a vacation plan that gave one paid day for each two hundred and fifty hours worked during the previous calendar year.[35] Longshoremen also had the choice of receiving five cents per hour in lieu of holidays. Gangs took a one-week holiday together in the summer, staggered over selected start times. In spring every year, a lottery was held, names literally pulled from a hat at times, to decide which gangs received which time slots. Chance rather than individual choice was the determining factor. Members also left with permission at intervals for personal reasons, but had to continue paying dues and remain in good standing. Members staying absent or 'disappearing' for lengths of time could be deemed delinquent and placement on particular gangs or even acceptance back into the membership was never assured.

In the United States, the ILWU negotiated and arbitrated the principle of paid holidays into the master agreement with the Pacific Maritime Association, the waterfront employers' body, though actual details in implementation were frequently contested. Local 502, along with other Canadian ILWU locals, expected to see some movement from the Shipping Federation, which opposed any improvements from existing arrangements. New Westminster longshoremen still had Sundays and Saturday afternoons free from work each week and were paid overtime if called in for dispatch those days. Recognized statutory holidays were subject to federal and provincial legislation and labour codes. Certain dates such as Christmas, Boxing Day, and New Year's were off, while overtime rates applied to hours worked on Empire (Victoria) Day, Dominion (Canada) Day, and Labour Day, when approved by the Shipping Federation.

The Shipping Federation consistently favoured paying incremental cash instead of granting paid time off or not paying extra at all. An employment system based on accumulation of seniority encouraged many longshoremen to work more hours and days. Regular vacations and time off from work, however, were crucial for the maintenance of health, motivation, and life balance off and on the job. New Westminster longshoremen maintained families and other pastimes outside the workplace. The Shipping Federation authorized no work to be done on the annual picnic day in July, even when New Westminster did not organize one of its own, which effectively meant a day off for the city's longshoremen.[36] The demands of a hard and, at times, physically-exacting job on the waterfront made personal free time and vacations especially sought after. Longshoremen jealously guarded the provisions surrounding vacation, while with the American example in mind, they pressed whenever possible for betterment of terms and conditions. Local 502 and the ILWU agreed that paid vacation was important to members.

Solidarity

In relations within the broader ILWU organization, ILWU Local 502 represented a relatively stable and free-thinking labour body looking out for its members. New Westminster longshoremen proved a loyal bunch. When the C.I.O. (Congress of Industrial Organizations) suspended the international union from its ranks on the grounds that Harry Bridges and the top leadership were too Communist, the membership of ILWU Local 502 reaffirmed "its affiliation to the International Longshoremen's and Warehousemen's Union and that we stand solidly behind our International Union in any hostile action against it by the C.I.O."[37] Other locals were not so quick and unquestioning. Harry Bridges and the ILWU fended off the accusations and emerged stronger than ever with the support of memberships like ILWU Local 502 along the Pacific coast.

	1950	1951	1952	1953
January	305	350	352	354
February	340	298	331	352
March	345	352	315	327
April	337	337	328	353
May	320	311	360	324
June	381	326	385	330
July	314	324	303	335
August	331	324	310	308
September	319	331	388	319
October	339	375	325	328
November	310	315	327	314
December	342	304	309	299

**Reported regular dues-paying union members
in ILWU Local 502, not including casuals**
Source: Library and Archives Canada, MG 28 I103 Canadian Congress of Labour vol. 30 files 11–13

A wide-scale railway strike occurred in August 1950, affecting traffic and transportation of commodities. New Westminster's port stayed open and longshoremen continued loading lumber and metals kept in storage until the transportation routes resumed operating.[38]

Though gangs were reduced to meet lower demand, the numbers employed on the docks remained relatively constant due to selective dispatch. New Westminster was second in the province only to Vancouver, which had nearly three times the number of members. Monthly statistics from year to year indicate a relatively stable membership in ILWU Local 502 that went up and down within a set range.

Employment, and in turn membership, was tied to steady trade through the port and satisfactory relations with employers. At the conclusion of a new collective agreement going into 1951 giving longshore workers an eighteen cent increase, John Berry attributed success to good labour relations between the employers and the ILWU, which "marks 16 years without conciliation, threats, or animosity on either side."[39] The talents of the Shipping Federation's general manager, George McKee, a war veteran and experienced master mariner, came out in tough negotiations with the joint committee from the locals, as well as a fairness in day-to-day dealings. Longshoremen respected the cigar-smoking McKee, though he always looked after the interests of the employers and not labour in general. Lack of unity and divisiveness amongst the larger IWLU locals in British Columbia complicated affairs.

Dean Johnson reflected on the long tradition of member involvement within ILWU Local 502:

Those guys were really dedicated to unionism and they argued different points of view and stuff like that. And it was a real democracy. It was really good. The union then was really tough, really tight. When it comes to union meetings, they would put whatever they had, all sorts of points of view. People were pretty passionate about the points of view. At the meetings, you could talk. I haven't worked with other unions. But I have heard a lot of them are run from the top down. The longshore union has always been run from the bottom up. And we at times have disagreed with our presidents and stuff. And everybody said, "You are out. You're impeached. We will elect a new president right now, off the floor."[40]

Such individual outspokenness in the local could cause some difficulties at times amongst themselves and with other parts of the ILWU.

Relations between the New Westminster and Vancouver locals reached a low point when ILWU Local 502 president, Fred Jackson, attending the Canadian Congress of Labour convention in Winnipeg, condemned actions aimed against Communists and unions branded with that ideology. As a telegram back to ILWU Local 501's president, William Henderson, described, Stewart McKenzie representing the

BC District Council "took to the floor and said [the] ILWU do not accept his [Jackson's] statements and [was] certainly not in favour of Communism."[41] Jackson, feeling betrayed and unsupported, lashed out at Berry and McKenzie once he returned to New Westminster. He wrote ILWU regional director, William Gettings, in Seattle giving his version of events and ended, "Regarding my future activities in ILWU, I am very much at sea just now. Whether I am a mere rank and file member or an officer of the local, I cannot at present see how I can in any way work in harmony with John Berry. I feel sure that I will fight him in every way I can. How this will affect the organization in British Columbia I cannot tell."[42] The sparring between rival local presidents and the ILWU international representative — John Berry was still technically a Local 502 member though he attended few meetings — showed the differences in attitudes at opposite ends of the union, one conservative in outlook and the other ready to question progressively the status quo. Whether they actually liked Communism or not, ILWU Local 502's general membership squared solidly behind Jackson for speaking out.[43] At the time, ILWU Local 502's stance was probably closer to the base in San Francisco, though, Harry Bridges showed a remarkable ability to adapt to any situation.

Despite the best efforts of prosecutors in several American courtrooms, no one could actually pin down if Harry Bridges was ever Communist. It was the innuendo and labour turning against itself that Fred Jackson questioned. Jackson's popularity in New Westminster, backed by hundreds of staunch members ready to support the ILWU and its leadership wholeheartedly, was genuine. George McKee felt little loss when the union leader decided, in protest, not to seek reelection on the ILWU Local 502 executive, telling his directors, "You will note that Jackson's name does not appear. It is understood that he did not even run for office. From a political standpoint, the above slate [William Lawrence, president; Merle Monssen, vice president; Roland Cope, secretary; Wilbur Scott, business agent; Alva Currie, dispatcher] seems to be a considerable improvement over last year."[44] John Berry, on the other hand, had to defend spending in his office, expensive travel, and lacklustre results achieved from the regular assessments given for organizing in British Columbia. As he focused on those parts of Vancouver Island and Victoria still not belonging to the ILWU,

Local 502 undertook its own organizing efforts in New Westminster at Pacific Coast Terminals Company Limited.

President	
William Lawrence	1947–1948, 1951
Fred Jackson	1949–1950, 1955
Leo Labinsky	1952–1954, 1956–1958
Elof Blixt	1959–1960
Vice President	
William Oakes	1947, 1952
Leo Labinsky	1948
Emilien Hammond	1949, 1955
Merle Monssen	1950–1951
Henry Sabourin	1954
Elof Blixt	1953, 1956
Guy Haymond	1957–1958
Fred Gibson	1959
Benjamin Sparks	1960
Business Agent	
Wilbur Scott	1947–1959
Fred Gibson	1960
Secretary-Treasurer	
Charles Peter Latham	1947–1948
Roland Cope	1949–1960

**Elected executive members leading
ILWU Local 502 between 1947 and 1960**
The individuals elected annually into these leadership positions enjoyed the support of the membership. Turnover was highest for vice president, while the remaining positions reflected considerable continuity. ILWU Local 502 benefited from solid and competent leadership during these years.
Source: ILWU Minute Books

Organizing at Pacific Coast Terminals

Pacific Coast Terminals represented a bastion outside the Shipping Federation, in more ways than one. The turnaround company, which started paying dividends to shareholders, was profitable as shipping and business steadily picked up in the years after the war. The following table shows the extent of that profit in each year, based on the revenue generated from dock operations on the New Westminster waterfront.

	Revenue	Net Profit	Capital Expenditure
1946	$720,012	$2,754	$153,244
1947	$1,019,368	$32,245	$106,587
1948	$1,052,114	$69,680	$71,228
1949	$1,005,092	$115,672	$10,686
1950	$840,728	$82,493	$76,553
1951	$1,048,391	$115,748	$1,963
1952	$1,296,328	$202,195	$30,213
1953	$1,055,696	$141,944	$12,458
1954	$1,201,589	$173,172	$13,152

All figures in Canadian dollars
Source: Library and Archives Canada, Pacific Coast Terminals Company Limited director's report ending 31 December 1954, RG30 A-1-c vol. 13039 file 1820-5 pt. 3

Pacific Coast Terminals was firmly under the control of the Canadian Pacific Railway and its subsidiary, Consolidated Mining and Smelting, which used New Westminster as a primary port of export for its metals, nitrates, and other commodities. Geoffrey Warren replaced William Blackstock Lanigan as company president in 1950, after Lanigan advocated opening a second terminal at another waterfront location unrestricted by conditions on the Fraser River, specifically Port Moody on Burrard Inlet.[45] As a consequence, relations with the mayor and city were not particularly cordial, which meant Pacific Coast Terminals had to pay out of pocket for capital expenditures and facility renovations on the leased harbour land, and was thwarted in proposals for expansion.

New Westminster taxpayers were still covering interest on the now-profitable company's debentures under the guarantee given twenty years before. The less-than-subtle threat to move business activities from the city hardly ingratiated Pacific Coast Terminals with civic leaders and the harbour commissioners. Warren faced a very uphill public relations battle in making Pacific Coast Terminals a good corporate citizen. The company's labour practices, which left the ILWU on the outside looking in, added to the discomfort.

Although a principal waterfront employer in New Westminster, Pacific Coast Terminals only formally came under the ILWU's purview after considerable effort and discussion, not only with the company but also with workers employed on the docks outside ILWU Local 502. The situation was in part the union's own making. When longshoremen refused lower rates for unloading railway cars and moving goods into warehouses and insisted on standard longshore rates, the company hired new men who would do the work. This group of individuals went from being non-union to certified as the Pacific Coast Terminals Independent Employees Association, affiliated with the Amalgamated Union of Canada, and to having their own signed agreement with the company.[46] On shipside work handling cargo from sheds or rail cars, regular longshore rates were paid, whilst unloading and transfer into the sheds was paid at eighty-six cents an hour, the going freight handlers' rate. ILWU Local 502 objected that all work properly belonged to longshoremen and claimed that Pacific Coast Terminals was not respecting the standard nine-hour work day.

Wilbur Scott, the business agent, approached both individual dockers and the Pacific Coast Terminals Independent Employees Association's executive about coming into Local 502 and the ILWU. Four workers appeared ready to do so and force the issue, though the majority were still undecided. Pacific Coast Terminals and the Shipping Federation treated the whole matter as an inter-union matter to be decided among organized labour, for which they stood on the sidelines. As lawyer John Stanton advised, existing labour law and precedent favoured the smaller union in any prospective legal challenge. The only alternative was to sit down and talk with the association's representatives at Pacific Coast Terminals through back channels.

What they learned really surprised them, since president Geoffrey

Warren and general manager Walter Brown ran and operated the private company discreetly. If Pacific Coast Terminals continued paying differentials, joining ILWU Local 502 was somewhat problematic, and the larger membership might even rebel against accepting lower hourly wage rates for everyone. The eventual answer was that the international union in San Francisco chartered the new ILWU Local 511, once the dock workers at Pacific Coast Terminals were convinced of the benefits that would accrue to them and applied for certification in May 1953.[47] This separate union local negotiated its own agreement with the management of Pacific Coast Terminals, while looking to ILWU Local 502 for advice and cooperation for mutual benefit on the New Westminster waterfront.

Port Improvements

Plans for the expansion of industry and shipping along the Fraser River were well under way. Fred 'Toby' Jackson (not the ILWU Local 502 president of the same name) was successful in attracting business and money for harbour purposes during his long tenure as mayor. Jackson was first elected in 1951, beating out harbour opponent and incumbent George Sangster, and remained in the top job at city hall until 1958. As mayor, he bought into and sincerely believed in the vision of his predecessors for a prosperous, independent city with the port and international trade as the centrepieces. The realization of 'Canada's Liverpool' on the Fraser River, first mooted in the 1920s and 1930s, appeared to be within grasp.[48]

New industrial concerns located inside and outside city limits. The harbour commissioners granted leases of varying lengths to prospective tenants of waterfront lots. The wealthy Duke of Westminster bought Annacis Island, a natural slough that, through Mother Nature and sandfill from river dredging, turned into land stable enough to establish a large industrial estate on a British model.[49] The federal government funded a $150,000 causeway from Lulu Island to Annacis to accommodate rail and automobile traffic, and planned dockage on the south side facing the river for deep-sea ships. Jackson backed the idea to diversify New Westminster's industrial and manufacturing base, though Annacis Island actually belonged to the municipality of Delta.

Lafarge Cement of North America Limited, a new industrial concern, established a plant with a dock near Annacis to handle limestone shale and gypsum rock. Canada Rice Mills, with its existing dock and large warehouse in Richmond at Woodward's Landing, was worked by longshoremen from Vancouver's ILWU Local 501 rather than ILWU Local 502, a festering sore point from a New Westminster perspective. The federal government, through a bill sponsored by Senator Thomas Reid, authorized the New Westminster harbour commissioners to borrow up to $1.25 million for dock extensions along the city's main waterfront, eastwards toward the Pattullo highway bridge.[50] This serviced land was from the start to be leased to private concerns. It provided additional capacity and flexibility to handle anticipated increases in shipping.

The overall commercial trade numbers for the decade bear out that deep-sea ships arriving in New Westminster were greater in number. The volume of exports and imports remained strong with some year-to-year fluctuations.

	Ships	Exports (in tons)	Imports (in tons)
1951	394	854,454	81,866
1952	397	1,035,162	93,363
1953	396	904,162	48,826
1954	439	910,240	45,322
1955	435	882,109	27,470
1956	407	796,984	93,502
1957	493	879,979	141,766
1958	451	884,526	119,914
1959	460	836,324	167,379
1960	591	991,833	124,089

Source: New Westminster Harbour Commissioners annual reports

These yearly statistics, however, only tell part of the story. The port of New Westminster and longshoremen working the ships and docks benefitted from a healthy demand for commodities and a positive economy at least until mid-decade, when the business fundamentals began to change and an economic recession set in after 1957. Due to price and currency sensitivities, primary customers in the United Kingdom began buying more lumber from Scandinavian countries, and the growing ports of Vancouver and Seattle gradually drew business away from the Fraser River. British investment and interest, especially after the Duke of Westminster's death, also slowed. ILWU Local 502 called upon the harbour commissioners and the federal government to explore trade with China, anticipating a turn to the Pacific. The 'build it and they will come' mentality, which underscored confidence behind New Westminster's master scheme for waterfront industrial development, typified the creation of the Overseas Transport Company.

Overseas Transport Company

Overseas Transport Company Limited, an employer of longshoremen from ILWU Local 502, was a general dock and warehouse operator that handled freight between ship and railway. The company, formed by the ever-resourceful Valentine Quinn with private capital, was locally based in New Westminster. Land and existing docks on the waterfront were leased from the city and rehabilitated, allowing berthing of two ships. The ILWU Local 502 hall dispatched longshore gangs as required for work at prevailing wage rates, though the company eschewed any formal agreement and could have employed non-union men if it wanted. The ILWU, however, was given preference. Following in their father's footsteps, sons Douglas Quinn and Edward Quinn became general manager and secretary-treasurer respectively; the former taking over as president and the latter as general manager in due course. In that sense, Overseas Transport was a local family business.

With Pacific Coast Terminals out of favour in civic circles, Overseas Transport assumed an advantaged position in the plans for port expansion. The city transferred ownership of the eastern part of the main waterfront to the New Westminster harbour commissioners for the token amount of $1, which in turn used the $1.25 million borrowed from the federal government to build dockage, receiving cargo sheds, and other improvements. A five-year lease, dated 15 September 1955, between the harbour commissioners and Overseas Transport provided for payment of $45,000 the first year, $55,000 the second year, $65,000 the third year, and $75,000 in each of the last of two years, as well as payment of city taxes.[51] The City of New Westminster essentially accepted a smaller revenue stream in exchange for being relieved of the burden of capital expenditure and maintenance, while at the same providing business stimulus through a reliable local company known to the city council and harbour commissioners. At least, that was how Mayor Toby Jackson and Alderman Stuart Gifford justified the controversial transaction. Gifford later became mayor in 1964 and remained enthusiastic about the harbour being an economic engine for the city's prosperity. Only a few years later, however, the building phase would give way to the first indications of decline on the main waterfront.

After the expansion, Overseas Transport possessed a total of five docks on the city waterfront — No. 2, No. 4, No. 5, No. 6, and No. 7 — with 3,300 tons of general storage and four million board feet of lumber storage. ILWU Local 502's Fred Jackson, before stepping down as president on account of ill health, met with Douglas Quinn about certification of the union on the docks and discussions toward a signed agreement. Overseas Transport joined the Shipping Federation in late January 1956.[52] The company and union agreed to the same wages and conditions effective at Pacific Coast Terminals. ILWU Local 502 longshoremen handled both dockside and freight handling from the rail cars and sheds at Overseas Transport, ILWU Local 511 still working the neighbouring Pacific Coast Terminals by separate agreement.

Relations between Two Waterfront Locals

The good times and steady employment of the 1950s were a high point for the union. ILWU Local 502, in terms of dues-paying members, available resources for pressing its viewpoints, and bargaining power in relations with employers, virtually controlled the whole New Westminster waterfront on the labour side.

Joe Breaks described the essential difference between members in Local 511 and Local 502:

Local 511 was dock work. And they worked at [Pacific Coast Terminals] where the Westminster Quay is now. And they did what we call dock work. They drove lift trucks, jitneys, they unloaded railcars, unloaded trucks, loaded railcars, loaded trucks with whatever. They cleaned the dock. And they did the maintenance work, the canning, carpenters, electricians, whatever. [Local] 502 was the deep-sea. We did the ship work. And the difference was fifty cents an hour. We got fifty cents an hour more. And we had basically one rate. Now, there were skill differentials. Side-runners got twenty cents an hour more, winch drivers got twenty cents an hour more, hatch tenders got thirty cents an hour more, everybody else got the base rate. On the dock, there were three different rates. If you were feeding the hook — that is, bringing cargo say from the dock to the ship — you got the longshore rate. Or if you were taking cargo from the ship out to the truck, you got the longshore rate. If you were working on the dock just loading the railcars, unloading the railcars, cleaning the dock, doing any of that, unloading trucks, you got fifty cents an hour less. And maintenance mechanics got something, I can't remember what they got. They got less again.[53]

	Local 502			Local 511		
	1954	1955	1956	1954	1955	1956
January	280	344	348	70	80	71
February	337	359	322	82	73	70
March	375	344	332	81	79	70
April	338	350	335	81	74	70
May	327	350	348	81	73	64
June	332	349	347	65	74	67
July	345	349	348	65	65	65
August	348	349	330	80	76	70
September	334	349	302	80	74	82
October	332	341	321	80	74	67
November	342	339	351	80	71	67
December	357	349	336	74	71	76

Number of reported dues-paying regular members in ILWU Local 502 and ILWU Local 511, not including casuals.
Source: Library and Archives Canada, MG 28 I103 Canadian Congress of Labour vol. 30 files 11–13

A breakdown from month to month over a three-year period shows the disparity in numbers between the two ILWU locals resident in the city. The established ILWU Local 502 had roughly four times the number of members. As the smaller and newer entity, ILWU Local 511 utterly relied on the support and backing of ILWU Local 502, including use of the hall for its meetings. When conciliation with Pacific Coast Terminals appeared inevitable, Henry Sabourin from the ILWU Local 502 executive "assured [secretary M.] Kendrick should trouble arise, this Local would not go through a picket line."[54] Financial assistance in the form of loans was advanced to keep ILWU Local 511 in the fight.

For small and large locals alike, conciliation and strikes were very expensive propositions on both sides. George McKee, from the Shipping Federation, was quick to raise the costs associated with conciliation and almost taunted the ILWU to take strike or legal action. ILWU Local 502 gained a deserved win against the Shipping Federation in a court case that ruled in the union's favour against New Westminster longshoremen working ordinary time Saturday evenings. The legal decision handed down read:

It was contended by the [Shipping Federation] that in any case it was not necessary to insert the Clause 10(e) in the new collective agreement because of other provisions. Mr. Justice McInnes [of the Supreme Court of British Columbia] did not accept this contention. Without Clause 10(e), if a man had commenced working Saturday morning and was called back in the afternoon, he would not be entitled to the minimum three hours' pay for the work done in the afternoon inasmuch as the time worked in the morning would be counted as part of the three hours.[55]

George McKee decided an appeal of this decision was not worthwhile. The legal route, however, represented a gamble which could never be a sure thing for the expense incurred, as small ILWU Local 511 found out in another unsuccessful legal case subsidized by ILWU Local 502.[56] Going to conciliation and court too often could exhaust a union's bank accounts and force special assessments from members.

There were also winners and sore losers. During the next round of negotiations, the Shipping Federation treated delegates from ILWU

Local 502 roughly and appeared bound and determined to reverse the judge's legal decision through the agreement. Strike or the threat of strike was not to be taken lightly, particularly with a potential adversary like the Shipping Federation. On one occasion when some younger members brashly talked about strike during a negative membership vote, long-timer Jack Adie wisely cautioned, "[He] spoke of past experiences with the employer and different strikes he has been through, namely 1923 and 1935. His remarks regarding strikes was that after each strike, the worker had to rebuild the union."[57] ILWU Local 502 faced losing everything, including its privileged position and gains on the New Westminster waterfront, by being drawn into major confrontations with the employer body. The ILWU had so far not gone on strike since coming to British Columbia. Any decision to do so came down to priority issues of vital importance to all members in ILWU Local 502, for which the Shipping Federation either opposed in some measure or wanted existing terms and arrangements revisited.

Union Dispatch

Union control over the dispatch system through the ILWU Local 502 hall was very important. In New Westminster and on the Fraser River, the dispatch had always belonged to the longshoremen themselves.

Dennis Buckle described the dispatch in 1956:

> When I started, when you went in for dispatch, it was just a matter of you stood there. The dispatcher would look out and say, "Do you want a job?" or "Come on up, you have a job." Otherwise, you just sat there and waited. Maybe you sat all day and went home at night without anything. And then it started to improve in the system after awhile. We went to different systems. Yeah, it was sit and wait and hope you get picked.[58]

The job of dispatcher required a special type of individual able to meet the demands with fairness and sense of humour. On a typical day, long-time dispatcher Alva Currie arrived at 7 am, went for lunch from 11:30 am to 1 pm, worked until 5 pm, then continued to dispatch from home by telephone in the evening. Saturdays started at 7 am and ended at 2 pm.[59] Wilbur Scott, in addition to his business agent duties,

ILWU Canada international representative John 'Jack' Berry, 1893–1969
Born in Wales, Jack Berry joined the Canadian Army in 1914, winning the Distinguished Conduct Medal in January 1916. By 1926, he had become the business agent for the Fraser River Longshoremen's Union. He moved on to the Canadian Longshoremen's Association in 1939, where he served as Secretary-Treasurer. He eventually joined ILWU, becoming the international representative for its Canadian section in 1948.
Source: Frank Kennedy

Large lumbers being dragged to a ship docked at Fraser Mills in Coquitlam. These ships, common up to the 1960s, typically carried cargo and some passengers to the United Kingdom and Australia.
Source: Port Metro Vancouver

A tugboat takes an empty scow back to Fraser Mills after loading a ship at Pacific Coast Terminals berth 1B. The gear tackle and booms used to load from the side of the ship are prominent in the foreground.
Source: Port Metro Vancouver

Loading boxed apples out of rail cars in the 1930s, Pacific Coast Terminals berth 1B. The apples probably came from the Okanagan Valley, for export across what was then the British Empire.
Source: Port Metro Vancouver

Trucks deliver loose lumber to a ship docked at Pacific Coast Terminals berth 1D. Prominent waterfront landmarks in New Westminster, the Brackman-Ker Milling Company building and the Pattullo highway bridge, are in the background.
Source: Port Metro Vancouver

Royal Mail Lines MV *Durango* at the main New Westminster docks taking on crated produce from railcars and dollies. Launched by Belfast's Harland and Wolff under private contract in 1944, the 9,800-ton *Durango* was originally intended for the chilled meat trade from South America and had special gas-sealed fruit compartments for longer voyages. It sailed regular routes between the North Pacific

and London until Royal Mail Lines was bought by Furness, Withy & Company in 1965 and the ship transferred to another shipping line under the new name *Ruthenic*. Besides cargo, the ship also carried twelve passengers.
Source: Port Metro Vancouver

Aluminum ingots being loaded onto a ship by derricks in a very narrow and tight space. The ingots typically came to New Westminster in gondola cars, not the boxcars shown here dockside. The hatch tender looking down is likely Thomas Render. A properly placed 'save-all net' hangs from the side of the ship, which prevented stray cargo from falling into the water or onto the dock.
Source: Port Metro Vancouver

Ship loading facilities at Fraser Mills, upriver from nearby New Westminster, at Coquitlam in August 1958. Canadian Western Lumber Company, acquired by the American Crown Zellerbach Corporation in 1953, owned this wharf where longshoremen on the ships and millworkers on the docks handled cut lumber and wood pulp. The MV *Besseggen*, and a sister ship MV *Rondeggen*, were a new class of gantry ship built in Norway and chartered by Crown Zellerbach to carry newsprint from British Columbia to California. The specialized design and equipment allowed an increase from fifty to three hundred rolls of newsprint per gang hour.
Source: Port Metro Vancouver

Unloading sacks of flour or rice at the Canada Rice Mills Limited wharf at Woodward's Landing in Richmond, near Highway 99 and the future site of the George Massey Tunnel. Members from ILWU Local 502 worked here on the lower Fraser River many years before the opening of Roberts Bank. The SS *P&T Trader*, pictured here, was a standard wartime C3-S-A2 type ship built for the United States Maritime Commission in 1944 and subsequently sold to American shipper Pope & Talbot Incorporated.
Source: Port Metro Vancouver

A collapse at Overseas Transport's berth 7 when a load of skelp (metal ribbon used for making pipes rolled onto a disc for shipping) was too heavy for the wharf and tipped over the lift truck carrying it. The terminal tried taking this type of work away from Fraser Surrey Docks across the river, without appreciating the full implications of the weight load. The lift truck's operator, Phillip Plamonden, escaped unscathed, though he reportedly lost his lunch bucket in the water during the surprise collapse.
Source: Wilf Hinshaw

This aerial view shows the close proximity of the Overseas Transport shed and Pacific Coast Terminals to New Westminster's downtown core. The main streets, starting from the river, are Front, Columbia, Carnarvon, and Agnes. Overhead parking above Front Street suggests that this picture was taken sometime in the late 1970s or early 1980s. The cold storage building is still prominent next to the ships at berths 1C and 1D.
Source: Port Metro Vancouver

performed a stint as dispatcher until Currie returned once again and Scott later took over the elected position of dispatcher. Alva Currie spent a total of twelve years as dispatcher until his retirement in June 1960, in a role that Roland Cope called at times 'thankless'.[60]

Brian Ringrose remarked on the social function of belonging to a dispatched gang:

> *The gang structure kept you together, where nowadays you don't have a gang structure. And I found that the gang structure was good, a good learning process, especially when I was young. You were told then what to expect. You didn't need a foreman basically in those days because the guys were your boss in a sense. They were very self-regulating. If you didn't pull your weight, you heard about it or you got the hell out of there. You know, you were sent. I never did. But I saw them basically tell a guy, "You're not cutting it buddy, get out of here." It wasn't the foreman. And they were gone. And if they didn't do it the next day, they might be in a different gang. They eventually would leave the waterfront. . . . you know what I mean. They were virtually pushed out in a sense because if you can't do the job, you're not staying down there, buddy.*
>
> *You are doing a lot of hard work. If you didn't pull your share, the other guys weren't going to do it for you. A lot of it was you're just not physically capable. But there was some that just didn't want — you know, slackers — just didn't want to do it. If you don't want to do it, don't hang around here, find another job. A lot of people leave the waterfront, a lot. I would have no idea but we registered so many hundreds of people. And they would come back years later. And sometimes their work number would still be active and start again. But now you can't do that. Once your number is deregistered, you're virtually gone. In those days, it was allowed maybe to come back. You hadn't worked for three years and your number was still active, you came back and tried it again.*[61]

Registered gangs were sent to jobs together, and additional longshoremen were assigned from boards, according to seniority and trade classification. The dispatcher telephoned the hatch tender with "orders for work from the Dispatch office, and in turn he has to notify each of the other ten men on the gang what the work orders are."[62]

Remaining dispatching was done directly from the floor of the hall. A person could be skipped over if he did not respond when his name was called several times or for some reason had ran afoul of the system; for instance repeatedly refusing jobs or using impolite words toward the dispatchers. It could be, at times, a modified union version of the old shape-up, according to Joe Breaks.

	Day Gangs		Night Gangs	
	Required	Available	Required	Available
1950				
November	15.0	23.0	-	-
December	25.4	26.4	3.9	3.4
1951				
January	21.4	27.2	5.0	5.6
February	14.3	38.1	2.2	17.2
March	16.7	35.7	2.6	12.6
April	16.2	34.0	1.9	10.9
May	13.4	30.8	2.4	10.6
June	14.0	33.5	2.0	14.4
July	13.0	29.3	1.3	12.0
August	15.1	32.8	3.3	13.7
September	10.6	33.1	1.8	14.8
October	17.4	33.5	2.4	11.1
November	15.8	33.2	2.1	11.2
December	20.0	28.4	2.3	7.1
1952				
January	18.8	35.2	1.9	12.3
February	16.7	31.7	3.3	9.3
March	14.0	36.2	2.4	17.2
April	18.1	31.7	3.3	9.3
May	22.6	34.5	1.6	8.6
June	19.8	28.8	3.0	8.0
July	3.8	33.9	0.3	24.6

	Day Gangs		Night Gangs	
	Required	Available	Required	Available
August	14.7	26.2	1.8	8.2
September	22.2	29.0	3.6	6.3
October	17.1	30.7	2.2	9.5
November	11.0	31.8	1.1	14.1
December	15.0	31.1	1.4	8.3
1953				
January	18.3	28.5	2.6	7.8
February	12.3	33.9	1.4	16.1
March	16.5	31.2	2.2	10.8
April	15.0	31.1	0.9	12.4
May	14.1	28.4	1.3	10.0

The orchestration of daytime and night gangs dispatched through ILWU Local 502 in New Westminster on behalf of the Shipping Federation
The presented figures disclose some interesting highlights. There were usually more gangs available than needed, so the dispatch needed to spread the work around. Surplus gangs were sent to Vancouver as required, or longshoremen in whole gangs simply did not receive work until their turn came up. The graveyard shift, or the 'gravy train' as longshoremen liked to call it because of night time pay rates, lasted six hours with no meal break and only one smoking break.

The Shipping Federation's policy was to keep an over-abundance of gangs to prevent congestion and tie-ups to shipping. Demand for gangs was also highly susceptible to external events that affected trade and shipping, beyond the control of ILWU Local 502. For example, the International Woodworkers' strike in summer 1952 clearly impacted the dispatch of gangs, which fell to a very low level. Since earnings were directly tied to work, longshoremen were directly affected.

Source: City of Vancouver Archives Monthly circulars "Deep Sea Longshore Gang Situation in Vancouver and New Westminster" AM 279 Shipping Federation of BC 520-F-7 files 4-6 and 520-G-1 files 1–4

Though complaints about dispatching done in New Westminster were rare, the Shipping Federation wished to take control over the dispatch away from ILWU Local 502. It did not see why all dispatching couldn't be done from the employer-run hall in nearby Vancouver.[63] By an existing arrangement, New Westminster gangs travelled to work in Vancouver harbour and on Vancouver Island and vice-versa. Empire Stevedoring complained when dispatching of the standard thirteen-man gangs had no hatch tender, winch men, and other topside workers.[64] The reasons were often straightforward: telephone calls were missed, automobiles broke down on the way, and family emergencies intervened.

Fraser River dispatch was more popular with most longshoremen residing in or near New Westminster. In September 1956, the Shipping Federation increased its monthly contribution toward dispatch salaries and office expenses at New Westminster to $550 from $460.[65] The question of value for money was always a point thrown in the face of union officers during informal meetings and discussions at times of collective bargaining with the Shipping Federation. The greatest danger was that ILWU Local 502 would surrender the union dispatch willingly for some other consideration, by trick or enticement.

Without the union dispatch, the likelihood of ILWU Local 502 losing its autonomy and being subsumed altogether was all too real. When pressure mounted to amalgamate the Vancouver ILWU locals into Local 500, it was the dispatch which chiefly saved ILWU Local 502 from a similar fate. Responsible executive members like Leo Labinsky communicated to longshoremen that losing the dispatch meant giving up the independent local. The Shipping Federation and even other parts of the ILWU never tired of putting forth persuasive arguments as to why New Westminster should act differently in the name of progress, efficiency, and productivity.

Brian Ringrose emphasized the importance of union control:

Dispatch is a big key of our local. It is something we have always cherished. Vancouver has a company dispatch, where we have a union dispatch. So we've cherished that for a lot of years. It has been threatened by the employer to want to take it away or amalgamate with the other locals, things like this. But we have been able to keep what we have, and it is something that we cherish. To be able to dispatch yourself is quite a good thing.[66]

ILWU Local 502, through the strength of its own convictions and in the best interests of members, held the union dispatch sacred, not subject to negotiation. Control over the dispatch was one of the few issues really worth striking for.

John Alfred 'Jack' Smith, hatch tender for Gang No. 13, going for lunch with his winch driver and close friend on Columbia Street

Smith, as someone who "paid his dues in the hold and as a union man bringing the ILWU to New Westminster," believed in the importance of a strong union according to his stepson, now living in California.
Source: Chris Madsen

Welfare Plan

Longshoremen under the Shipping Federation's purview received group benefits described as a welfare plan as part of the 1953 collective agreement, even though coverage actually did not come into effect until March 1954. The welfare plan, administered by a private insurer, was a pooled trustee fund with contributions split between employers and employees. The Shipping Federation paid three cents per working hour and longshoremen five cents into the plan. To be eligible, an individual had to work at least one hundred hours in a month; otherwise contributions were forfeited to the plan for mutual benefit. The welfare plan provided $2,000 life insurance in case of death, a sick allowance of $25 per week for a maximum of twenty-six weeks, as well as health and accident benefits. An equivalent American welfare plan, negotiated into the ILWU master agreement back in 1949, was better funded and more generous in payouts.[67] The Great West Life Assurance Company was involved in early consultations with ILWU Local 502, but the Traveller's Insurance Company in due course became the private administrator. The Shipping Federation, initially compliant, grew progressively uncooperative, bringing in experts to claim that the current plan was too rich to either justify cutting down benefits or raising contributions by longshoremen (but not the employer body).[68]

New Westminster longshoremen welcomed the security of group benefits. Before and after the welfare plan's introduction, they still took up private collections for individuals and survivors in need, or exhausted the limited amounts provided by the union's sick fund. The union looked after its own, as Don MacIntosh recalled:

The waterfront was good to our family. And to me. I always appreciate earning a good living and having good conditions, and my dad before me. And my dad got arthritis in his late 40s. All his joints swelled up and he couldn't do physical work anymore. That is how he became a first-aid man. There are very few industries where if something happened to you, you wouldn't be in poverty because if you couldn't work, you wouldn't get the kind of money you got on the waterfront, you know. So that was really nice.[69]

Indeed, the welfare plan was perhaps a little too popular as a fair number of members were drawing on the plan at any one time. By June 1956, ILWU Local 502's available funds dropped from $18,000 a year before down to a mere $1,000, which called into question the viability of the self-funded plan without some change in formula or calculation.[70] The primary culprit for the drop was lower contributions from fewer working hours, as employment slackened along the Fraser River due to changes in shipping patterns and other factors. Longshore gangs lucky enough to get the minimum monthly hours stayed on the welfare plan, while those who did not fell off. The Shipping Federation resisted various proposals to make improvements to the welfare plan and its funding structure, as ILWU Local 502's members grew increasingly frustrated with what should have been a straightforward group of benefits. The membership was growing older with a variety of health issues and looking toward retirement.

Pensions upon Retirement

If the welfare plan was frustrating, the Shipping Federation's stingy stance on pensions was downright shameful. Longshoremen, for a long time, had no pension to collect at the end of working lives, relying instead on savings, equity in property, and their children. They usually worked until no longer able to, some individuals well into their seventies. The breakthrough came in the United States when the ILWU negotiated a pension scheme into the master agreement.[71] Wishing similar consideration, ILWU Local 502 joined with the other Canadian locals on a dedicated committee to meet and discuss with the Shipping Federation proposals and counter-proposals which, due to disagreements and stalling tactics, lasted years.

Finally, a plan watered down from what was originally proposed was tabled. An invited guest from Vancouver "spoke of the Pension Plan down south, but he also spoke of the Canadian Plan and while it was not what we hoped for, he was going to go along with the Canadian Plan because in Local 501 there were many brothers hanging on in the hopes of getting a pension. He said three of them died in the last year and he believed if a pension plan had been in force, in all probability these departed brothers would still be living."[72] Judging that something was better than nothing, longshoremen accepted the

Shipping Federation's lowball offer by a vote of eight hundred and seventy-seven to seventy-eight, with seven spoiled ballots across the Lower Mainland locals.

The pension scheme came into effect on 1 April 1953, with the first payment at the end of that same month. The Shipping Federation's president handed out cheques at a departure reception in Vancouver to the first forty-five longshoremen retiring on pension. Wilfred Amero and James Burgess from ILWU Local 502 were allowed to postpone retirement for another year, and the Joint Pensions Administrative Committee considered applications from Israel Goodwin (sixty-five years old), Joseph Paquette (sixty-seven years old), and Henry Richards (sixty-eight years old).[73] Each longshoreman in the union was required to provide proof of age within six months.

The pension plan paid $60 per month for twenty-five years service or a lower amount for twenty years, the minimum time required for pension eligibility. By comparison, the American pension plan paid $100 monthly after retirement at age sixty-five. ILWU Local 502 continued pressing for better entitlements and changes but the Shipping Federation was careful to keep the issue separate from negotiations surrounding the year-to-year agreement. According to president Leo Labinsky, who sat on committees and attended numerous meetings, in the area of revisions to the pension plan "nothing has been accomplished."[74] Pensioned longshoremen, including the handful in ILWU Local 502, gradually lost ground with rising prices because the Canada Trust Company-administered plan fell behind inflation and the Shipping Federation adamantly refused to pay higher.

Some individuals hardly had time to enjoy 'golden' retirement. Ward Judson Barnes and Joseph Lavery died in June 1954, a little more than a year after the pension scheme came into effect, while Charles Fraser died in March 1957.[75] Many other older longshoremen in New Westminster held off retiring, hoping for better payouts. The ILWU made pensions part of negotiations for the agreement set to expire on 30 April 1958 and when rebuffed again, applied to the federal government for conciliation.[76] The results of that conciliation provided a jumping board for a month-long strike in late summer 1958, the first major longshore disruption on the New Westminster waterfront since 1935.

Gerry White described how union members vaguely remember the strike, its causes, and people involved:

Prior to 1958, there was no pension benefit on the waterfront. They had a major strike and slowdown in 1958 because the work practices before that — as tough as they were when I started, and it was pretty tough work in some cases — was really bad before that. And there was no protection for the guys who got hurt. You had to do it or you got fired. So after 1958, all that lesson I guess became easier to — well not easier, but I guess more safety practices were put in place so that you did not have to lift as much or get more equipment to do it, that sort of thing. You have to understand that the people that made up the workforce then were a lot of veterans from World War II who had been on the waterfront before and had come back, a lot of people from logging camps which were their own horror story themselves before that, and there were lots of guys from the Prairies, farmers and farmer families that had worked hard. There were lots of strong people, in both mindset and strength.[77]

The Strike in 1958

While not eager to strike, the ILWU Local 502 membership was ready and prepared to confront the Shipping Federation. Going into negotiations, the ILWU committee sought a sixty-one-and-a-half cent wage increase to the prevailing $2.57 hourly wage, a better pension plan under shared trusteeship, an eight instead of nine-hour working day, improved vacation with pay, and the 'call out' minimum increased from two to four hours. The Shipping Federation considered pensions outside collective bargaining and therefore not up for discussion. Federal conciliation officer, George Currie, brought in to find some common ground between the two sides, made little progress.

The impasse was referred to a conciliation board established under the *Industrial Disputes Act*. As late as June 1958, Leo Labinsky told ILWU Local 502 members that he did not favour striking and believed the "Shipping Federation did not want any strike, but he informed [the Shipping] Federation that our demands were reasonable, but if we had to strike, we would."[78] A majority report from the conciliation board, received on 1 August, recommending a ten-cent increase to deep-sea longshoremen wage rates, which was promptly turned down by the Shipping Federation. The membership of ILWU Local 502 was put into the quandary of either voting to reject the conciliation board's report as well or facing a potential lockout in a replay of 1935.[79]

The choice was made. With one hundred and ninety-nine members crowded into the Legion hall on the evening of 18 August, a special general meeting nominated a strike committee, chaired by vice president Guy Haymond and given an extraordinary financial assessment from the general fund.[80] Longshoremen in the five deep-sea ILWU locals, including New Westminster, voted eighty-four percent in favour of striking when the ballots were finally counted.

Last-ditch talks with the Shipping Federation's labour manager, George McKee, led nowhere. At 6 pm on 21 August 1958, three hundred and forty-three longshoremen from ILWU Local 502 stopped work on the New Westminster waterfront.[81] The outcome was uncertain and the road to an end likely to be long, but they were cheerfully resolved to act together. They did so on behalf of the old-timers who still remembered the last big strike and also for themselves. The 1958 longshoremen's strike in British Columbia was mostly over pensions, wages being incidental.

During the strike, ILWU Local 502 members maintained an orderly and committed presence on the New Westminster waterfront in order for discussions to proceed toward a final settlement. Pickets appeared at Fraser Mills, Overseas Transport, BC Electric Railway, Pacific Coast Terminals, Searle grain elevator, and the Lafarge gypsum plant. Signs and placards carried by strolling longshoremen prominently read, "ILWU 502 on strike only against Ship. Fed. of B.C."[82] A few half-empty ships cleared the port before the strike started, but at least three were stuck in New Westminster with no means of loading. ILWU Local 502 issued printed passes to ILWU Local 507 grain liners and ILWU Local 511 warehouse dock workers to pass through the picket lines and continue working, since they were sympathetic though not formally on strike with the deep-sea longshoremen.

Owners of ships stranded in New Westminster went into court to get cargo loading moving with available labour. Justice Alexander Manson of the Supreme Court of British Columbia, a former provincial

**Local 502 deep-sea members picket in front of
Pacific Coast Terminals during the 1958 strike**

The strike was predominantly over pensions for older longshore workers. Union secretary Roland 'Doc' Cope is second from the left in the striped shirt. Besides his other duties, he was editor of ILWU Local 502's *Gang Plank* newsletter.
Source: ILWU Anne Rand Library, San Francisco

attorney general and minister of labour, issued an injunction to prevent picketing and interference with the Danish freighter, SS *Rondo* at Overseas Transport.[83] Manson also granted an injunction to Pacific Coast Terminals because the company was not a member of the Shipping Federation and its ILWU warehouse workers were outside the deep-sea longshoremen's strike. The Shipping Federation appealed to the federal government to intervene by compulsory arbitration, but the Minister of Labour, Michael Starr, declined and demanded that negotiations with the ILWU resume.

MR. AVERAGE LONGSHOREMAN

You have been idle since August 21st because of a strike called by your Union principally on the issue of pensions. Consider these facts:

1. Since 1953 you have had a Pension Plan paid for wholly by the Shipping Federation. This plan pays benefits almost twice those paid to longshoremen at Montreal and Halifax.

2. In 1956 the Union requested the Federation to consider establishing a contributory pension scheme which would provide increased pension benefits.

3. After detailed study, the Federation offered a contributory Pension Plan which compared favorably with any of the major industrial pension plans in the Province and in Canada and was MORE generous than most.

4. Your committee rejected this offer and has steadily refused to re-consider it.

Pension plans are a field for experts, not amateurs.

WHY DO YOU OBJECT TO A MEDIATOR?

SHIPPING FEDERATION OF BRITISH COLUMBIA

William Henderson, the ILWU's strike spokesperson, made clear the union's distaste for any attempt at compulsory arbitration. The ILWU Local 502 executive consulted lawyer John Stanton about the applicable law and wrote a letter to Starr objecting to compulsory arbitration backed by legal argument.

George Currie brought the parties together on 29 August 1958 for more discussions, but no headway was made. George McKee declared that a conciliator more familiar with the intricacies of pensions was needed; apparently part mediator and part actuary. A series of Shipping Federation advertisements in the local New Westminster newspaper targeted the 'average' waterfront worker on the pension issue and openly taunted the union.[84] All the while, the longshoremen strike was costing British Columbia ports an estimated $7 million per day in lost business and the effects were being felt faraway, in Canada and internationally.

Friendly American and Canadian visitors to a special meeting at the Legion hall on 3 September pledged financial assistance and moral support. Upon returning to Seattle, ILWU regional director William Gettings wrote Harry Bridges directly:

I did not hear one single member say a word in either meeting or on any of the picket lines we visited in a way of complaint. The strike and membership at this point is solid. The outside support is good, the public seems to understand that what the Union is asking is only fair. All the Union publicity to date has centred around a decent Pension Plan, which the Union members stand ready to pay their part, [and] the eight-hour shift, which is a condition enjoyed by all workers in B.C. including non-union people . . . It is 25 years since the ILWU has had a strike in B.C. and in some ways that is helping the situation. The Government is in no position to step in right away and force arbitration, the Press can't yell about former strikes. On the other hand, this is something new to 90% of our membership, to be on the bricks, and therefore it must be handled right. The morale is important. There must be good understanding among the ranks and I have impressed upon all the Officers that they must keep the members informed at all times and above all keep them busy and in a fighting mood.[85]

The American union locals stood in solidarity with the Canadian deep-sea longshoremen strikers. In a letter communicated to ILWU Local 502 and the public, Harry Bridges promised "an immediate program of action will be instituted in all US ports if the BC Shipping Federation attempts to operate with scabs behind picket lines."[86] This show of resolve appeared to have the right effect. Local 502 and the other ILWU striking locals dug in for the long haul from a position of strength.

Pressure grew on the federal government to do something to end the Pacific coast longshoremen's strike. On 9 September 1958, Minister of Labour, Michael Starr, announced that Eric Taylor, from Toronto, was appointed industrial inquiry Commissioner to mediate "in view

	New Westminster	Vancouver	Victoria	Chemainus	Port Alberni
1949	$976,125.70	$2,299,484.09	$309,238.54	$244,630.97	$231,541.93
1950	$1,087,145.17	$2,838,478.12	$413,811.34	$434,433.36	$250,717.53
1951	$1,163,891.14	$3,352,692.96	$472,173.76	$522,176.04	$336,254.16
1952	$1,297,069.74	$3,872,859.64	$481,052.98	$544,327.05	$402,286.68
1953	$1,318,814.63	$3,362,160.96	$594,584.58	$722,782.37	$504,638.54
1954	$1,505,188.29	$3,675,448.40	$610,230.20	$849,030.02	$509,972.66
1955	$1,486,354.55	$3,934,301.73	$584,645.16	$874,587.15	$537,498.69
1956	$1,326,849.84	$4,080,061.64	$453,534.29	$730,421.79	$396,525.38
1957	$1,650,174.95	$4,400,849.50	$505,288.70	$804,370.05	$594,964.18
1958	$1,792,301.60	$4,429,251.53	$633,966.11	$951,725.02	$758,133.97
1959	$1,912,453.71	$4,807,251.55	$593,461.40	$1,046,981.14	$837,351.04
1960	$2,549,603.20	$5,563,261.72	$793,297.89	$1,436,497.57	$1,218,110.64

Total yearly deep-sea payrolls for longshoremen in principal southern British Columbia ports
All figures in Canadian dollars.
Wage rates were paid in all ports under jurisdiction of the Shipping Federation, as negotiated in the collective agreements. New Westminster was second only to Vancouver in dollar value of longshore earnings, though the three Vancouver Island ports showed significant gains toward the end of the decade. The effect of the 1958 settlement also served to increase the dollar value of payrolls.
Source: Yearly statistical information and president's reports, AM 279 Shipping Federation of BC, City of Vancouver Archives

of the increasingly serious economic effects of the dispute between the International Longshoremen's and Warehousemen's Union and the Shipping Federation of British Columbia."[87] Taylor met with the two sides in Vancouver four days later and after an intensive week of back-and-forth, obtained signatures on a memorandum that offered to settle the strike. Leo Labinsky signed on behalf of ILWU Local 502.

In the end, the Shipping Federation and ILWU negotiated a deal without resort to compulsory arbitration, just what the federal government and Minister of Labour, Michael Starr, wanted. Leo Labinsky presented the settlement terms to ILWU Local 502's membership on 22 September for a vote, commending Taylor's mediation skills and personal commitment to making a settlement happen.[88] The gains were a ten-year pension agreement requiring the Shipping Federation to pay sixteen cents per worked hour into a joint trusteeship-administered plan with the option of voluntary individual contributions to boost later benefits, up to three more cents per working hour added to vacation with pay based on the principles of seniority, a twenty-one cent hourly wage increase to be effective in three equal installments by 1 November 1959 and five cents in the period between expiry of the last agreement and start of the strike, and an eight-hour instead of nine-hour day based on a forty-hour workweek. These gains were real.

Harry Bridges and other executive board members were delighted. A telegram sent to the ILWU central strike committee offered "congratulations on a magnificent victory. At a time when many unions are in full retreat and anti-union employers and politicians are driving hard, your victory deserves special acclaim. We are proud of the solidarity, understanding, and militant fighting spirit of British Columbia membership which brought the strike to its successful conclusion."[89] The Canadian arm had finally won its laurels in the pantheon of ILWU waterfront struggles. After a strike lasting thirty-three days in duration, longshoremen from ILWU Local 502 restarted work at 8 am on 24 September 1958.[90] ILWU Local 502 members rejoiced that everything had turned out so remarkably well.

Basking in Victory

The settlement, in effect until 30 April 1960, instilled a new confidence in Local 502 and ILWU ranks. On 6 February 1959, members voted to accept the pension agreement.[91] Older longshoremen, who had waited for the revamped pension scheme to kick in, rushed to retire, opening up spots for the induction of new members into the union. The Shipping Federation refused to consider boosting monthly payouts for previous retirees, who still received $60 or less under the earlier pension plan. John Stanton and the ILWU went into court to decide the disposition of $2,134,120 in funds still available in the old plan, in excess of the $479,600 actually needed for the still alive fifty-eight pensioners.[92] The Shipping Federation argued that the remaining balance should be applied to contributions for the newer pension plan, which the judge partly agreed to because the union had left the door open in negotiations leading to the strike settlement.

Justice Brown, of the Supreme Court of British Columbia, remarked in the legal decision:

> *At this point I may interpolate to remark that both [Leo] Labinsky and [George] McKee were excellent witnesses, and there is almost no inconsistency between them. The only reservation I have as to their evidence is that it was never made clear by either why the subject of the disposition of the 1953 fund which had been canvassed for months preceding and during the strike negotiations was suddenly dropped during the two final days of bargaining just before the strike ended.*
>
> *McKee says the federation always intended to use the surplus monies it had paid into the 1953 fund to finance the next fund, and I should think the curious wording of the pensions clause of ex. 17 (memorandum of terms of 1958 strike settlement) 'the Federation will direct to be paid into a Pension fund' etc. could hardly have escaped the notice of the union negotiators. I am afraid that all the evidence points to the fact that the antagonists, perhaps weary of long negotiations, deliberately refrained from mentioning the disposition of the 1953 fund at the time of the 1958 settlement: McKee admits quite frankly that the federation intended to use the fund and I think it is apparent that the union's silence at this point*

about the fund meant, unfortunately, that the subject would be raised litigiously at a later date.[93]

Members retiring from ILWU Local 502 enjoyed higher payments and greater security once they reached the end of careers. Retirement became compulsory at the age of sixty-five years old for longshoremen.

With the strike and ongoing struggle over pensions in mind, IWLU Local 502 also supported creation of a new ILWU Canadian regional body, to replace the BC District Council. Harry Bridges and the executive board in San Francisco allowed the devolving of authority, responsibility, and most importantly, finances to a Canadian area with its own elected officials. Craig Pritchett, a member of ILWU Local 507 who started as a wheat trimmer, was chosen Canadian Area president. Seven delegates from ILWU Local 502 attended the first Canadian Area convention, which convened on 31 January 1959. A member was nominated to sit on the area's executive board, as well.

Monies collected in British Columbia stayed in the province for organizing and the Canadian Area coordinated relations between the locals and negotiations with the Shipping Federation and employers. As the second-largest ILWU local by numbers in the province, New Westminster contributed heavily in leadership and support. Later, Donald Garcia, a colourful ILWU Local 502 member, was an active and brash Canadian Area president. According to Joe Breaks, Garcia was fond of saying, "To get apples one has to shake some trees", and sometimes during union meetings members in the back rows would humorously shout back, "Time to go get some apples." Garcia always had a high opinion of himself and his abilities. Longshoremen needed to be led, Garcia once told a former local president, and he was just the one to lead them.

On the Cusp of Change

By the end of the decade, the importance of the port to New Westminster and the role of longshoremen in the work environment were set to transition. Alderwoman Beth Wood became the city's mayor in January 1959, replacing the harbour and industrial booster Toby Jackson, who was later appointed chair of the Fraser River Harbour

Commission. Wood, like many of her constituents, was inclined to see the aging infrastructure along the river as a problem. Her attempts to get funds from the federal government for replacement of the old Queensborough bridge were fruitless, the Department of Public Works claiming it was an internal roadway and therefore a city responsibility.

Beth Wood personally headed a delegation to Ottawa to meet with government bureaucrats about the waterfront and docks.[94] Wharves needed replacement, and work began on a trifurcation project to make the Fraser River more amenable to larger ships. The Deas Island George Massey Tunnel, opened in 1959, already put limitations on water depth lower down the river. The federal government had passed on the cost of dredging to private companies like Pacific Coast Terminals and Searle, by requiring them to pay for a service previously provided at public expense. Even if commercially viable, the waterfront in New Westminster was just too cramped.

Ideas of expanding warehouses right up to Columbia Street ran up against efforts to revitalize the downtown retail core to former glory by the installation of elevated parking over Front Street. Roland Cope was wrong when he predicted, "it is my honest opinion in the years to come, and it won't be too long, you will see Front Street and Columbia become a warehouse extension of the waterfront."[95] Port activity simply went elsewhere.

In time, Pacific Coast Terminals moved operations to Port Moody, and suitable lands at the grain elevator site on the south side of the Fraser River and farther downstream were developed instead. The advent of containers would revolutionize the shipping business, requiring even more space and specialized equipment. The word that every longshoreman dreads — automation — was spoken. The American ILWU warned Local 502 that mechanization was coming to British Columbia and Harry Bridges already had a strategy to deal with that challenge, in the form of mechanization and modernization proposals.[96] The ILWU sought protections for the existing workforce and special dedicated funds to ease the transition. Mechanics, technicians, and operators serving the machines were classed as longshoremen. ILWU Local 502 had to adapt in order to survive and prosper on a changing waterfront.

Watching the Waterfront

**New Westminster police investigate a break-in at
the union hall office on 9 November 1957**

Quantities of cash and lack of police response time attracted professional safe-crackers, sometimes with inside help. Nitroglycerine was frequently used to blow off doors, though on this occasion, the heavy safe was knocked over on its side and cut open with tools to avoid the noise and shock of an explosion. Such occurrences afforded police opportunity to poke around union affairs, as government worries about organized crime activity on the waterfront first began to be raised. In 2015, thieves just took the entire safe and its contents away in another break-in at the ILWU Local 502 hall in Surrey.

Source: New Westminster Museum and Archives IHP 138700-001 Croton Studio

Watching the Waterfront

The state, represented by federal and municipal police forces, customs and immigration officials, and domestic intelligence agencies, has a long interest in unions and other groups active on the Fraser River. After 1919, the criminal intelligence and special branches of the Royal Canadian Mounted Police (RCMP) collected information for files on persons in the labour movement with known or suspected socialist ties, before and after the Communist Party of Canada was officially banned. The search for political subversives deemed a threat to the capitalist system and government, given the widest possible interpretation, happened in concert with ordinary policing of waterfront-related crime and times of labour unrest within 'E' Division encompassing British Columbia.

Drug smuggling through the port started on a larger scale in the 1920s, predominantly from Asia. Opium dens operated illegally in New Westminster's Chinatown, and at least one chief constable in Vancouver was mired in serious public allegations of looking the other way and corruption. Police upheld the laws of the time, some of which criminalized certain political associations and non-conforming acts. Labour unions were specifically targeted under the infamous Section 98 of the Criminal Code of Canada.

The RCMP worked closely with the Federal Bureau of Investigation of the United States, sharing information and tracking individual union members passing across the international boundary between the two countries. One former longshore worker was surprised that a US border guard knew so many personal details about him during a secondary referral examination, information which could have only come from Canadian sources. The ILWU and Harry Bridges, said by American authorities to be under Communist influence, as well as general paranoia and scares about the reach of the Soviet Union into Canadian society during the Cold War, brought Local 502 and its top officials into the sights of the RCMP. A former local president recounted how a couple RCMP plainclothes members interviewed his wife and neighbours while he was away at work, mainly for background purposes.

Growing concerns about the levels of organized crime related to port operations focused attention on the criminal side. The classic 1954 black-and-white film *On the Waterfront*, starring Marlon Brando, tells the story of ordinary longshore workers standing up to corrupt and murderous union officials. In the United States, longshore workers of Irish and Italian backgrounds were heavily involved in petty theft, racketeering, and the underground economy. High-profile investigations and trials into relations between unions and organized crime in the ports of New York and Montreal spilled over onto the west coast. Dishonest people skimmed membership dues, hijacked cargoes, smuggled contraband and people, imported restricted weapons, and intimidated other members into criminal activities.

The first concerted effort to tackle the problem started in the late 1950s with the formation of a task force, an early type of integrated enforcement team — known today as the National Port Enforcement Team and the local Waterfront Joint Forces Operation, funded in part by Port Metro Vancouver— that put aside jurisdictional lines and involved numerous participants from the federal level right down to the municipal. From the purpose-built Green Timbers 'E' Division headquarters in Surrey, the RCMP performs federal, provincial, and community policing functions for certain municipalities (Surrey, Richmond, Coquitlam, Burnaby, and North Vancouver), coordinating closely with separate city police departments in New Westminster, Delta, and Vancouver. Many official entities are watching the Fraser River waterfront and building domain awareness through a whole-of-government and integrated approach.

The lead agency depends on the nature and geographical location of the criminal activity. The Ports Canada Police (the National Harbours Board Police before 1983) handled policing inside Canada's federal port system, though it was too small in numbers and specialized to handle major crimes and criminal activity effectively. The province's Ministry of Attorney General undertook a review and made recommendations in regard to policing Greater Vancouver waterfronts prior to the RCMP taking over tasks and duties from the Ports Canada Police in June 1997 as part of the federal government's announced port divesture plan. That same year, Vancouver's port contracted out patrolling and basic security to a local private company named Securiguard. The Minister of Transport has statutory authority to make marine transportation security regulations. An interdepartmental marine security working group meets regularly in Ottawa. The Waterfront Joint Forces Operation, specific to Vancouver and area, involves law enforcement acting in conjunction with the RCMP and the Canada Border Services Agency.

In *On the Waterfront*, safes and documents mysteriously disappeared when union officials were subpoenaed to testify, in advance of police coming with search warrants. During the 1970s, the RCMP's Security Service entered offices of labour unions illegally, as well as a number of other dirty tricks. On one occasion, the Canadian Area office was searched after hours, though nothing of obvious value was taken, including a Polaroid camera left in plain sight on a desk. The administrative secretary said files were misplaced and out of order. In May 2015, a safe holding documents and other important materials from ILWU Local 502 was stolen and removed entirely during a break-in.

Police forces today use search warrants issued by the judiciary on a case-by-case basis along with expanded police powers given under federal legislation in the guise of anti-terrorism measures and battling organized crime for collection of signals intelligence (SIGINT) and human intelligence (HUMINT). The Department of National Defence's Communications Security Establishment of Canada in Ottawa and the regional office of the Canadian Security Intelligence Service (CSIS) assumed larger roles in cooperation with national security police forces and other government departments. Ports, as points of entry, and the people who work in them received special scrutiny. ILWU Local 502 and other waterfront unions resisted initial implementation of the Marine Transportation Security Clearance Program, which required all longshore workers to apply for mandated security screening and background checks.

The drug trade in hashish, heroin, and cocaine brought bigger money into the picture as well as the arrival of biker gangs in the late 1970s. Bikers took a smart, methodical, and long-term approach to the elimination of rivals and infiltration into union ranks. The local chapter of the Hell's Angels had a clubhouse at 1041 Brunette Avenue in Coquitlam, all signed up and under constant surveillance, occasional raids, and threatened seizure by police under the *British Columbia Civil Forfeiture Act*. Various East Asian, South Asian, and Hispanic gangs in Surrey challenged the Hell's Angels for turf dominance over the waterfront, on occasion putting aside their differences to work together.

Federal and municipal police investigations of gangs and organized crime eventually took them to the waterfront and ILWU Local 502. A Senate committee report in 2007 and more recent RCMP confidential intelligence reports suggest critical vulnerabilities and the presence of persons with close family and other associations within the union who sponsor other known gang members. In the search for possible biker elements, the police have for many years used informants and undercover operatives inside ILWU Local 502 and its casual workforce. This type of HUMINT is critical to intelligence gathering and building legal cases for arrests and prosecution under the Criminal Code of Canada.

The police are remarkably well-informed most of the time, notwithstanding the limits of investigatory technique, legal authorities, resources, and analysis.

Running a strong union requires integrity and leadership. Dishonest people and cheaters eventually get found out. When a secretary-treasurer was discovered to have embezzled funds from the union to cover a gambling habit, ILWU Local 502's executive called the RCMP and won a $1.3 million civil suit in court against the individual and his wife for sharing in the proceeds. The response of the union to such lapses of moral judgment has to be consistent and reflect the best interests of the membership. It is very hard to remove members, even after criminal convictions. One longshore worker killed another longshore worker outside work hours, served a sentence in prison, and then went back to work on the waterfront upon his release. Sensational media stories about organized crime and the purported involvement of ILWU Local 502 thrive on such salacious content, and the union needs an effective communications strategy rather than giving a wall of silence and denial.

— *Chris Madsen*

Sources: Reg Whitaker, Gregory S. Kealey, and Andrew Parnaby, Secret Service: Political Policing in Canada from the Fenians to Fortress America (Toronto: University of Toronto Press, 2012); Gregory S. Kealey, "The Early Years of State Surveillance of Labour and the Left in Canada: The Institutional Framework of the Royal Canadian Mounted Police Security and Intelligence Apparatus, 1918–26", Intelligence and National Security vol. 8 no.3 (1993), 129–148; Gregory S. Kealey, "Spymasters, Spies, and Their Subjects: The RCMP and Canadian State Repression, 1914–39", in Gary Kinsman, Dieter K. Buse, and Mercedes Steedman, Whose National Security? Canadian State Surveillance and the Creation of Enemies (Toronto: Between the Lines, 2000); Larry Hannant, The Infernal Machine: Investigating the Loyalties of Canada's Citizens (Toronto: University of Toronto Press, 1995); John Sawatsky, Men in the Shadows: The RCMP Security Service (Toronto: Doubleday Canada, 1980); Dwight Hamilton, Inside Canadian Intelligence (Toronto: Dundurn Press, 2006); William J. Neill and Ted Matthews, Ministerial Review of Ports Policing in Lower Mainland Seaports (Vancouver: Ministry of Attorney General, 1997); Public Safety Canada, Economic Sectors Vulnerable to Organized Crime: Marine Port Operations, RDIMS No. 538909 (January 2011); British Columbia Maritime Employers Association v. International Longshore and Warehouse Union Local 500, Local 502, Local 514, and Local 517, 2007 CIRB 397; Standing Senate Committee on National Security and Defence, Canadian Security Guide Book — Seaports (March 2007); Julian Sher and William Marsden, The Road to Hell: How Biker Gangs are Conquering Canada (Toronto: Vintage Canada, 2004); International Longshore & Warehouse Union Local 502 v. Ford, 2014 BCSC 65; Mary R. Brooks, "Maritime Security in Canada", in Khalid Bichou, Joseph S. Szyliowicz and Luca Zamparini (eds), Marine Transport Security: Issues, Challenges and National Policies (Cheltenham, UK: Edward Edgar Publishing, 2013)

Chapter Notes

1　"Meeting of Harbour, Shipping & Navigation Committee", 31 July 1947, AM 440 New Westminster Board of Trade reel M 8-9, CVA.

2　Special general meeting, 31 July 1946, ILWU Local 502 minute book.

3　Interview with Joe Breaks by Andrea Walisser, 9 July 2013.

4　Interview with Bruce Briggs by Dean Johnson, 13 May 2013.

5　"Card Playing in the Hall", 11 December 1945, AM 279 Shipping Federation of BC 520-F-6 file 2, CVA.

6　J.T. Thompson to Shipping Federation, 20 March 1946, AM 279 Shipping Federation of BC 520-F-2 file 1, CVA; "B.C. District Council is Established", *The Dispatcher* vol. 4 no. 1 (11 January 1946), 5.

7　"Minutes of a Board of Directors Meeting of Shipping Federation of British Columbia, held in the Federation Offices, Vancouver, B.C., Tuesday, 8th January, 1946, at 2.30 p.m.", AM 279 Shipping Federation of BC 73-F-8 reel M 17-5, CVA.

8　Edward Wennerlow, "Organizational Report from 20th March 1946 to 28th February 1947", AM 332 ILWU Local 501 541-C-6 file 9, CVA; "Organizational Survey — Canada", ILWU — Organizing — Canada, box 4 file "General", ILWU Library.

9　Interview with Brian Ringrose by Andrea Walisser, 11 July 2013.

10　"Minutes of a Joint Meeting of the Board of Directors and Ways and Means Committee of Shipping Federation of British Columbia, held in the Merchants' Exchange Board Room, Vancouver, B.C., Tuesday, 21st October, 1947, at 1:30 p.m.", AM 279 Shipping Federation of BC 73-F-8 reel M 17-5, CVA.

11　General meeting, 3 December 1947, ILWU Local 502 minute book; D.M. Cameron to members, "New Westminster Agreement", 16 January 1948, AM 279 Shipping Federation of BC 520-F-2 file 2, CVA.

12　John Berry to J.R. Robertson, "Organizational Report up to November 25, 1947", 25 November 1947, ILWU — Officials — Correspondence, file "Berry, John International Representative" (1), ILWU Library.

13　"Shipping Federation of British Columbia President's Report Year 1948", AM 279 Shipping Federation of BC 520-F-2 file 2, CVA.

14　D.M. Cameron to members, "Longshoremen's Strike United States Pacific Coast Ports", 10 September 1948, AM 279 Shipping Federation of BC 520-F-2 file 2, CVA.

15　D.M. Cameron to members, 14 October 1948, AM 279 Shipping Federation of BC 520-F-6 file 5, CVA; Ronald Magden and A.D. Martinson, *The Working Waterfront: The Story of Tacoma's Ships and Men* (Tacoma: ILWU Local 23, 1982), 138.

16 General meeting, 3 November 1948, ILWU Local 502 minute book; John Berry to J.R. Robertson, 15 September 1948, ILWU — Officials — Correspondence, file "Berry, John International Representative" (1), ILWU Library.

17 "Minutes of the Twelfth (1948) Meeting of the Board of Directors of Shipping Federation of British Columbia, held in the Shipowners' Association Board Room, Vancouver, B.C., Tuesday, 7th September, 1948, at 11:15 a.m.", AM 279 Shipping Federation of BC 73-F-8 reel M 17-5, CVA.

18 "Minutes of Meeting held in New Westminster at 71 10th Street on July 11, 1948", ILWU — Canada, file "Local 501 Vancouver (longshore) — general", ILWU Library.

19 General meeting, 8 September 1948, ILWU Local 502 minute book.

20 General meeting, 14 September 1949 ILWU Local 502 minute book.

21 John Berry to Robert Robertson, 19 October 1949, ILWU — Officials — Correspondence, file "Berry, John International Representative" (1), ILWU Library.

22 Unemployment Insurance Commission, "Coverage of Employment in Stevedoring: Proposed Method of Operation", 8 August 1947, AM 279 Shipping Federation of BC 520-F-2, file 2, CVA.

23 Minutes sub-committee meeting, 29 August 1947, AM 279 Shipping Federation of BC 73-F-8 reel M 17-5, CVA.

24 D.M. Cameron to secretary Local 502, "Records", AM 279 Shipping Federation of BC 520-F-6 file 3, CVA.

25 Executive meeting, 3 May 1948, ILWU Local 502 minute book.

26 PC 587, Unemployment insurance coverage for longshore and stevedoring workers, 24 February 1948; "Unemployment Insurance — Longshoremen", 12 March 1948, AM 279 Shipping Federation of BC 520-F-6 file 4, CVA.

27 Interview with Nick Feld by Dean Johnson, 4 March 2013.

28 Interview with Bruce Briggs by Dean Johnson, 13 May 2013.

29 D.M. Cameron to W.L. Hurford, "SS 'Riverside' — New Westminster 21st January 1948", 3 February 1948, AM 279 SFBC 520-F-6 file 4, CVA; D.M. Cameron to G.R. Currie, 4 February 1948, RG 27 reel T-4093 vol. 462 file 12, LAC; Theodora Kreps to W.H. Lawrence, 17 October 1947, ILWU — Canada, file "Local 502 New Westminster (longshore) — general", ILWU Library.

30 D.M. Cameron to members, "Nitraprills and Aeroprills", 11 February 1948, AM 279 Shipping Federation of BC 520-F-2 file 2, CVA.

31 Interview with Gerry White by Andrea Walisser and Michelle La, 2 July 2013.

32 Shipping Federation of British Columbia, "Safety Regulations Governing Waterfront Operations at British Columbia Ports", 1 December 1948, AM 279 Shipping Federation of BC 521-C-6 file 12, CVA.

33 Interview with Brian Ringrose by Andrea Walisser, 11 July 2013.

34 G.E. McKee to P.V.O. Evans, 30 March 1953, AM 279 Shipping Federation of BC 520-G-1 file 3, CVA.

35 D.M. Cameron to members deep-sea section, "Vacations with Pay", 11 December 1947, AM 279 Shipping Federation of BC 520-F-2 file 2, CVA.

36 G.E. McKee to members, "Longshore Annual Picnics", 22 June 1950, AM 279 Shipping Federation of BC 521-B-7 file 8, CVA.

37 General meeting, 5 October 1949, IWLU Local 502 minute book.

38 "Rail Strike Won't Close Ocean Port", *Vancouver Daily Province* (24 August 1950), AM 279 Shipping Federation of BC 521-B-4 file 22, CVA.

39 Jack McCaugherty, "On the Labor Front: Pay Hike This Week for Longshoremen", *Vancouver Daily Province* (20 September 1950); G.E. McKee to secretary Local 502, 18 October 1951, AM 279 Shipping Federation of BC 520-F-7 file 6, CVA.

40 Interview with Dean Johnson by Andrea Walisser, 18 July 2013.

41 Stewart McKenzie to W.A. Henderson, 26 September 1950, AM 332 ILWU Local 501 541-D-2 file 2, CVA; Henderson replied: "Local 501 endorses stand you have taken, according to your wire. Make it strong. Have talked to COPE [secretary of Local] 502 who will consult his committee. Jackson was not instructed! I do not believe he is presenting the opinion of his membership. You are instructed and as you are drawn into politics take strong and definite anti-Communist stand. Yet fight for straight trade unionism. Send full information night letter."; "Confidential Periodic Bulletin (No. 2) to Directors of the Shipping Federation, September 26th, 1950", AM 279 Shipping Federation of BC 521-F-4 file 2, CVA.

42 Fred Jackson to William Gettings, 30 September 1950, ILWU — Officials — Correspondence, file "Berry, John International Representative" (1), ILWU Library.

43 General meeting, 5 October 1950, ILWU Local 502 minute book.

44 G.E. McKee to directors, "Results, New Westminster Elections, Friday, December 8th, 1950", 9 December 1950, AM 279 Shipping Federation of BC 520-F-7 file 4, CVA.

45 Minutes executive council, 8 May 1950, AM 440 New Westminster Board of Trade reel M 8-10, CVA.

46 "Minutes of the Second (1948) Meeting of the Board of Directors of

Shipping Federation of British Columbia, held in the Shipowners' Association Board Room, Vancouver, B.C., Wednesday, 11th February, 1948, at 11:15 a.m.", AM 279 Shipping Federation of BC 73-F-8 reel M 17-5, CVA; John Berry to J.R. Robertson, "Organizational Report", 22 March 1948, ILWU — Officials — Correspondence, file "Berry, John International Representative" (1), ILWU Library.

47 Executive meeting, 4 May 1953, ILWU Local 502 minute book.

48 Brian Towers, *Waterfront Blues: The Rise and Fall of Liverpool's Dockland* (Lancaster: Carnegie Publishing, 2011).

49 Memorandum W.C. Hymus to H.A. Wood "Annacis Island, New Westminster, B.C.", 4 December 1952, RG 30 A-1-c vol. 13054 file 2400-11, LAC.

50 Minutes regular meeting New Westminster Harbour Commissioners, 6 June 1952, Fraser River Port Authority reel 2, NWPL.

51 J.E. Clayton to W.T. Bell, "Overseas Transport Lease & General Information", Fraser River Port Authority reel 11 file 49, NWPL.

52 General meeting, 8 February 1956, ILWU Local 502 minute book; "Agenda for a general meeting of Shipping Federation of British Columbia, to be held in the Merchant's Exchange Board Room, Vancouver, B.C., Tuesday, 24th, January, 1956, at 11 a.m.", AM 279 Shipping Federation of BC 521-F-2 file 1, CVA.

53 Interview with Joe Breaks by Andrea Walisser, 9 July 2013.

54 Executive meeting, 3 July 1956, ILWU Local 502 minute book.

55 *Labour Gazette* vol. 60 (1955), 959–960; *Jackson and Cope v. Shipping Federation of British Columbia*, (1954) 15 W.W.R. 311; John Berry to Louis Goldblatt, 22 July 1954, ILWU — Officials — Correspondence, file "Berry, John International Representative" (2), ILWU Library.

56 M. Kendrick to W.J. Desmarais, 1 February 1957, AM 332 ILWU Local 501 541-D-2, CVA.

57 Special general meeting, 6 October 1952, ILWU Local 502 minute book.

58 Interview with Dennis Buckle by Joe Breaks, 23 January 2013.

59 Executive meeting, 4 January 1954, ILWU Local 502 minute book.

60 "Al Currie", *Gang Plank* no. 27 (June 1960), ILWU — Canada, file "Publications — Local 502 New Westminster *Gang Plank*", ILWU Library.

61 Interview with Brian Ringrose by Andrea Walisser, 11 July 2013.

62 C.W. Train to R. MacPherson, 15 August 1952, AM 279 Shipping Federation of BC 520-G-1 file 2, CVA.

63 Stuart B. Philpott, "The Union Hiring Hall as a Labour Market: A Sociological Analysis", *British Journal of Industrial Relations* vol. 3 no. 1 (March 1965), 20.

64 G.E. McKee to secretary Local 502, 4 December 1952, AM 279 Shipping Federation of BC 520-G-1 file 2, CVA.

65 Executive meeting, 10 September 1956, ILWU Local 502 minute book.

66 Interview with Brian Ringrose by Andrea Walisser, 11 July 2013.

67 John Berry to Louis Goldblatt, 26 February 1953, ILWU — Officials — Correspondence, file "Berry, John International Representative" (2), ILWU Library.

68 President to members, "Welfare Plan", 13 April 1953, AM 279 Shipping Federation of BC 520-F-1 file 5, CVA.

69 Interview with Don McIntosh by Dean Johnson, 12 November 2013.

70 Executive meeting, 6 June 1956, ILWU Local 502 minute book.

71 *Pensions on the Waterfront: The Climax of an Era of ILWU Progress* (San Francisco: International Longshoremen's and Warehousemen's Union, 1952).

72 General meeting, 6 August 1952, ILWU Local 502 minute book.

73 G.E. McKee to secretary ILWU Local 502, 23 May 1953, AM 279 Shipping Federation of BC 520-G-1 file 4, CVA.

74 General meeting, 16 April 1958, ILWU Local 502 minute book.

75 "Agenda for a Joint Meeting of the Pensions Administrative Committee, to be held in the Shipping Federation Board Room, Vancouver, B.C., Tuesday, 5th October, 1954, at 2:00 p.m.", AM 279 Shipping Federation of BC 521-F-2 file 1, CVA.

76 John Berry to J.R. Robertson, 15 August 1958, ILWU — Officials — Correspondence, file "Berry, John, International Representative" (2), ILWU Library.

77 Interview with Gerry White by Andrea Walisser and Michelle La, 2 July 2013.

78 General meeting, 6 June 1958, ILWU Local 502 minute book; "President Labinsky report on Conciliation", *Gang Plank* no. 3 (June 1958), ILWU — Canada, file "Publications — Local 502 New Westminster *Gang Plank*", ILWU Library.

79 "Strike Fear Grows on Waterfront", *Vancouver Sun* (9 August 1958).

80 Special general meeting, 18 August 1958, ILWU Local 502 minute book.

81 M.A. Hambley, "Report on Industrial Dispute Commencement between Shipping Federation BC and International Longshoremen's and Warehousemen's Union Local 502, New Westminster", 22 August 1958, RG 27 reel T-4142 vol. 530 file 169, LAC; "Longshore Strike Paralyzes Shipping in Five B.C. Ports", *Vancouver Sun* (22 August 1958).

82 Bruce McLean, "Strike Idles Docks", *The Columbian* (22 August 1958).

83 "Injunction Allows Ships to be Loaded", *Vancouver Sun* (6 September 1958); Judy Fudge and Eric Tucker, "'Everybody Knows What a Picket Line Means': Picketing before the British Columbia Court of Appeal",

BC Studies no. 162 (Summer 2009), 64.

84 "Mr. Average Longshoreman", *The Columbian* (8 September 1958).

85 William Gettings to Harry Bridges, 5 September 1958, ILWU — Officials — Correspondence, file "Berry, John International Representative" (2), ILWU Library.

86 Clipping "Longshoremen's Strike", 5 September 1958, RG 27 reel T-4142 vol. 530 file 169, LAC; "U.S. Docker Chief Intervenes in B.C.: Bridges to 'Tie Up All Coast' if Strike Breakers Used Here", *Vancouver Sun* (4 September 1958).

87 Department of Labour News Release No. 5151 "Minister of Labour Appoints Industry Inquiry Commissioner to Mediate West Coast Longshore Dispute", 9 September 1958, RG 27 reel T-4142 vol. 530 file 169, LAC.

88 Special general meeting, 22 September 1958, ILWU Local 502 minute book; "Agenda for a meeting of the board of directors of Shipping Federation of British Columbia to be held in Room 404, 326 Howe Street, Vancouver, B.C., Wednesday, September 24th, 1958, at 10:30 a.m.", AM 279 Shipping Federation of BC 521-F-2 file 1, CVA; "Terms of Settlement", *Gang Plank* no. 7 (October 1958), file ILWU — Canada, file "Publications Local 502 — New Westminster *Gang Plank*", ILWU Library.

89 Harry Bridges, J.R. Robertson, Germain Bulcke, and Louis Goldblatt to ILWU Central Strike Committee Vancouver, 23 September 1958, ILWU — Officials — Correspondence, file "Berry, John International Representative" (2), ILWU Library.

90 M.A. Hambley, "Report on Industrial Dispute Termination between Shipping Federation and International Longshoremen's and Warehousemen's Union Local 502, New Westminster", 24 September 1958, RG 27 reel T-4142 vol. 530 file 169, LAC.

91 General meeting, 4 February 1959, ILWU Local 502 minute book,

92 *Jones et al. v. Shipping Federation of British Columbia*, [1963] D.L.R. (2nd) 274; "Agenda for a meeting of the board of directors of Shipping Federation of British Columbia, to be held in the Federation board room, Burrard Building, 1030 West Georgia Street, Vancouver, B.C., Thursday, April 14th, 1960 at 10:30 a.m.", AM 279 Shipping Federation of BC 521-F-2 file 1, CVA.

93 *Jones et al v. Shipping Federation of British Columbia, 1963 Dominion Law Reports (2nd)* 274.

94 Memorandum to file, 24 March 1960, RG 11 B-4-a vol. 5219 file 1024-192, LAC.

95 *Man Along the Shore!*, 124.

96 Louis Goldblatt and Otto Hagel introduced by Harry Bridges and J. Paul St. Sure, *Men and Machines: A Story About Longshoring on the West Coast Waterfront* (San Francisco: International Longshoremen's and Warehousemen's Union Pacific Maritime Association, 1963); Emil Bjarnason, "Mechanisation and Collective Bargaining in the British Columbia Longshore Industry", Ph.D. dissertation (Burnaby: Simon Fraser University, 1975), 1; Alexander C. Pathy, *Waterfront Blues: Labour Strife at the Port of Montreal, 1960–1978* (Toronto: University of Toronto Press, 2004).

Chapter 4

Transformation, Expansion and Conflict

1960–1979

Liam O'Flaherty

On January 1ˢᵗ, 1960, British Columbia had a population of roughly 1.6 million people, just less than a third the number of people who lived in the province in 2011.[1] John Diefenbaker was the Prime Minister of Canada and W.A.C. Bennett was the provincial premier. In New Westminster, still the epicentre of Fraser River shipping, Beth Wood was beginning her second year as New Westminster's first female mayor and her eleventh year on council, having been elected as its first female city councillor in 1949.[2] Though Progressive Conservative William McLennan was New Westminster's Member of Parliament that year, the city tended to elect New Democratic Party representatives both provincially and federally throughout 1960–1979 (and beyond). The #1 song on the *Billboard* Hot 100 chart was Frankie Avalon's "Why", and the CHUM hit parade in Toronto shows that Johnny Preston's "Running Bear" topped the chart that week.[3]

The waterfront landscape of downtown New Westminster was a steady row of industry, shops, and warehouses, part of an interconnected economy dependent on marine and rail-based shipping but also logging and fishing. What looks like an almost exclusively-white European culture today looked incredibly diverse in 1960: Poles, Italians, Hungarians, Scandinavians, Dutch, Greeks, Portuguese, and others.[4] This diversity was obvious to Canadians in 1960. By the early 1960s, some of ILWU Local 502's first non-white members had already begun what would become their lifelong careers on the beach.

By 1960, Local 502 was at its postwar peak. The union was relishing its moment in the sun, as it had just successfully won a 1958 strike whose central concern was pensions, and had also just signed a 'modernization and mechanization' (M&M) agreement with the employers in 1962, agreeing to certain aspects of mechanization so long as longshoremen received ample reimbursement. Ports along the Fraser River were seeing sizable growth in terms of the amount of cargo handled. This had no small impact on the employment outlook for longshoremen. It also allowed growth in the ranks of Local 502. Wartime growth in west coast shipping spurred activity along the Fraser River in the 1940s, then continued in full swing through the 1950s and well into the 1960s. Many of the retirees whose voices contributed to the content of this book were hired in the early 1960s and experienced the robust economy of what is sometimes referred to as a 'Golden Age' for labour.[5] Yet, the seeds of major technological changes, which fundamentally altered the nature and amount of longshore work at Fraser River port terminals, were sown at this time. The 1960s and 1970s, then, represent a moment of pivotal transformation for ILWU Local 502, which was intimately tied to local but also national and global trends.

One of the inspirations for this book was another book published in 1975 called *Man Along The Shore! The Story of the Vancouver Waterfront as Told by Longshoremen Themselves, 1860s–1975*, which was oral history, collected, written, and published by a committee of pensioners from ILWU Local 500 in Vancouver. That book compares the experiences of old-timers and the new longshoremen in the mid-1970s. Every generation, it seems, has its own old-timers, and each new generation of longshoremen along the Fraser River has had better wages and working conditions than the generation before it. This is one of the things that is revealed in the oral histories of the retirees who contributed their knowledge and history to this book. As the old-timers in the 1970s drew stark comparisons between the old days and the present at that time, so too do present-day retirees see the radical changes that have taken place since they started as markers between an older and younger generation of longshoremen. Many of these radical changes — the end of the 'modified shape-up', the opening of the Westshore terminal, the first back-to-work legislation of this era, the introduction of packaged lumber and containerization, the end of hand-stowing, larger ships, and increasingly formalized training — took place in the 1960s and 1970s.

Many longshoremen from Local 502 who were hired in the 1960s were hired at a time when new workers were expected to look at their own old-timers with a certain degree of deference and respect. In many respects this is still the case, though it was especially so in the early 1960s for a variety of reasons. First, many of the more senior longshoremen along the Fraser River around this time had seen combat in World War II and with their service record went a fair amount of both respect and clout. Second, in the early 1960s, there existed very little in the way of formal training. New workers on the docks had to learn on the job and learn quickly, and the way to do that was to establish a rapport with more seasoned longshoremen. Ron Noullett, a retired longshoreman who started working at age 16, described it as follows:

These old guys, you learnt from them. You never mouthed off to them. They were the guys that taught you whatever — they taught you how to do the job, they taught you what the safety rules were, they taught you what our union rules were. I guess it was like . . . a continuation. At least for me, because I started so young, it was a continuation of my growing up.[6]

For many younger longshoremen straight out of high school, this would have been their first job. Working with older longshoremen was about not only learning the job but also coming of age. Joe Breaks, another retired longshoreman, recounted his experience with a more senior fellow worker:

I remember one time I was with Cece Goodall, we turned out to be good friends after . . . So he would grab two of these 3 × 9s [pieces of lumber], twenty feet long, and he pushed them at me. [He said]

"Okay whippersnapper, I'm going to see how good you are." And it was the winter time, I had one of those heavy mac jackets on and he says, "I'm going to have that jacket off you today." And I didn't say anything because you wouldn't say anything. These guys were . . . you don't talk back. So, all day, we didn't run but we were walking really fast and, by the end of the day, I was so tired, I went home and went to bed. I didn't eat supper or anything, but I didn't take my jacket off. The next day . . . I see Cecee and he never took one [off me]. They were just testing you. That's the way it was.[7]

The older generation of more seasoned longshoremen looked out for the younger generation, but also tested them. It was not unusual for younger casuals to be pushed past their comfort zones by more experienced longshoremen. It was a way of ensuring work was getting done the proper way, but it also had the effect of establishing solidarity and camaraderie.[8]

The Crewman's Watch

Senior longshoremen often acted as mentors to younger longshoremen, but not all of them were perfect role models. One retired longshoreman recalls a time when he witnessed a tough longshoreman stealing a Seiko watch from a crewman. The now-retired longshoreman was very nervous at the time because he had to hand-stow lumber with the thief and he kept dropping the boards as he was not yet that strong. During the coffee break, a crewmember came down and wanted to sell his watch to this longshoreman for five dollars. He asked whether he could try it on to see how it looked, but after doing so, the longshoreman refused to give the watch back. The crewman then grabbed a knife, so the longshoreman grabbed a four-by-four and started chasing the crewman. The crewman ran back to the ship and the foreman investigated what was going on. The longshoreman told the foreman, "No, I paid him," and that was the end of it because the crewman couldn't do anything. A younger longshoreman who witnessed this event said his eyes were bulging from shock throughout the whole incident. It was the second shift of his entire career.[9]

— *MICHELLE LA*

Another retired longshoreman, Brian Ringrose, following in his father's footsteps, reported being told by his father on his first day on the job to "do three things: keep your head up, your mouth shut, and your ears open."[10]

Work was busy, tough, and sometimes dangerous. Indeed, just as *Man Along The Shore* emphasized the cramped working conditions, pitiful benefits, and lack of safety for longshoremen at the turn of the century, the early 1960s, though better by comparison in terms of working conditions, still saw a large workforce engaged in heavy lifting and manual labour. New workers were still expected to take on the most physically demanding tasks. The 1960s saw the expansion of mechanization processes which began in the 1950s[11] — mechanization in this context refers to the development of increasingly technologically-advanced ways of handling cargo. As a result of both the mechanization of work along the Fraser River and the more rigid safety standards that would come later as a result of union activism and provincial government legislation, the work steadily became more advanced and safe, though also in some respects more solitary.

Work and the 'Gang' System in the Era of Modernization and Mechanization

The evolution of 'gangs' of longshoremen who collectively took on work tasks aboard ships is indeed one of the central themes of work life in the oral histories of New Westminster longshoremen. These gangs allowed for efficient division of labour among an appropriate number of people per hatch. Prior to mechanization, the employer preferred gangs as well, as evinced by their continuing presence on the gang system "during the prewar period of company unionism."[12] In the age of mechanization however, gangs, which were also institutions that built camaraderie among longshoremen, were zealously defended by the ILWU as instrumental to longshore work life.[13] Longshoremen in New Westminster near-unanimously remember the earliest gangs as having thirteen members. With mechanization, the employer proposed to reduce gang sizes throughout British Columbia, increasingly viewing the thirteen-member gang as featherbedding and certain positions within gangs as redundant. Gang sizes, however, depended on the types of loading and unloading that were being done. Nevertheless, employers' proposals for 'manning relief' urged a further reduction of all gangs throughout BC around this time.[14]

Who comprised the gang? The original thirteen-member gangs included eight men down below in the hold of the ship (four on each side, each man handling the cargo), one hatch tender, two winch drivers, and two slingmen. The hatch tender was the leader of the gang, and gave signals to winch drivers. The winch driver operated the winches, which were used to lift cargo in and out of a ship.

**Longshoremen observe as zinc bars are being
loaded into the hatch at PCT Berth 1D**
Zinc was one of the most popular types of cargo to handle, due to its light weight and easy-to-manage shape. To the right, large pieces of lumber called 'timbers' are stacked on the deck.
Source: Pacific Coast Terminals

Slingmen stayed on the dock or barge where they would connect the slings to the cargo hook. The men in the hold of the ship were responsible for doing all of the manual labour, including unloading and stowing the goods that were about to be transported. In the hold of the ship, two groups of four men would handle the cargo. For each of the two groups in the hold, there would be a side-runner:

> [The side-runner] was responsible to tell you what to do, to show you, any new guys, what to do . . . and how to stow. You had to listen to him because he had the power to kick you off. What he would do is just tell the hatch tender, "Hey, this guy, get rid of him, he's not working." You know? And the hatch tender would say to the foreman, "Hey, kid, phone the hall," get a replacement for this kid, or this guy, or whoever it is, and you're gone . . . They would ditch you right in the middle of a shift sometimes, or, you would go for lunch and you'd come back and you'd be replaced.[15]

The side-runner thus commanded quite a degree of authority.

In older times, the hardest physical work was in the hold of the ship, and the physically easiest work was topside or the duties of the slingmen.

Of slingmen, Dean Johnson noted that:

> By the time a man got enough seniority to get a steady slingman's job, he was getting up in years. On the dock, it was a good job, but when the job was on the scow, it was hard and dangerous. They had to climb all around that pile of lumber sometimes over six loads high. They had to climb down the side of the ship to the scow by a 'Jacob's ladder' — that's what we called a rope ladder. They also had to wear a lifejacket — we called it a 'Mae West' — that was cumbersome. It made climbing up and down the lumber loads quite hard. When it rained or snowed, they had to put on raingear and that made it very dangerous climbing around the scow and up the Jacob's ladder. Also, whenever they went to coffee or lunch, they had to climb up that Jacob's ladder.[16]

Once the cargo was being moved about however, a slingman could often take a break for as much as a half-hour, sometimes more, as his work was done and now remained in the hands of the men down below.

The port of New Westminster was centred on lumber exports, so much of the work was handling and stowing lumber. As Geoff Clayton, an apprentice machinist recounted, "You'd have your deck, 'tween deck, and hold . . . the longshoremen would work in the holds." The standing gear of the ship would bring the loads of lumber into the hatch and the longshoremen "would have to get it from the hatch opening and [stack it in] the side of the ship." The lumber would also "have to be stowed so that it wouldn't shift [during transport]."[17] Gerry White further recounted how the New Westminster port was temporarily though significantly affected by the establishment of the Seaboard and Lynnterm Terminals on the north shore of Burrard Inlet.[18] According to him, this resulted in the transfer of most of New Westminster's lumber export activity to other parts of the Lower Mainland. What lumber remained to be exported in the jurisdiction of Local 502 was increasingly packaged lumber, meaning that it could be loaded and stowed onto ships using lift trucks rather than by hand.

Though retired New Westminster longshoremen near-unanimously remember the thirteen-member gang, some longshoremen recall that the original gangs had "twelve or thirteen", depending on whether there were one or two winch drivers.[19] The reduction in the gang size for certain ships at New Westminster went, as Joe Breaks noted, from thirteen, to eight, eventually to zero.[20] Longshoremen also note that with mechanization came not the elimination but rather the disaggregation of the gang structure whereby many types of gangs proliferated. The introduction of packaged lumber meant that a gang would thereafter be comprised of six members and one lift truck driver. Gangs that handled steel would comprise eight men. There were 'specialty gangs' of varying sizes that were appropriate for individual types of cargo and ships. Over the 1960s and 1970s, some ships no longer required gangs at all. This was particularly true of the 'roll on/roll off' or 'ro-ro' ships, including those ships that delivered cars to Annacis Island. For 'ro-ro' operations, it was typical for there to be a combination of 'operators' who operated the new and multiple types of machinery, such as cranes, forklifts, and so on, and 'spare men' who performed manual labour and whose number depended on their need.

These changes did not happen without a fight. Oral histories are replete with references to slowdowns and work stoppages in the early

1960s, as well as to long and bitter debates at the union hall among longshoremen about how they as workers should respond to the structural pressures that they faced. In 1960, the American branches of the ILWU signed M&M agreements. There, Harry Bridges, firebrand founder of the ILWU and its then-president, believed that the changes brought by mechanization and automation were inevitable and that the best way forward for workers was to accede to the employers' wishes on some matters such as gang changes and scheduling, in return for a "package of benefits and guarantees which would give the workers a 'share of the machine'."[21]

Harry Bridges

Harry Bridges (1901–1990) is one of the founders of the ILWU and led the union for over forty years. He was one of the most influential labour leaders in American history. Bridges was born in Melbourne, Australia. At the age of fifteen, he worked for a shipping line that sailed from Australia to Tasmania where he met militant Wobblies, members of the Industrial Workers of the World or IWW, who had the union motto "an injury to one is an injury to all."

A few things shaped Bridges' political views: the Wobblies, one of Bridges' uncles, and the slums he saw in East Asia and India while working as a sailor. In 1920, Bridges moved to San Francisco and worked as a sailor until the Sailors Union of the Pacific was dismantled in 1921. He then began longshoring and disliked the exploitative working conditions set by the employers. Longshoremen had no job security, were overworked, had to endure the 'shape-up' hiring system, and were paid very low wages.

After the union was formed in 1937, Bridges advocated for racial diversity amongst the union membership and emphasized the importance of rank-and-file unions. The federal government of the United States failed to deport him numerous times. He retired from his position as the President of ILWU in 1977. He made several trips to Western Canada and at every convention, he gave a keynote speech.[22]

— *MICHELLE LA*

However, many in Local 502 viewed the M&M agreement as selling out and some old-timers are mad about it to this day, according to some longshoremen. Harry Bridges, himself, was reportedly almost impeached for it.[23] Incidentally, longshoremen in Canada had been arriving at the same conclusion, as evinced by old issues of the *ILWU Canada Waterfront News*, where the editor spelled out "the ILWU approach" to modernization. BC's longshoremen argued that the principle of this alternative approach to dealing with mechanization is to "protect the workers who actually suffer the effects of mechanization, by guaranteeing a certain definite amount of employment to the basic work force." In those times when there was a shortage of work, the fund would kick in and pay for retraining but also help fund earlier retirements until the ILWU's supply of manpower equalled the employers' demand for it again.[24] The 1962 M&M agreement of the Canadian Area thus followed the American lead and was itself followed by 1963 terms of settlement that established a reserve fund to "shore up pension, life insurance, and other welfare programs," and to provide a guaranteed number of work hours for longshoremen whose time spent working was negatively affected by mechanization.[25]

Mechanization often meant machines replacing the labour of longshoremen. An article in the *Globe and Mail* newspaper bragged that:

> *The most startling changes are in ship design. A vessel specifically built to carry newsprint now is running between the Pacific ports and two Crown Zellerbach Corp. paper mills in British Columbia. One shift of 25 men can unload what would take two shifts of 72 men each.*[26]

It is, nevertheless, difficult to determine the rate with which mechanization affected longshoremen in terms of job losses (or creation). The introduction of one machine did not necessarily mean one lost job or ten lost jobs. Technology advanced unevenly throughout these two decades and did so in ways that often created new opportunities for the continued employment of longshoremen as well. Indeed, the M&M agreement helped in this regard, in that it gave the union breathing room to retrain workers for the new shipping processes and get soon-to-retire longshoremen to retire sooner so the union might better meet labour demand.

However, technological change had measurable impacts on the type of work that longshoremen did, but it also impacted the culture

Three-wheel lift fork-truck at Overseas Transport terminal
This was a unique piece of equipment. One time, this machine was backed through the wall of the Overseas shed, with the single back wheel inside the shed, and the double wheels outside. The operator reportedly said, *"I didn't do it,"* as he sat in the cab!
Source: Port Metro Vancouver

of Local 502. The gang system did not wither away, but it did start to dissipate and that moment can be traced to the 1960s. One retiree noted that the more expansive use of the lift truck in the 1960s was crucial to the destabilization of the twelve or thirteen-member gang.[27]

The lift truck was necessary and useful for newer forms of cargo in the 1960s, including packaged lumber. The introduction of packaged lumber — which Lorne Briggs remembered happening in the mid-1960s[28] — rather than loose lumber, meant that there was less need for longshoremen to handle individual pieces of lumber. In this way, the number of workers required on a gang faced a direct threat from advances in technology. Sometimes workers themselves faced a direct physical threat as a result of these advances in technology too! A machine known as 'the assassinator' was one such new piece of technology that has become legendary in longshoremen's lore for how dangerous it was to operate.

The Assassinator

The assassinator was the nickname of a machine that was used when packaged lumber was first loaded into wings of ships. The assassinator was three feet long and eight inches high, and had a twenty-foot rope attached to it. It had four rollers on the bottom, four on top, and a lock on the side. The lock only locked the top roller. A gang member put the packaged lumber in the centre of the assassinator. When the assassinator was pushed into place, one gang member pulled the rope with great care after unlocking it, after which it immediately shot out under the load. A few longshoremen got hurt, earning it the name 'the assassinator'.

— *Michelle La*

Longshoremen were right to be wary of changes to the gang structure. The issue of mechanization was of foremost concern to the union and to its employer, the Shipping Federation of British Columbia, and often became the focus of controversy between both sides. One such dispute arose between the Federation and Locals 503, 504, and 508 of the ILWU, all on Vancouver Island, when the introduction of packaged lumber was said to have made the second winch driver unnecessary. The Shipping Federation felt that only one man was needed to operate either a single or double winch. Local 502, and the other mainland locals of the ILWU, felt that two winch drivers were even more necessary with mechanization, the second being someone who could act as both a backup winch driver and a safety enforcer.[29] The issue of the winch drivers became so heated that, as Joe Breaks remembered, "when they tried to get rid of the one winch driver, we had a slowdown for a month — it was terrible."[30] Many longshoremen, nonetheless, look back on this time period reflectively. One concluded that the effect of mechanization was largely mitigated by the continued though now-specialized employment of many longshoremen, even in the lean years that typified the late 1970s and early 1980s, and the rise in cargo volume thereafter.[31]

This drawing by Fred Wright appeared in the *ILWU Canada Waterfront News*, the newsletter for the ILWU Canadian Area, on April 20, 1963. It reflects an early unease with automation and mechanization among longshoremen — processes that were just starting into full swing at the time.
Source: UBC Archives, ILWU Canada Waterfront News, April 20, 1963, ILWU records, file 13-14

New technology also created new opportunities for longshoremen. The skills that longshoremen acquired in their lifetimes are referred to as 'ratings'. In the early 1960s, there was no formal training. Longshoremen learned on the job. This meant that, as part of a gang, one would be informally shown what to do by other more experienced gang members, or, as one former longshoreman noted, you were self-taught. At the dispatch hall in those days, a casual would volunteer to take on tasks for which he might not have had any previous experience.

Doing so would add to one's ratings. This even included on-the-job, largely self-taught ways of using the new heavy machinery such as lift trucks when they came on board in the mid-1960s.

Retired longshoreman Jack Singh described his first day working at Westshore Terminals when he and one of his coworkers were assigned to operate a machine neither had ever used before:

Herman Chrysler and I, we had never been to the coal dock at Roberts Banks. Went in the hall, only two jobs, two Cat [Caterpillar machine] drivers. I looked at Herman and Herman looked at me. Herman said, "Let's go check that place out." [I asked] "Have you ever drove a Cat?" He says, "No. Did you?" I say no. So away we go. We get the slip [from the dispatcher]. "Okay, we'll take it." . . . Lots of piles, three, four piles [of coal], two big Cats sitting there, uglier than hell. I never drove one in my life. Neither did Herman . . . You know, we did the wrong things. We did not know how to start . . . Anyway after trial runs, dips, and bumps . . . [the] foreman for the maintenance, he says, "How you boys making out there on the coal pile?" Herman says, "All the holes have been dug, you plant the potatoes anytime." That was one of his funniest lines ever. Well, anyway, they wanted to shovel so much coal in, and we were finished, so they got it done and they go to a 4,200 ton of coal or something . . . But we got it done early, earlier than the rest of them, so it worked out for a couple of rookies, huh? Never been on a Cat before. It worked.[32]

The more ratings one had, the more jobs one was able to do. This was ideal for a longshoreman, as it would increase opportunities for getting work if you were a casual, but it would also give you more choice later on when you became a member and could pick the jobs you wanted to do. With technological change came more opportunities to acquire particular ratings.

Prior to automation, most longshoring was hard manual labour. Not surprisingly, longshoremen who worked in the 1960s preferred handling certain cargo over others. One favourite cargo was zinc, which retired longshoremen said was fairly easy to lift, handle, and stow:

We used to handle lead and zinc. Lead was 110-pound bars, and zinc was 60-pound bars. Because the bars were about 20" long, 4" wide, and 6" high and they had a handle on either end, you could only work two guys at a time of the four. You'd work two loads. You'd do two, the other guys would rest, then they would do two, and you would rest . . . It was a good job, it was clean. Zinc was really good, because it got so you could throw them and they would slide right into place . . . you didn't even have to walk! [33]

There was a consensus among many retired longshoremen who worked in this era that the worst job was handling animal hides. The hides smelled and were often covered in maggots.[34] One retired longshoreman vividly recounted what it was like to handle hides:

We used to load hides coming from mid-Canada — Alberta, Saskatchewan . . . They used to ship them out in boxcars, tied up skin-side out. And in the summertime, it was just terrible with the maggots and the smell and what-have-you. I'll never forget one time I wolfed and went to Vancouver, and the foreman said to me, "You got to finish this container of hides." I said, "I am only working until six." He says, "If you're not working past six, you'll never work in Vancouver again." Well, I was kind of cute, I did leave the job, right . . . Funny part was that, though, I went to the bus stop — I didn't drive a car in them days — I got on the bus. You got to remember this is hides, this is one of the smelliest jobs that I have ever encountered. When I got on the bus, I walked back to the bus and it was packed. Before the bus went two more blocks, I just had the whole back of the bus to myself and it looked like a whole can of sardines up to near the bus driver. [35]

Longshoremen also reported that the handling of large sacks, such as those containing fertilizer or coffee, was difficult work. The fertilizer would often cause burns or skin irritations. Sacks of flour weighing 112 lbs. were described as particularly difficult to handle, though much worse were the coffee sacks weighing 240 lbs., which would require two men to lift them. Other heavy items that longshoremen disliked included lead bars, which weighed 110 lbs. The heaviest items, as well as animal hides, or any items that were difficult to carry, stack, or sling were the cargo that longshoremen favoured the least.

Gerry Cooke stowing flour
Note that the paper along the side of the ship prevents the sacks from touching the steel sides of the ship.
Source: H Langill

The Evolution of the Dispatch System

Longshoremen who wanted to work would go to the hall on Tenth Street in downtown New Westminster and arrive by 7 am. Members were given priority, and most members belonged to a gang. Once all members had the opportunity to get work, the casuals — the new longshoremen who had not yet been sworn in with the union — would go next. Casuals, like members, could be on a 'spare board' or be in regular gangs. Once you were in a gang, you tended to stay with the same gang for a period of time. Gangs were named after the hatch tender, who was usually the one with the most seniority. Each gang would be assigned to work in a hatch of the ship.

One thing that existed in practice at the dispatch hall (though no longer in the Shipping Federation's rules after 1952) was a 'preferred casuals' list. This list tended to be made up of the children (in those days, the sons) of union members. Some longshoremen were frank in recalling the preferential treatment members' children would often receive. For example, a casual might get, on average, one day of work a week, but someone whose father was a member might get two days of

**The former location of the ILWU Local 502 dispatch
hall at 71 Tenth Street, New Westminster**
The location is now occupied by a produce store. Since the year 2000, the
dispatch hall is located at 11828 Tannery Rd, Surrey. The union moved locations
to better accommodate a larger membership as well as to move where most of
the work was going: the other side of the Fraser River.
Source: Larry Kalish

work a week. Joe Breaks described where this 'preferred list' was located
in the order of preference relative to the other boards:

> *[The dispatcher called out] "Are there any members that want to
> work?" And there were only three guys that weren't in gangs —
> everybody worked in gangs in those days. And then there was a
> spare board, which was the highest level of casuals, and then you
> [the dispatcher] say, "Spare board available?" And then those were
> in gangs too. There were only a couple of those. And then there
> was a preferred casual list of fifteen people, and he would say, "Is
> anyone on the preferred list?" Nobody. Then he would go down
> to card men, and then he would say, "Anybody want to work?"
> If you haven't been registered, you were in the 'anybody want to
> work' group, so then you would go up to the wicket and they would
> register you.*[36]

The dispatcher's continued use of a preferred casuals list eventually
fell out of practice in the sixties.

Further down the hierarchy, after the spare board, were the 'card men'. Card men were new employees who had just gotten a registration or 'man number' from the dispatcher. If the work was sufficient that card men were required for work, those men were expected to go to the wicket — once called upon to do so by the dispatch officer — where they would register and receive a credit-card sized card with an identification number. They would then graduate to the spare board, and then ultimately to union membership.[37] As with today, many new employees had to work for several years as a casual longshoreman before becoming full-fledged members of the union. This amount of time varied. One narrator said it took four-and-a-half years to become a member.[38] For others it was longer, and still others it was shorter.

As noted in *Men Along the Shore*, mechanization "brought the specialists, Crane Operators, Ship Loader Operators, Fork Lift and Straddle Carrier Operators." This resulted in the decline of the gang structure.[39] For this reason, many longshoremen saw mechanization as a threat not only to their job security but also to the internal solidarity that created a sense of fraternity in the workplace. In part because of the way that mechanization undermined the gang structure, the union experimented with several dispatch systems.

In the mid-1960s, Local 502 tried a pegboard. Casuals would have white pegs that looked like a chalk sticks and members had clear plastic pegs. Workers would arrive in the morning and place their pegs in a slot on a board on the wall near the dispatcher on a first-come-first-served basis. Longshoremen who witnessed this dispatch control system reported that, on occasion, some longshoremen would physically whack the board, causing the pegs to fall out. Then there would be a riot of longshoremen trying to put their pegs back into the dispatch board.[40] Curly Smith was infamous for knocking pegs off the board. In the 1960s, the work was so plentiful that casuals' and members' cars and trucks would be lined up all the way up Tenth Street in New Westminster.[41]

After the 1960s and 1970s, the dispatch system moved toward a 'job pick' system where longshoremen got to pick the type of job they wanted to do, though eventually the jobs they would be dispatched to were guided by the ratings they held. A telephone-based pre-dispatch system was implemented for Deltaport when it opened in 1997.[42]

As noted, the union controlled the dispatch of longshoremen. In fact, the dispatcher was someone who was elected to that position by the members of Local 502. The union-controlled dispatch remains a point of pride for many members of Local 502, who see this as a singular achievement that gives workers a modicum of independence and also separated the local from longshoremen elsewhere in BC including most notably Vancouver, where the employer operated and still operates the dispatch system. This relative independence had spin-off effects on the culture of Local 502.

The union typically handled grievances internally and did so either formally or informally. Of course, the employer could still get involved, but the union tried to handle disciplinary matters internally. Sometimes the business agent or another member of the executive would try to convince the employer to let the union keep a disciplinary matter in-house. A business agent or president could, with cause, suspend a member for a short period of time for insubordination, for example. In addition to giving the local more internal power, it gave it a higher sense of professional responsibility to its members and to its executive.

Shifting Westward and Southward: From New Westminster to Delta and Surrey

1960 also marked the beginning of several changes to the New Westminster waterfront that set into motion a chain of events that affected the geographic location of Local 502's work sites. But first, where did Local 502's members and casuals work?

According to one former longshoreman, a gentleman's agreement between Local 500 and Local 502 in the 1960s, which later made its way into the constitution of the Canadian Area ILWU, had resolved that Local 502's jurisdiction would encompass all those longshoremen who worked on sites bounded by Mission in the east and all territory south of Fraser River's North Arm, but including the port of New Westminster and the newer Pacific Coast Terminals (PCT) site that would come to be developed in Port Moody. In a trade-off, Local 500 ended up taking over the Port Moody PCT terminals, and Local 502 acquired the rice mills in Richmond. There were, however, numerous work sites for Local 502. Each terminal was named after the stevedoring company that leased the land from the Harbour Commission and operated terminals on it.

Some of the biggest terminals for Local 502 in the 1960s and 1970s were the PCT at what is now New Westminster Quay, the Fraser Mills lumber site, the Fraser Surrey Docks, and Overseas Terminals Ltd. The New Westminster Harbour Commission opened Fraser Surrey Docks in 1964, eventually replacing the Searle Elevator, an old grain elevator that had existed on the site and was finally demolished in 1970.

Searle's Grain Elevator, Surrey, c. 1970s
This is now the site of Fraser Surrey Docks (FSD), approximately Berth #4. For the time, the ship depicted in the foreground was fairly modern from dock to scow. Note the five upright hatch covers which can be opened by the ship's crew without being handled by longshoremen. The small boat at the bottom of the picture is a safety boat. The long shed to the left is the Mount Baker shed, formerly a plywood mill, then a maintenance building for FSD, and then a gear locker for Empire Stevedoring.
Source: Port Metro Vancouver

PCT opened its new location at the eastern edge of Burrard Inlet in Port Moody in 1960. The Pacific Coast Bulk Terminal's location at Port Moody, selected because of its proximity to the Port Coquitlam

Pacific railyards, moved just a thousand tons of cargo an hour in 1960, compared with three-thousand tons of cargo an hour as of 2005. In 1964, the facility expanded even further. By 1981, the PCT on the New Westminster Harbourfront, which had four berths at the site of what is today the Westminster Quay, closed up.[43] Other important docks included the Gilley Brothers docks, the Brackman & Ker (B&K) docks, the Johnson Terminals, and the Evans, Coleman and Evans docks. Each dock served different purposes. For example, the Gilley Brothers docks were primarily a supply dock for fishers, but they also supplied coal.

The establishment of Local 502 can be traced all the way back to July 1944, when New Westminster's longshoremen, following on the heels of a "unanimous vote of the members of the Vancouver Waterfront Workers Association"[44] in March 1944, voted to join the ILWU. Nine years later in 1953, as the ILWU grew and began to organize other parts of British Columbia such as Port Alberni, Prince Rupert, Chemainus, Victoria and so on, Local 511 was established among warehouse workers in New Westminster, primarily at the Pacific Coast Terminals site on the New Westminster Harbourfront.[45] This local coexisted with Local 502 until 1966 when they merged.[46]

ILA/ILWU

In North America, most longshoremen are unionized members of the International Longshore and Warehouse Union (ILWU) or the International Longshoremen's Association (ILA). The ILA was founded in 1892 and operates on the East Coast of the United States and Canada, the Gulf Coast, and Puerto Rico.[47] During the 1934 West Coast Waterfront strike in San Francisco, Harry Bridges, who led the ILA Pacific Coast District up to the strike, rebelled against the ILA. In 1937, he helped form the ILWU. The ILWU operates on the west coast of Canada and United States, including Hawaii and Alaska, and the Panama canal. [48]

— *MICHELLE LA*

In addition to this merger, the stage was set for Local 502 to organize workers at a new terminal outside of the traditional areas in which the local had jurisdiction, namely, the Westshore Terminals at Roberts Bank.

The politics of British Columbia's historically-strained relationship with Ottawa is a factor here. This can be traced all the way back to intergovernmental disputes over Prime Minister John A. Macdonald's National Policy, a federal program that mandated national tariffs and the building of a railway to connect east and west. British Columbia had been urged into Confederation in 1871 on the promise of being linked up with the rest of Canada, only to face numerous delays in the building of the railway, causing deep resentments in the new province.

Likewise, it is within this milieu of intergovernmental conflict that the idea of a superport at Roberts Bank came into being. In 1967, a dispute arose between the provincial and federal governments regarding the inability of the Crow's Nest mine near Fernie to export coal to Japan as part of a lucrative ten-year deal. The Canadian Pacific Railway, the mine operators alleged, was charging too much for freight. The mine, with the support of the provincial government of W.A.C. Bennett, sought to instead ship its coal through the now-defunct Great Northern Railway, a primarily American rail network that operated in parts of BC as well. The CPR president and federal ministers, threatened by the possibility of the provincial government independently building a superport at Roberts Bank and usurping CPR's monopoly at Burrard Inlet port facilities, proceeded to build the superport itself.[49]

The following year, Kaiser Coal Ltd., a subsidiary of Kaiser Steel Corporation of California, inked a deal with a Japanese consortium to export coal,[50] a deal only made possible as a result of the federal government intervention into the Roberts Bank superport proposal. The provincial government responded by developing a BC port authority with the aim of expropriating the land around Roberts Bank, but here too, the federal government beat the province to it.[51] Development of the port took place immediately and the first shipment of coal left the terminal on 15 June 1970.[52]

How Westshore Terminals Ltd., operating the new terminal on behalf of Kaiser, came to be in the jurisdiction of Local 502, or indeed ILWU at all, is a question that is fraught with politics. On the one hand, Westshore clearly fits within the territorial boundary of the areas of jurisdiction agreed upon by the union's two nearby locals, 500 in Vancouver and 502 in New Westminster. On the other hand, as with Deltaport over two decades later, when there were questions about

The newly-constructed Westshore terminal receives its first shipment of coal.
May 1970
Source: Port Metro Vancouver

which union or local would represent its workers, there was initially some intrigue surrounding who would work at Westshore. The owners at Westshore did not want to be part of the BC Maritime Employers Association (BCMEA). It is unclear from oral histories why this was the case, but what is clear is that Westshore's stance caused Local 502 to make a tough decision: sign a separate agreement with Westshore, thus dividing 502's members into two different agreements, or back out altogether. Doing the latter would have meant that Westshore would have given the jobs to the International Union of Operating Engineers, something company owners had purportedly said they would do. Local 502's executive agreed to proceed and sign a separate contract. People from other locals worried that Local 502 signing a separate agreement with Westshore was the beginning of the end; a deal being made outside the existing structure, the prevailing way of doing things, was too risky, and could pit longshoremen with different agreements against each other. "You don't always know in advance if these side deals or capitulations are going to backfire and hurt the union or benefit," said Joe Breaks.

The consensus among longshoremen of Local 502 seems to be that signing the contract with Westshore turned out well for them. Westshore was a different sort of place to work, as compared to the already-established ports further up the Fraser River. At Westshore, longshoremen were dealing with coal all day long. Because it was salaried, they would do a standard full day's work, then went home. This made it distinct from some of the other jobs longshoremen tended to do in other terminals on the Fraser River, where sometimes you could do four hours' work and get paid for a full shift, for example. At Westshore, the "guys were older, you were way out in the ocean, you were away from the bars . . . you got paid for your lunch, you worked your full shift . . . 8am–4pm, 4pm–12am, 12am–8am . . . guys there were settled down."[53] The notion of steady work attracted more family-oriented men who wanted the stability.

Strikes, Lockouts, and 'The Time We Almost Lost the Union'

In addition to being a time of growth in shipping, the waterfront also saw a great deal of industrial conflict in the 1960s and 1970s. One of the 1960s' first big industrial conflicts between longshoremen and the employer was a strike in 1966 over the bargaining rights of foremen, who had formed Local 514. While certification of the foremen would remain an issue that long outlasted the 1966 strike,[54] the 1966 strike morphed into one that encompassed other issues, including the right to take Victoria Day as a statutory holiday. At the time, the ILWU was often subject to court injunctions when it took industrial action that was perceived by the employer, the BC Maritime Employers Association,[55] as illegal. The employer's use of judicial means to quell industrial action was highly controversial, though the use of injunctions to quash union militancy was so common that union leaders, the presidents of the locals, got used to them. Ignoring an injunction gave the union an option: pay a hefty fine or have its leadership thrown in jail. In 1966 for example, the union — again, arguing that its members had the right to take

Victoria Day off — instructed them to take the day off. The employer had, previous to this, been granted a court order restraining the union from treating Victoria Day as a statutory holiday. When the union failed to abide by the court order, the employer went back to court and advised the judge that it had not heard back from the union. Fines were issued to the ILWU Canadian Area president and the presidents of the nine locals.

"This Is What Jail Looks Like"
Union presidents are sent to mock jail as a stunt to celebrate defying the court order. Back row — left to right: Les Copan (Local 501, Vancouver), Laing Mackie (Local 503, Port Alberni), Roy Smith (Canadian Area), Bill Foster (Local 507, Grain Liners), Vince Shannon (Local 510, First Aid).
Middle, kneeling: Bill Laurillard (Local 506, Marine Checkers).
Front row — left to right: Ed Pilford (Local 505, Prince Rupert), Don Garcia (Local 502, New Westminster), Stan Ball (Local 504, Victoria), Dave Mason (Local 508, Chemainus).
Source: International Longshore & Warehouse Union, August 12, 2008, accessed November 22, 2015, http://ilwu500.org/wp-content/uploads/2008/08/08-08-12-The-Presidents-Go-To-Jail-Education-Comm.pdf

Because the leadership had failed to appear before the court, arrest warrants were issued for all ten men, after which each of them had offered themselves up to the sheriff and were released on bail.[56] Those men were Les Copan (Local 501, Vancouver), Laing Mackie (Local 503, Port Alberni), Roy Smith (Canadian Area), Bill Foster (Local 507, Grain Liners), Vince Shannon (Local 510, First Aid), Bill Laurillard (Local 506, Marine Checkers), Ed Pilford (Local 505, Prince Rupert), Don Garcia (Local 502, New Westminster), Stan Ball (Local 504, Victoria), Dave Mason (Local 508, Chemainus).

The matter went all the way to the House of Commons where the federal Minister of Labour, John R. Nicholson, faced questions from NDP leader, Tommy Douglas, about whether or not the federal government should intervene in the case. At the time, Nicholson took a hands-off approach to the conflict, noting:

> *It is not so much a question of interpretation but whether an order of the court has been obeyed. In my opinion that is not a question for the Minister of Labour, it is a decision for the court or judge who is involved. What representations should be made to the court on that occasion will be for the respective sides to decide, but I understand that it is a straight question of whether an order of the court has been obeyed.*[57]

Though Douglas was incensed at the notion that BC longshoremen were "threatened with jail sentences when they seek to exercise the right which Parliament gave them," the union could not have been surprised. As early as the 1950s, opinions expressed in the *Gang Plank* newsletter of Local 502 congratulated a group of ironworkers in a separate union who had recently succeeded in getting an injunction and a series of fines overturned at the Court of Appeals.[58] The Local 502 newsletter went on to make a series of remarks that suggested the use of injunction against it and brothers in other locals and unions was very much part of a class-based political attack on trade unionists.

By 1962, the unnamed writer or writers of the *Gang Plank* newsletter remarked, "It appears to me a judge will issue an Injunction to a Firm without getting the Unions [sic] version of it."[59] In a story titled "Justice for the Unionist?", the author provided a radical critique of the use of injunctions against workers in the province of BC:

In Port Alberni, the I.W.A. have an agreement with the lumber tycoon Mac. B. & P.R. Co. regarding seniority. This was broken, and a strike was the outcome. They go to court, again the men were given the option of paying a fine or go [sic] to jail, because some magistrate said they were guilty. So I say Unionists will never get a square deal from magistrates or judges as long as the system of appointment of magistrates or judges prevails.

The author went on to say:

You might ask yourself, how are they appointed? First of all, you may be sure no lawyer who belongs to [the New Democratic Party] will . . . be chosen in spite of his capability. The appointment is usually a member of the Bar Association who belongs to either the Liberal, Conservative or Social Credit, and the party in power makes the appointments, and you can be sure it is for the past services rendered. Now stop and think how much sympathy for labour has any of the above mentioned group? So brothers, under this system workers will have to suffer by being fined or jailed to uphold a principle, and that's what some magistrates do not understand at least, I don't think so.[60]

The events of 1966 thus marked a pivotal moment in the policies of the trade union movement in British Columbia toward the use of injunctions by the courts. The *ILWU Canada Waterfront News*, the official newsletter of the Canadian Area of the ILWU, noted at the time that longshoremen were leading the fight for a "strong and militant stand" against injunctions in both the New Westminster and Vancouver regions.[61] The effect of the union's militancy in the 1966 affair, which was aimed at winning the right to statutory holidays but also to take a stand against injunctions, was that the federal parliament would in November of that year pass the *Statutory Holiday Act*.[62]

After 1966, which saw other changes, such as the name change of the Shipping Federation of BC to the BC Maritime Employers Association, and the successful negotiation of the first coast-wide longshore contract, Local 502 was becoming stronger and sharing membership growth with other locals. From 1959 to 1967, membership in the Canadian Area jumped from 2,100 to 3,200.[63] Local 502 was growing both in membership and in militancy as a result of these developments, particularly in a context of anxiety about mechanization.

There were two sets of strikes that fundamentally altered Local 502. The first was a set of two strikes (and three contract votes) that took place between 1969 and 1970. The second was a strike that took place in 1972 that has gone down in local history as the first that resulted in federal government intervention and back-to-work legislation. Longshoremen recall these two conflicts as being critical for the survival of the union. One described the events of 1969–70 as the moment when "we almost lost the entire caboodle." Some longshoremen had to turn to food banks to survive, and others went to regular banks to see if they could, for instance, delay mortgage payments on their houses. Brian Ringrose picked up work driving a taxicab. Frank Cobbaert, who started longshoring in 1968, spoke about how he coped with a lack of work during the slowdowns and strikes that epitomized the next few years:

> In my days, it took me six-and-a-half years to get into the union and I had an unemployment claim opened for the whole six-and-a-half years. And there was tough times, especially when I first started. There was some strikes and other things, and I remember there was absolutely no work.[64]

Of the strike in 1972, longshoremen remember it in deeply personal ways. For the employers and politicians, these were just strikes by rowdy entitled dockworkers but for individual members of ILWU, this was the moment when "Trudeau forced us back."

In 1969, the ILWU and the BCMEA engaged in a protracted dispute over a number of issues including pay, gang size, shifts, and modernization. The employers wanted to reform the gang system, to reduce the size of a gang from eight to six, and to allow it to vary according to the new types of ships and cargo being brought in. They also wanted to end the ability of longshoremen to receive a day's pay for doing less than a full eight-hour shift.

In a report published by the Employers' Council of British Columbia, the authors pinpoint the existence of what they called "archaic work rules" whereby workers could "virtually pick and choose the type of work they would do and select shift work with shorter hours to their own monetary advantage."[65] Winch drivers, for example,

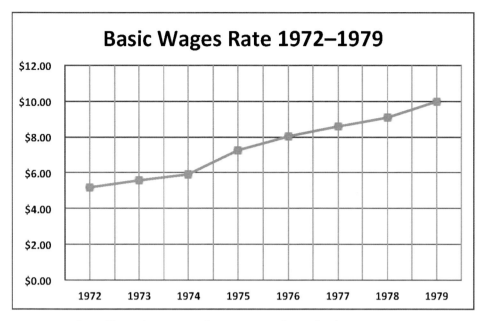

Basic Wages Rate 1972–1979

Source: http://www.bcmea.com/CMS_Content/CABB/39/BCMEA_LONGSHORE_
CA_FINAL.pdf, Collective agreement 1982–1984

would work a four-hour shift and receive pay for a full eight-hour shift. Longshoremen also remembered that loading sacks at PCT could sometimes be completed before noon, and in one instance, Dean Johnson finished up at 10 am, allowing him and the rest of the crew to have the day off.[66] In such a case, a longshoreman would get paid for the entire shift. The employer considered this unreasonable and attempted various measures to alter the situation.

Sometimes the employer arbitrarily increased the quota of goods to be loaded. The employer also pushed to reallocate longshoremen to other jobs if one was completed early. Longshoremen responded by pointing out that certain jobs, including winch-driving, required such focus, repetition, and attention that it was the equivalent of an eight-hour shift of doing other tasks. One longshoreman would do a shift at 8 am and another would do one at 12 pm. A winch driver would never double up by doing both four-hour shifts. Wages were another issue, in many ways a related one. The union wanted a base pay rate of $51 per shift, which was the equivalent of $6.37 per hour, $2.49 higher than the base pay of what was then $3.88 per hour.[67] The union emphasized shifts, whereas the employer worked with hourly numbers. Nevertheless, the BCMEA capitulated and agreed to a base rate of $49 per shift. The president of the ILWU Canadian Area, Andy Kotowich, supported it, but the executive was split and the membership voted against it.

The matter first went to a conciliation board. This board found that both the employers and the union were unreasonable. For its part, the employers were recommending a pay increase of the base rate to a figure that was only 3¢ more than the average pay on the docks. The ILWU had already made concessions by agreeing to the creation of a 24/7 schedule whereby ports would be open, where the employer wished, all seven days a week and with three shifts each day. The shift times ran 8 am to 5 pm for day shift, 5 pm to 1 am for the afternoon shift, and 1 am to 8 am for the graveyard shift. The union felt that this concession alone was worth their asking price on the wage front.

Nevertheless, the impasse resulted in the ILWU rejecting the conciliation board's proposal by 90% and a six-week strike began on 25 September 1969. In that time, the federal government kept a watchful eye over the events. The federal Labour Minister, Bryce Mackasey, intervened by publicly asserting that grain would continue to ship regardless of the strike, but longshoremen agreed to handle the grain.

For this, the head of the Canadian Labour Congress congratulated the union for its "social conscience,"[68] not because the grain was aid on its way to feeding hungry populations, but because the longshoremen were moving goods whose export was relied upon by farmers from the Prairie provinces.

The 1970 report by the Employers' Council of BC identifies Simon Fraser University professors and their influence on ILWU members. The professors were purported to have held "meetings with rank-and-file longshoremen at their local hall" and to have distributed information showing the profits of BC shipping and stevedoring companies. Even Maoist and Trotskyist elements were reported to have influenced longshoremen, given that the prolonging of the conflict was seen as potentially ushering in the federal nationalization of ports.[69]

On 1November 1969, there was an additional proposed new agreement. Local 502 overwhelmingly rejected it — as did the locals in Vancouver and Port Alberni, but not those in Victoria, Prince Rupert, and Chemainus — totalling just 58% for the 'no' side. There remained much confusion over job losses as a result of modernization and proposals to computerize the dispatch system. Andy Kotowich, the chief negotiator and president of the ILWU Canadian Area, had previously revealed that it was likely that as many as one-third of the current longshoremen would no longer be needed in a few years, as a result of the modernization of the waterfronts in BC.

Why would striking longshoremen want to ship goods during a strike?

Longshoring work is so deeply interconnected to every other sector of the economy that when a labour dispute happens on the docks, everyone is affected. The railways delivering raw product from Western Canada to the Pacific coast for shipment are the first to feel the pinch, followed by farmers. In 1997, "coal, forest products, minerals, and machinery" were all more valuable than grain, which accounted for only 1.8% of the value of Canada's exports at the time. Still, the ILWU recognized that when the grain doesn't ship, the employer is able to "bring political heat and draw Ottawa into the dispute," thus getting longshoremen legislated back to work. Under ordinary circumstances, a union would rarely agree to exceptions to their withdrawal of labour. In most contexts this would be seen as weakening their bargaining position, or worse still, a form of 'scabbing'. But the ILWU always backed federal initiatives to allow grain to flow during a strike, including during the industrial conflict of 1969–70. This forced the employers to "negotiate more seriously rather than wait for Ottawa to step in to resolve disputes."[70]

— LIAM O'FLAHERTY

This third rejection caused chaos. Kotowich attempted to resign. Then, having his resignation rejected by the Canadian Area executive, he promised to run again at a special convention held by the ILWU. At that convention, he was voted out, as were many of the other members of the executive. Longshoremen remember this as a time when all the leadership of their union was cast out to make room for new blood. A further vote resulted in another rejection of the proposal, resulting in a second strike. At this point, the employers pointed out that in each year of their proposed pay hike schedules, BC longshoremen would be paid higher rates than those in Seattle, Montreal, and New York. By 1972, the base rate of pay would be $5.03 an hour, making it the highest in North America. In February 1970, longshoremen approved the contract with 55 percent in favour.[71]

Longshoremen remember this was the strike (or rather, strikes) that almost broke the union. The main issue, despite the multiple rejections, was not about monetary gains but rather how workers were hoping to address the twin issues of "the opening up of the ports" — that is, establishing a 24-hour port operation — and containerization. The container clause, which the longshoremen ultimately won, turned out to be a win for the union, one whose importance they would not fully realized for years to come.

Industrial action by the local took other forms too. The changes in the gang structure, which were ushered in by mechanization, happened over the course of many arduous contract negotiations and slowdowns over the years. Slowdowns were necessary because if the longshoremen conducted a work stoppage, the employers were within their rights to fire the entire gang. Firing was, as we shall see, not necessarily the end of one's career as a longshoreman, but it was nevertheless preferable to do a slowdown and avoid being fired than to stop work altogether and be fired. That sometimes did not stop the foreman from disciplining workers in the event of a slowdown.

One Local 502 longshoreman tells the story of a 1960s slowdown he participated in when he was working in Vancouver:

We [had] a contest to see which gang could do the least, but you couldn't stop because if you stopped, they'd fire you. So you had to keep moving, so you'd carry the same board back and forth, back and forth, back and forth. Yeah, it was, it was terrible but that's what we did . . . You can't stop. Because they'd be waiting to see if anybody'd stopped, just stood there. They'd fire you, right? They'd fire the whole gang, not just you, the whole gang. So . . . I remember once in Vancouver, a slowdown, I can't remember what the issue was now, but anyways it was in the winter, Christmastime, Japanese oranges. So, it was a foreman's strike — yeah, because they had all these office workers out there. So when it was oranges, we would rig these tents because it was raining in the wintertime, Christmastime. Because you couldn't get the oranges wet, so we'd rig these tents. So this young guy came out from the office someplace.

And there was a big hullabaloo about which gang went to which hatch. Finally, he got that sorted out, so he said, "Yeah, rig the tents." We said, "Yeah, okay, fine." So, we rigged — it took us 'til about 2 pm to rig the tents. But instead of rigging the tents for the dock, we rigged 'em all for the water. So when he found out that . . . he fired the whole ship, the whole ship was fired, you're all gone. [laughs] So and then, we had to get — because Vancouver . . . they would provide you with transportation to and from, but if they fired you, [you] had to get out on your own. So we all had to get our own taxis back [to New Westminster and Surrey].[72]

This epitomizes the spirit of the age when it comes to longshoring in the 1960s. The longshoreman was at once fiercely self-governing and also ready to take on the task of labour struggle. So little did one care about getting fired in the event of a slowdown that one's only concern was having to arrange a taxi home.

The 1971 ILWU American strike

A retired longshoreman remembers that during the 1971 ILWU strike in the United States, he held the special position, which he had only one time, of the "assistant banana inspector." He remembers due to the strike "these liquor barges [came] or else you had, like, the stuff coming from Hawaii, and sometimes it was bananas" which were docked at Pacific Coast Terminals. This longshoreman assisted the banana inspector by bringing the bananas for the inspector to look at. He recalls that when the liquor barges came in due to 1971 strike, "the party was on then 'cause there was no real policing of those things." Some longshoremen would get drunk as they were unloading these barges. He remembers bottles being all over the place. Sometimes on ships, he would find bottles left from the longshoremen who worked on the ship from the previous ports, often on ships that had nothing to do with liquor.[73]

— *MICHELLE LA*

The events of 1969–1970 were not the only bitter years for Local 502. The events of 1972 also proved to be a time of acrimony between longshoremen and the employer. 1972 was, incidentally, also a year remembered for disputes with other unions, as longshoremen and teamsters disagreed over work

Bureau du Greffier des Parlements

I, Robert Fortier ——, Clerk of the Parliaments, Custodian of the Original Acts of the Legislatures of the late Provinces of Upper and Lower Canada, of the late Province of Canada, and of the Parliament of Canada, certify the subjoined to be a true copy of the original Act passed by the Parliament of Canada in the Session thereof held in the twenty-first years of Her Majesty's Reign, and assented to in Her Majesty's name by the Governor General, on the first day of September one thousand nine hundred and seventy-two remaining of record in my office.

Given under my Hand and Seal at the City of Ottawa, Canada, on the first day of September one thousand nine hundred and seventy-two.

Je, Robert Fortier ——, Greffier des Parlements et gardien des originaux des Lois des Législatures des ci-devant Provinces du Haut et du Bas-Canada, de la ci-devant Province du Canada et du Parlement du Canada, certifie que le texte ci-joint est une copie conforme de l'original de la loi adoptée par le Parlement du Canada en sa session tenue en la vingt-et-unième annéex du règne de Sa Majesté, et sanctionnée au nom de Sa Majesté par Son Excellence le Gouverneur Général, le premier jour de septembre mil neuf cent soixante-douze et fait partie des archives de mon bureau.

Donné sous mon seing et sceau en la ville d'Ottawa, Canada, le premier jour de septembre mil neuf cent soixante-douze.

This is a parliamentary certificate from 1972, verifying the authenticity of the copies of the *West Coast Ports Operations Act* of that same year. Copies of that act were sent to union officers after the ILWU was forced back to work by that same legislation.
Source: Joe Breaks

jurisdiction at Pacific Coast Terminals and the Annacis Auto Terminal.[74] But it was the 1970 contract, now up for renewal, that produced the most acrimony for longshoremen in 1972. This time however, we do not see the use of the courts and injunctions, but rather the federal government using executive authority against longshoremen. A conciliation board was convened in the summer of 1972 to deal with outstanding points of contention between the union and the employer related to the 1969 agreement. On September 1, 1972, the union was forced back to work after a little over a week of picketing (over three weeks for the Vancouver local) due to passage of the *West Coast Ports Operation Act*, 1972, known at the time as Bill C-231. The same thing happened again in 1975 when negotiations broke down and the federal government passed the *West Coast Ports Operation Act*, 1975, and again later in 1994 when the federal government also compelled the parties to final-offer selection.

In 1975, the federal government of Pierre Trudeau also passed the *Anti-Inflation Act*, which established wage and price controls and also the Anti-Inflation Board (AIB), to which parties in industrial conflicts were required to submit proposals. This restricted labour rights by forcing unions like the ILWU to keep monetary demands within prescribed amounts when engaging in collective bargaining. If the rule for one year was that the monetary demand could not be more than, for example, a six-percent increase, the union would not be able to seek anything more than six percent — this included not only wage increases but also benefits as well. This put the union in the position of having to do something that neither it nor the employer ever did before: monetize all non-monetary demands. In other words, everything in the proposed collective agreement had to be converted into monetary terms so that the AIB could verify that the cost of all demands did not exceed the limits set out in the act. Retired longshoremen agreed that this counter-intuitively turned out to have some benefits for the union, as it taught the union how to cost its contract proposals better, but the 1979 contract that was approved by the AIB also ended up giving the ILWU in British Columbia a better deal than they had anticipated.

Class Consciousness, Politics, and Newsprint Media

Workers in Local 502 had, around this time, developed a clear class-consciousness and sense of brotherhood, but they also had a spirit of independence. This manifested in many ways.

First, despite the editorial line of the *Gang Plank* and a loose consensus among longshoremen in Local 502 in favour of pro-labour policies and political parties, the union was largely non-partisan. Some longshoremen who were around in the 1960s and 1970s remember that throughout this period, the local would, from time to time, invite provincial election candidates to come discuss their ideas and platforms, and often contribute to the campaigns of candidates who were pro-labour. Some members cringed at the idea of their local giving money to political parties or candidates for whom they did not intend to vote.[75] For its part, the *Gang Plank* echoed the thoughts of ILWU president Harry Bridges, who famously told the AFL-CIO that the "rank and file would support the party, or parties that labour could get the most out of, and that's the way it should be."[76]

"How Harry Bridges saved my bacon"

Joe Breaks, one of the retired longshoremen who contributed oral history for this book, had a story about a time when Harry Bridges intervened to help and saved the day. One time, when Joe was president of Local 502, he shut down a ship, meaning that he ordered his fellow longshoremen to cease work. He quickly realized that he was in the wrong and that the BCMEA were within their rights to sue the ILWU over the work stoppage. Other than going on a legal strike, the only other time longshoremen could stop work was under '7.03', the section of the collective agreement that permitted longshoremen to refuse unsafe work. This particular work stoppage did not fall under that provision.

So Joe headed to the Canadian Area office on Hastings Street to let them know what he had done. There were no Canadian Area officers around, though Harry Bridges was present. So Joe told Harry about what he had done. Joe was sure he was going to get a "call from the lawyers" at BCMEA pretty quickly. He waited, but the call never came. Days later, still no call came. Years later, Joe discovered from a Canadian Area officer that the day Harry was set to fly back to San Francisco after that trip to Canada, he had made a stop into the BCMEA office to speak with the general manager, Ed Strang, about the incident. "I don't know what he said," said Joe, but Harry talked Strang "out of doing whatever [the BCMEA] wanted to do."[77]

— *Liam O'Flaherty*

I.L.W.U., Local 502			I.L.W.U., Local 502	
BALLOT			**BALLOT**	
Friday, October 25th, 1963			Friday, October 30th, 1964	
For President			**For President**	
Vote for One				
BROOKS, H. A.			CRANE, Robert	270
GARCIA, D.	*Elected*	29	GARCIA, Donald P.	60
		166		
STEIGENBERGER, R.		105	**For Vice-President**	
For Vice-President			FORD, Glen	103
Vote for One			MONSSEN, Merle	222
ERICKSON, O. C.	*Elected*	152	**For Secretary-Treasurer**	
FERGUSON, C. N.		139	MAAREN, Otto	244
For Secretary-Treasurer			McFADYEN, Stewart	80
Vote for One			**For Business Agent**	
COPE, R. R.	*Elected*	200	KOTOWICH, Andy	303
McFAYDEN, S.		93	PETRIE, Keith	22
For Business Agent			**For Dispatcher**	
Vote for One			AMERO, Leo	83
ALLEN, F. L.		48	LESTER, Gerry	241
BURTON, W. K.	*Elected*	129	**For Relief-Dispatcher**	
KOTOWICH, A.		126	Vote for One	
For Chief Dispatcher			BENTLEY, Don	62
Vote for One			BUCKLE, Denny	15
LESTER, G.	*Elected*	262	BROOKS, Harry "Bill"	10
PURDIE, J.		40	FOORT, Eddie	12
For Relief Dispatcher			McKAY, Sidney	23
Vote for One			PENNELL, Joe	25
BOLEN, L. A.		24	RICHARDS, Harvey	35
FORD, G. E. (Jr.)		20	STEIGENBERGER, Robert	115
MAAREN, O.	*Elected*	227	TAYLOR, Len.	25
MULLEN, E.		28		
Mark All Ballots by an X			Mark All Ballots by an X	

Elections to the Local 502 executive were annual and competitive
These vote tallies from the 1963 and 1964 elections show how easily an incumbent could get voted in and then voted right back out again.
Source: ILWU Local 502 Minute Books

Secondly, before modern-day arbitration laws came in, longshoremen reported quitting *en masse* in solidarity with workers in dispute with the boss. If a longshoreman had a dispute with a foreman, oftentimes the longshoreman would just quit, or worse, be fired by the foreman. The remarkable thing about this period, however, is that because labour laws and protocols were relatively lax and because there was always a demand for hard-working and skilled longshoremen along the waterfront in those days, a longshoreman who had quit or been fired would very likely be hired back that week, or, in more rare cases, the same day. This would especially be the case when a solidarity strike happened and the whole gang would quit in protest. In this way, longshoremen stood out in the world of unionized workers — the gang structure, which Joe Breaks called "mini-unions"[78] was a site of worker solidarity but also formed the basis of independent, worker-led industrial activism.

Third, Local 502 members were deeply involved in the politics of their local and the wider Canadian Area of the ILWU. Early final tallies of Local 502 elections reveal that all positions in the local executive saw fiercely competitive election battles and rarely any acclamations.

Local 502 elections

Elections for the local executive happen annually. The positions are: President, Vice-President, Secretary-Treasurer, Business Agent, Dispatcher, and relief-dispatchers. Elections also happen for the Canadian Area executive. Retired longshoremen remember how "the VP wasn't that active" and how it was primarily the President and Business Agent(s) that were most active — in the 1960s, there was only one business agent, but nowadays there are two. Additionally, while the presidency of the local was not ordinarily a full-time job, it is now.

— LIAM O'FLAHERTY

For longshoremen, it was the union above all else, including the egos of executive office holders and their competitors. Often, well-known and well-respected local presidents, business agents, dispatch officers, and others would be bounced out of office in a union upheaval for any number of reasons. This was the case in the years 1963 and 1964, when one local president, who had just been elected in 1963, was turfed the following year. It was also the case in the aftermath of the 1969 strike when the entire executive was voted out and replaced.[79]

For as long as Local 502 has existed, it has zealously defended its independence and particular interests from the affairs of neighbouring longshoring locals, especially Local 500 in Vancouver. This spilled over into the politics of the Vancouver District Labour Council (VDLC). The VDLC was the constituent local council of the Canadian Labour Congress and covered the greater Vancouver area. As early as the late 1950s, the thought arose that New Westminster and the surrounding area should have its own labour council. The reasons given were that it took delegates at the VDLC from New Westminster area too long to travel to Vancouver. It was also argued that as a separate city and regional area with a distinct local industrial base, including the waterfront, the unions and their locals which existed in the New Westminster area were outnumbered at the VDLC and not getting the representation they deserved.[80] The proposed new district council would eventually come to cover not only New Westminster but Burnaby, the Tri-Cities area (Coquitlam, Port Coquitlam, and Port Moody), Surrey, Delta, Langley, and as far east as Maple Ridge.[81] As a local of the ILWU, which already stressed its independence from Vancouver, Local 502 was at the forefront of leading this evolution away from the VDLC towards the eventual New Westminster District Labour Council (NWDLC), which first met in 1966.

Internationalizing the Union: Longshoremen Look Beyond BC

Shipping on the west coast of North America puts longshoremen in a unique position at the heart of Pacific, and indeed global, trade. As a result, and in a more direct and evident way than labour in other sectors, longshoremen are constantly confronted with international aspects of their work. This also spilled over to the status of New Westminster as a 'hub of the area' with a global flair. It was "the place to go, it was where the action was," said one former millworker and carpenter, Bill Zander. It was a place where, he noted, you could always check out the ships tied up at dock. Zander continues, "we were always interested in the flag, what country they came from, because it gave us the feeling that this was an international place, pretty exciting, and it was — a busy, busy little town."[82] Longshoremen also saw these international connections in the goods and materials that were coming and going from the ships they loaded and unloaded, as well as with the people who worked aboard those ships. Local 502 members started visiting, through trade missions, those same countries from which the goods were coming or to which they were going. They encountered seamen from other countries who worked aboard the vessels. They attended conferences of the ILWU, most of whose locals were and are in the United States. Finally, they occasionally had the opportunity to work in those countries. Through all this, Local 502's international complexion is revealed in these encounters across the globe.

The early 1960s was a period of major global upheaval. Local 502 was no stranger to international affairs. Indeed, as the name of the union suggests, it was an international union which, depending on the era, had varying degrees of formal or informal connections with the ILWU head office in San Francisco. According to a pamphlet published on the twenty-fifth anniversary of the founding of the Canadian Area, the ILWU was "exceptional" among U.S. internationals in that its Canadian locals were "democratically run" and, in the words of Harry Bridges, the Canadian Area of the union was "Canadian . . . for the Canadians [and] without interference from the labour fakers in the United States."[83] This was echoed in the preamble of the first constitution of the ILWU Canadian Area, drawn up in 1959 — a year after the union had won major concessions regarding such things as vacation pay and pensions — where it stated:

> *We, the men and women, working under the jurisdiction of the ILWU in Canada, recognize the need for autonomous expression of Canadian conditions while maintaining international solidarity with the workers of all parts of the world, to the mutual advantage of all.*

Here, the Canadian locals of the ILWU, all in British Columbia, were attempting to strike a balance between ensuring that they had autonomy from the American headquarters while also maintaining the internationalist spirit of fraternity.[84]

Many retirees of Local 502, some of whom had spent time as business agents, local presidents, or in other positions in local leadership, fondly remember Bridges. But separate from the inherently international nature of the union structure, constitution, and links with Americans, members of Local 502, as well as their brothers in nearby locals, were quite involved in the global trade union movement. This involved small-scale things, such as agreements with locals elsewhere on the west coast, namely those in Victoria, Seattle, San Francisco, and Los Angeles, whereby longshoremen could work temporarily at each other's work sites.

Travelling cards

Up until the early 1960s, longshoremen were able to get travelling cards that permitted them to travel to other ports on the west coast of North America for three months in a year. One of the longshoremen did this over two years for a total of six months in California. He and his best friend worked the ports of Long Beach, San Pedro, and Wilmington. The longshoreman states, "We worked down south there and we had a ball down there. Everyone treated us a hundred percent." The longshoreman recalls that in California they had different versions of jobs that the longshoremen did in New Westminster, particularly 'run and drop'. This longshoreman did not just work on this trip with his partner, as he states, "we went all over." They visited places such as Disneyland and would go to Santa Anita racetrack every weekend to watch races. Another longshoreman recalls spending his childhood summers in California. His father, who was a longshoreman, had a travelling card, and moved the family down while he worked there.[85]

— *Michelle La*

Taking a global view also meant involvement in the big political issues of the day. Local 502 paid witness to the rise of the Cold War, the beginnings of decolonization in the third world, and the postwar growth of international trade more generally, in very unique and distinct ways. One moment when BC longshoremen were involved in international politics can be seen in the decision by Canadian locals of the ILWU to support trade with Cuba and to send longshoremen there as part of a trade union delegation.

After the Cuban Revolution in 1959, the world's attention turned to the rise of Fidel Castro and the Cuban Communist Party after the fall of right-wing dictator, Fulgencio Batista. The labour movement was divided over its position on the results of the revolution. Some either supported the revolution or believed, as the federal government of Progressive Conservative Prime Minister John Diefenbaker did, that the revolution was an internal matter for Cuba. Others sympathized with vigorous American and Cuban-exile opposition to Castro. In 1960, the British Columbia Federation of Labour proposed plans to send a delegation of its workers to Cuba. Craig Pritchett, then the president of the Canadian Area of the ILWU, wrote to E.P. O'Neal of the BC Federation of Labour to express longshoremen's interest in participating in the delegation.[86] O'Neal responded by indicating that he had asked the International Affairs Department of the CLC to assist with making these plans.[87] The response from the CLC was that:

> It is important that affiliated and chartered organizations of the Congress should be familiar with the conditions under which trade union organizations function in [Cuba]. It should be emphasized at this point that the C.L.C. is not opposed to the maintenance of normal diplomatic and trade relations with Cuba, which is in conformity with our attitude towards all totalitarian countries. The Congress, however, cannot become a party to any expression of sympathy or active fraternization with organizations and institutions which follow a policy of suppressing the free trade union movement.[88]

It would be wrong to overstate the degree to which longshoremen in the Lower Mainland influenced federal government policy. Still, it is worth noting that the ILWU was instrumental in supporting the BC Federation of Labour's delegation, which contradicted the CLC's veiled caution that it not express sympathy with the Cubans. To this end, Pritchett stressed that Vancouver-area locals, including 502, made their own decisions on such matters. He even went so far as to telegram the Prime Minister to express his union's support for trade with Cuba.[89] In so doing, he noted that the ILWU was, unlike its counterparts in the ILA in Saint John and Halifax, not controlled or influenced by their American brothers who had come under pressure to oppose the new Cuban regime, nor would it boycott the handling of cargo destined to or from Cuba to BC ports.[90] For this, Pritchett was sent a letter from the leadership of the Cuban longshoremen's union thanking the BC longshoremen for supporting trade with Cuba.[91]

To this end, the ILWU, and Local 502 in particular, has a history of acting autonomously from the larger organizations to which it belonged, whether it was the wider ILWU federation, the BC

Federation of Labour, or the Canadian Labour Congress. This was particularly true in the 1960s. There was a limit to the local's support for such causes, however. Solidarity was important to the union but union members understood the need to balance such causes with the very real financial costs of supporting such international delegations, as such costs were borne by the union itself. The rank and file of Local 502 members were reported to have grumbled that the sending of a second delegation to Cuba in 1961 was a 'waste of money' given that a delegation had been sent to Cuba just a year prior.[92] In any case, one Local 502 member was reported to have gone to Cuba of his own volition in 1962, the following year, to pay witness to the post-revolutionary changes firsthand.[93] Members of Local 502 very much had an international spirit. Their international solidarity was expressed in a multitude of ways.

As early as 1947, the ILWU,[94] following an initiative from Australian dockworkers and led by other BC unions, planned to boycott ships from the Netherlands to protest atrocities being committed in Indonesia by the Dutch colonial forces at the time.[95] Longshoremen struck or informally idled ships from certain countries for any number of reasons, sometimes not as an authorized union activity but simply through individual actions. In the early post-World War II years, some of the men on the shore who had been prisoners of war in Hong Kong refused to work on Japanese vessels and instructed younger longshoremen to follow their lead.[96]

Old-timers/War Veterans

Not all longshoremen had positive experiences with crewmen, especially the longshoremen who served in World War II and the Korean War. These men were called the 'old-timers' and had a reputation for their heavy drinking and being tough. The younger longshoremen avoided conflicts with these men.

A couple of these old-timers had been captured in Hong Kong by the Japanese, and were held as prisoners of war. There was a longshoreman, who was over 200 pounds when he signed up for the army but came back 93 pounds from being in a prisoner-of-war camp for four years. Some longshoremen remember that when Japanese ships were docked in New Westminster, this particular old-timer would yell obscenities in Japanese to the Japanese crewmen, who would go back inside and not leave their quarters.

A longshoreman remembers a ship docked at the port which had flown the Canadian flag — at that time, the Red Ensign — upside-down by mistake. He was about to board the ship to work, until one of the old-timers warned him to not get onto that ship until they put the flag right.

One longshoreman also recalls an *older* old-timer who said to a foreman that was trying to get him to work, "For five years, the Japanese with a bayonet couldn't get me to work. You think *you're* going to get me to work?"[97]

— MICHELLE LA

Likewise, some longshoremen remember in the early years of the Cold War some men either refusing to load or unload Russian or Russia-bound ships, or at least having moral dilemmas about it.[98] While longshoremen's refusal to work aboard vessels of certain countries was most often motivated by sympathies for or solidarity with their fellow workers or otherwise oppressed people, their memories of participation in full boycotts of certain countries is limited. Few remember the politics around the ILWU or the BC Federation of Labour's stance against handling South African ships during the Apartheid era, though this may simply have been due to a possible lack of South African ships coming up the Fraser River. The sort of politically-motivated coast-wide work stoppages that sometimes animated American branches of the ILWU — from those during the Vietnam War all the way up to the May Day strike in 2008 against the War in Iraq — tended not to be as pronounced nor as frequent in Canada, at least among Local 502's workers.

Nevertheless, longshoremen in Local 502 often looked beyond the immediate tasks of their workday or their own interests and engaged in the politics of international solidarity. Indeed, the very nature of longshoring work necessarily owes itself to an international orientation. This is expressed most eloquently by archival documents that show longshoremen were enthusiastic about trade, but it is also revealed in the stories that retired members of Local 502 share about their encounters with sailors and ship crews from foreign countries that worked aboard docked ships in Local 502's jurisdiction.

Interactions with Sailors

Longshoremen would often have interactions with crewmen aboard visiting ships. Sometimes crewmen would invite the longshoremen to eat with them. A retired longshoreman recalled being on a Norwegian car ship and, as soon as he heard the lunchtime whistle, he saw a Norwegian crewman with a nice cold twelve-pack of beer and some sandwiches to share with the longshoremen. If the longshoremen were finished work and the crewmen were off-call, sometimes the longshoremen would take the crewmen to the beer parlours in New Westminster and sometimes back to their houses to continue partying. The crewmen would often sell their foreign liquor to longshoremen, which was much cheaper for the longshoremen compared to buying in-province. PAD ships from Australia that came into the port were very popular amongst the longshoremen, as these ships had a bar and the longshoremen would enjoy a couple of drinks. When ships from the Soviet Union came, some of the longshoremen received USSR memorabilia from the crewmen as gifts. However, some longshoremen recalled that those crewmen would be under surveillance by Soviet officials to ensure that they would not defect.

Sometimes, the crew's English was very limited and even the crewmen themselves would not understand each other, as sometimes the crew was made up of sailors who came from different places around the world. This made hand-signal communication very important. Occasionally, there would be communication difficulties between the longshoremen and crewmen.

Longshoremen empathized with the crewmen and felt like they had a lot in common, as they were all family men. Some gangs got to know the crewmen really well. The gangs would sometimes get called back to work on the ship for over two weeks. Through that, continuing friendships were made between the crewmen and the gang. Sometimes, the longshoremen would help the crewmen out by giving them food and money or taking them home for dinner. Some longshoremen even partied with them.

When retired longshoremen look back, they take pride in the hard work they did before automation and mechanization were introduced. However, when longshoremen talk about the hard work of crewmen, it is often with a tone of respect. Crewmen now have better living conditions on these ships, but the longshoremen recall the horrible and cramped living conditions that crewmen lived in for months at a time a couple decades ago. Sometimes these crewmen faced abuse from their employer; often, crewmen would not be paid their salaries for months at a time and would get fined for any little infraction. The ship's food was also terrible. Longshoremen recall that sometimes when these crewmen spoke up about their working conditions to the employer, the crewmen's families might get punished back home in retribution.

A lot of the ships that came through the Local 502 during the 1960s and 1970s were Liberty Ships that were used in World War II. The shipping magnate, Aristotle Onassis, purchased these old war cargo ships by the thousands to deliver cargo around the world. In those decades, it was the crewmen who were the ones who had to repair the ships. Some of the ships were in deplorable and unsafe conditions. Longshoremen recall that some of these ships, nicknamed 'rustbuckets', were rusted out so much you could see the ocean through them. During the 1960s, Local 502 had a generation of young longshoremen who were very safety-conscious during this period of expansion, and they would always inspect the ships for safety before they worked on them. This often led to fights with the shipping lines due to the unsafe gear and booms on their ships. Sometimes, the shipping companies would fire the longshoremen if they said conditions were unsafe — the issue then went to arbitration and the longshoremen always won because the arbitrators would not want them working in unsafe conditions. The longshoremen would not work until the ship was fixed and safe. As a result, Local 502 gained a reputation for safety and there was the saying "if a ship can work in New Westminster, it can work anywhere."[99]

— MICHELLE LA

Short-term solidarity or sympathy strikes with international workers also occurred, and their presence along the Fraser River tended to occur as a result of those moments of encounters between ship crew and longshoremen, sometimes even when there were language barriers. Such actions involved longshoremen refusing to work aboard ships where the crew was on strike.

Crewmen Strikes

Whenever the crewmen decided to strike against their employer, the longshoremen always supported them. Crewmen preferred to strike at British Columbian ports because they had the reputation for supporting crewmen strikes, as ILWU longshoremen never crossed their picket lines. If crewmen's strikes could not be settled immediately, which most would be, Tom McGrath, official representative for the seamen's union would be called upon for assistance, as he understood maritime law and contracts. Most of the time, strikes would be settled through negotiations with the ship's captain or agent.

However, there was one strike where ambassadors got involved. During the 1970s, there was an incident with Filipino crewmen from a Greek ship who struck at Fraser Surrey Docks. As soon as they docked, the crewmen had a picket line at the foot of the gangplank due to the horrid conditions on the ship and because they had not been paid wages for six months. The shipping company hired a law firm to intimidate the crewmen, but they continued striking.

Local 502 put a little pressure on the shipping company by putting up water pickets, which trapped the ship because longshoremen would not release it, therefore tugboats could not escort it out. After a week or two, the Greek and Filipino ambassadors visited the ship and McGrath got involved in the bargaining process. The process was complicated as significantly different parties were involved. The crewmen eventually won and all thirty sailors were compensated around $1,000 USD and received business-class tickets back to the Philippines.

The consequence of the strike was that the crewmen were blacklisted. Local 502's president at the time kept in touch with the crewmen's leader, who, unlike the rest of his crew, eventually sailed again.[100]

— *MICHELLE LA*

Helmer West (right) feeding an elephant transported in a container on the *Paralla* (a 'PAD' or Pacific Australia Direct ship). The elephant, Suze, liked the fall apples from Helmer and Lena West's garden. Suze was flown down to Australia for a movie and was brought back on the Paralla. Suze's handler is in the background. *Source: Lena West*

Looking Towards the Eighties

We began this chapter in 1960, examining a local, national, and international context represented by big wins for the union. Though this was still a time of hard manual labour and union struggle, Local 502 was the beneficiary of economic growth in the Fraser River region and successes from union-wide contract negotiations in 1958, resulting in the formal establishment of the Canadian Area a year later. Even so, worries about mechanization were in the air and big changes were yet to come, not the least of which was the 'opening up' of the ports, that is the creation of an around-the-clock or 24/7 port schedule.

Despite the influx of containers and a decreasing reliance on traditional gangs of workmen, Local 502 survived. The first cracks in New Westminster's deep connection to ports and longshoring began to materialize. Nevertheless, New Westminster — the area of the Lower Mainland by which Local 502 still distinguishes itself despite the current lack of ports there — was, to paraphrase many longshoremen, "one of the only places where the ports shut down but the union has grown."

Local 502 showed itself to be skillful at adapting to structural changes in the economy, but it also profited from a fair bit of luck. Longshoremen often remarked at the fortunate alignment of circumstances that gave Local 502 breaks when they were most needed. These include Kaiser's decision to stay outside the BCMEA, the union constitution giving jurisdiction of Westshore to 502, the union's survival of the devastating 1969–70 strikes, and so on. As we will come to see in chapter 5, these events were, in retrospect, welcome interventions that buoyed the local and its members during a period of hard times from roughly 1978 to 1985.

Chapter Notes

1 "Population of British Columbia, 1800–2006," Ministry of Forests, Lands & Natural Resource Operations, accessed 6 August 2015, http://www.for.gov.bc.ca/hfp/sof/2006/figures/fig06.pdf.

2 "Mayors of New Westminster," New Westminster Heritage, accessed 6 August 2015, http://www.nwheritage.org/heritagesite/history/content/mayors.htm and "Mayor Beth Wood," New Westminster Parks, Culture & Recreation, accessed 6 August 2015, http://www.newwestpcr.ca/database/files/library/Mayor_Beth_Wood.pdf.

3 "The Hot 100–1960 Archive," Billboard Charts Archive, accessed 6 August 2015, http://www.billboard.com/archive/charts/1960/hot-100 and "CHUM Hit Parade, 1960," 1050 CHUM Timeline, accessed 6 August 2015, http://chumtribute.ca/timeline/.

4 Bill Zander interview, 21 March 2013.

5 Michael J. Webber and David L. Rigby, *The Golden Age Illusion: Rethinking Postwar Capitalism* (New York: The Guildford Press, 1996); Alec Cairncross and Frances Cairncross (eds), *The Legacy of the Golden Age: The 1960s and their consequences* (London: Routledge, 1992); and Lawrence Black and Hugh Pemberton (eds), *An Affluent Society?: Britain's post-war 'Golden Age' revisited* (Burlington: Ashgate, 2004); see also Herb Mills, "The San Francisco Water Front: The Social Consequences of Industrial Modernization, Part One: 'The Good Old Days,'" *Journal of Contemporary Ethnography* 5 (July 1976), 222–223 (of 221–250).

6 Ron Noullett interview, 29 January 2013.

7 Joe Breaks interview, 26 June 2014.

8 Michelle La, "The Effects of Automation, Mechanization, and Formalization on Camaraderie within ILWU Local 502, from the 1960s to Present," Undergraduate thesis, Simon Fraser University, 2014.

9 Frank Cobbaert interview, 1 May 2014.

10 Brian Ringrose interview, 19 June 2014.

11 *I.L.W.U. Canadian Area: 25th Anniversary, 1959–1985* (Vancouver: International Longshoremen's & Warehousemen's Union Canadian Area, 1984), 26.

12 *I.L.W.U. Canadian Area: 25th Anniversary, 1959–1985* (Vancouver: International Longshoremen's & Warehousemen's Union Canadian Area, 1984), 25.

13 La, 2014.

14 UBC Rare Books and Special Collections, letter from Shipping Federation of British Columbia to various recipients, 13 February 1962, International Longshoremen's and Warehousemen's Union (Canadian Area) fonds box 13, file 19.

15 Dean Johnson interview, 18 July 2013.

16 Dean Johnson, personal correspondence, 9 March 2015.

17 Geoff Clayton interview, 27 June 2013.

18 Gerry White, unpublished typescript, 1 March 2006.

19 Brian Ringrose interview, 19 June 2014.

20 Joe Breaks interview, 9 July 2013.

21 *I.L.W.U. Canadian Area: 25th Anniversary, 1959–1985* (Vancouver: International Longshoremen's & Warehousemen's Union Canadian Area, 1984), 25.

22 "Waterfront Workers History Project — Harry Bridges: Life and Legacy," Harry Bridges Center for Labor Studies, University of Washington, accessed 6 August 2015, http://depts.washington.edu/dock/Harry_Bridges_intro.shtml

23 Joe Breaks, personal communication, 6 March 2015.

24 *UBC Rare Books and Special Collections, ILWU Canada Waterfront News*, 6 June 1960, International Longshoremen's and Warehousemen's Union (Canadian Area) fonds box 13, file 14.

25 Warren Tucker, "Pacific Mechanization Contract Delights U.S. Dockers, Shippers," *Globe and Mail* (26 March 1963), p. B3.

26 *Ibid.*

27 Brian Ringrose interview, 19 June 2014.

28 Lorne Briggs interview, 31 May 2013.

29 UBC Rare Books and Special Collections, "Memorandum re Winch Drivers," 19 July 1961, International Longshoremen's and Warehousemen's Union (Canadian Area) fonds box 13, file 19.

30 Joe Breaks interview, 9 July 2013.

31 *Ibid.*

32 Jack Singh interview, 18 February 2013.

33 Joe Breaks interview, 9 July 2013.

34 Bobby Labinsky interview, 20 May 2014.

35 Anonymous interview, 2 January 2013.

36 Joe Breaks interview, 9 July 2013.

37 *Ibid.*

38 Gerry White interview, 2 July 2013.

39 *Man Along the Shore!*, 98.

40 Joe Breaks interview, 9 July 2013.

41 *Ibid.*

42 Brian Ringrose interview, 19 June 2014.

43 "PCT Newsletter: Channels (Spring 2005, Vol. 21, No. 1)" Pacific Coast Terminals, accessed 6 August 2015, http://pct.ca/wp-content/uploads/2014/12/PCTNewsletterSpring2005.pdf

44 *I.L.W.U. Canadian Area: 25th Anniversary, 1959–1985* (Vancouver: International Longshoremen's & Warehousemen's Union Canadian Area, 1984), 5.

45 *Ibid.*

46 *ILWU Canada Waterfront News*, vol. 3, October 2009, p. 11.

47 Executive meeting, 4 May 1953, ILWU Local 502 minute book.

48 "Waterfront Workers History Project — Harry Bridges: Life and Legacy," Harry Bridges Center for Labor Studies, University of Washington, accessed 6 August 2015, http://depts.washington.edu/dock/Harry_Bridges_intro.shtml.

49 "No Need to Bluff, with Province's High Cards: B.C.-owned Super-Port Proposed Answer to Crow's Nest Coal Impasse," *Globe and Mail* (28 March 1967), B5; and "Ottawa's Port Decision Shows Lack of Rapport with B.C. Government," *Globe and Mail* (21 October 1967), 18.

50 "Kaiser Coal Completes $650 Million Deal with Japanese for Coking Coal Exports," *Globe and Mail* (1 February 1968), B4.

51 "Bennett Attacks Ottawa Policies on Roberts Bank," *Globe and Mail* (8 May 1968), B1.

52 Peter V. Hall and Anthony Clark, "Maritime Ports and the Politics of Reconnecting," in *Transforming Urban Waterfronts: Fixity and Flow* eds. Gene Desfor, Jennefer Laidley, Quentin Stevens, and Dirk Schubert (New York: Routledge, 2010), 25.

53 Dean Johnson interview, 18 July 2013.

54 The Canada Labour Relations Board did not accept Local 514's certification until their third attempt in 1974; see *I.L.W.U. Canadian Area: 25th Anniversary, 1959–1984* (Vancouver: International Longshoremen's and Warehousemen's Union Canadian Area, 1984), 37–38.

55 The Shipping Federation of BC altered its constitution and changed its name to the presently used British Columbia Maritime Employers Association in 1966.

56 "10 Union Officials Choose Jail Over Fines," *Globe and Mail* (18 June 1966), p.3.

57 Hansard record 17 June 1966, Commons Debates, Inquiries of the Ministry, page 6542 (image 1010 in online edition, accessed online on 19 June 2014) http://parl.canadiana.ca/view/oop.debates_HOC2701_06/1010?r=0&s=1

58 *Gang Plank*, no. 21, December 1959, 2.

59 *Gang Plank*, no. 56, December 1962, 2.

60 *Gang Plank*, no. 57, January 1963, p.2.

61 *ILWU Canada Waterfront News*, 5 October 1966.

62 Ken Bauder, *History ILWU Canada: a draft document from 1800 to 2007*, p.7.

63 *Ibid*

64 Frank Cobbaert interview, 1 May 2014.

65 Employers Council of BC, "Anatomy of a Strike: A Case Study of a Dispute in B.C. Ports 1969–1970."

66 Dean Johnson interview, 14 January 2014.

67 "Anatomy of a Strike," p.2.

68 "CLC Official Praises British Columbia Longshoremen for Social Conscience," *Globe and Mail* (10 October 1969), p. B3.

69 "Anatomy of a Strike," 7.

70 "Bill on Gain Shipping Panned," *Globe and Mail* (24 February 1997); "Anatomy of a Strike," 15.

71 "Anatomy of a Strike," 7.

72 Joe Breaks interview, 9 July 2013.

73 Frank Cobbaert interview, 1 May 2014.

74 "B.C. Longshoremen Agree to Arbitration," *Globe and Mail* (28 March 1972), B2; "Longshore Decision Reserved," *The Columbian* (26 July 1972), 23.

75 Brian Ringrose interview, 19 June 2014.

76 *Gang Plank*, no. 50, June 1962, p2.

77 Joe Breaks interview, 25 May 2015.

78 Joe Breaks interview, 9 July 2013.

79 *Ibid.*

80 *Gang Plank*, no. 9, December 1958.

81 "About Us," New Westminster & District Labour Council, accessed 6 August 2015, http://www.nwdlc.ca/aboutnwdlc.html

82 Bill Zander interview, 21 March 2013.

83 *I.L.W.U. Canadian Area: 25th Anniversary, 1959–1985* (Vancouver: International Longshoremen's & Warehousemen's Union Canadian Area, 1984), 8, quoting Bridges from the Canadian Area Convention proceedings, February 1963.

84 *I.L.W.U. Canadian Area: 25th Anniversary, 1959–1985* (Vancouver: International Longshoremen's & Warehousemen's Union Canadian Area, 1984), 14, 42.

85 Jack Singh interview, 18 February 2013; Joe Breaks interview, 26 June 2014.

86 UBC Rare Books and Special Collections, letter to E.P. O'Neal, 23 November 1960, International Longshoremen's and Warehousemen's Union (Canadian Area) fonds box 13, file 22.

87 UBC Rare Books and Special Collections, letter to C. Pritchett, 25 November 1960, International Longshoremen's and Warehousemen's Union (Canadian Area) fonds box 13, file 22.

88 UBC Rare Books and Special Collections, letter from Donald MacDonald, Secretary-Treasurer, 10 January 1961, International Longshoremen's and

Warehousemen's Union (Canadian Area) fonds box 13, file 22.

89 UBC Rare Books and Special Collections, telegram to PM Diefenbaker, 16 December 1960, International Longshoremen's and Warehousemen's Union (Canadian Area) fonds box 13, file 22.

90 "Longshoremen in BC Okay Shipments to Cuba," *The Province* (9 December 1960); Harold Boyer, "Canada and Cuba: A Study in International Relations" (PhD Thesis, Simon Fraser University, 1972), 190.

91 UBC Rare Books and Special Collections, letter from Julio Montero Corzo and Rene F. Baro, 9 January 1961, International Longshoremen's and Warehousemen's Union (Canadian Area) fonds box 13, file 22.

92 *Gang Plank*, no. 42, October 1961.

93 *Gang Plank*, no. 52, August 1962, p2.

94 Referred to by the author at the time as the Royal City Waterfront Workers Association. The ILWU had been established in the port of New Westminster three years prior and both names had been in use.

95 "Longshoremen Meet Tonight: May Boycott Dutch Freighters," *The Columbian* (4 August 1947).

96 Brian Ringrose interview, 11 July 2013.

97 Bill Wilson interview, 29 January 2013; Dean Johnson interview, 13 June 2014.

98 Brian Ringrose, interview, 19 June 2014.

99 Information from various interviews, including several each with Dean Johnson, Brian Ringrose, and Joe Breaks.

100 Joe Breaks interview, 26 June 2014.

Chapter 5
Continuity and Contradiction in the Container Age 1980–2010

Liam O'Flaherty

"We as workers have nothing in common with the employers."

— Harry Bridges, former president of the ILWU,
to an audience at the University of Washington in the mid-1930s[1]

"The Director of Corporate Development . . . [is] very enthusiastic on the quality relationship that is developing between the union and ourselves and our various customers."

— minutes of a 1991 meeting
of the Fraser River Harbour Commission[2]

A summer stroll along the westernmost part of Westminster Quay, a promenade in downtown New Westminster running adjacent to the Fraser River, gives pedestrians and cyclists a sensory overload. First, the sights: families walking and laughing, cyclists zipping through the pedestrian throng, and the scenery. On a clear evening, the sunset rivals that of any urban waterfront boardwalk. The pink, yellow, and white condo towers just north of the walkway are shielded from passers-by by an array of palm trees and potted plants. The floral scents combine with the aromas emanating from nearby bars and restaurants. Tourists might be forgiven for being unaware that this idyllic environment replaced what was once a busy industrial and manufacturing area that, in 1966, the City of New Westminster itself referred to as "unsuitable and blighted".[3] The Westminster Pier Park, completed in 2012, is a recent extension of the esplanade to accommodate a growing desire that downtown New Westminster be modern, green, and resident- and tourist-friendly.

This new, redeveloped landscape along the riverfront belies a past whose primary features were not condos and walkways but industry- and primary-resource-oriented work. The greens and pinks of the 'revitalized' waterfront scene act as a sort of mirage, intentionally or otherwise obscuring what, to longshore workers of Local 502, are very real memories of waterfront work and life. There are still the vestiges of yesteryear. Ships and floating logs can still be seen offshore from the quay and a steady stream of railway cars, whose signals can be heard from as far away as Eighth Avenue, are a reminder of what was once the heavy industrial landscape of a 20th Century British Columbian port city.

The pleasant irony for longshore workers in the 1980s and beyond is that, despite the deindustrialization of New Westminster and the closing of its riverfront to longshore work, their union local not only survived these changes but grew. The 20th Century saw the development of shipping facilities from New Westminster to Surrey and further down the Fraser River, then later still to Roberts Bank in Delta, along the coast of the Lower Mainland. The survival of Local 502 depended on its ability to traverse these geographical changes, a radically altered and mechanized workplace, and the ensuing changes in work culture.

Yet it is no simple thing for those of us in the present to understand the early part of the 1980s for longshore workers in Local 502. Even the data suggests multiple, competing, and often seemingly contradictory trends. Statistics compiled from the annual reports of the Fraser River Harbour Commission (FRHC) show that the amount of cargo tonnage handled was on a rather steep upswing at the beginning of the 1980s. After reaching a peak of roughly 3.7 million tons loaded in 1966, there was a decline that did not see recovery until 1979 and 1980, suggesting a steep decline and, later, an improvement in exports. Likewise, the tonnage unloaded from ships docking within the jurisdiction of the FRHC remained fairly constant from as early as 1960 until 1979–1980 when there was again a sharp upswing. The editor of *The Columbian*, New Westminster's newspaper, pointed out that port officials across Canada, including in Vancouver, were optimistic as the 1970s drew to a close.[4]

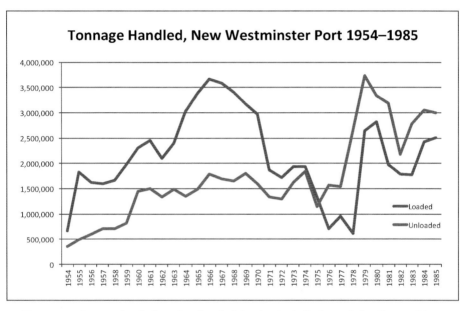

Tonnage of cargo loaded and unloaded in the jurisdiction of the Fraser River Harbour Commission, formerly the New Westminster Harbour Commission (now Port Metro Vancouver), 1954–1985.
Source: Annual Reports of the New Westminster Harbour Commission/Fraser River Harbour Commission

Yet, the number of vessels berthing in ports under the FRHC's jurisdiction experienced a particularly drastic drop that took a big bite out of business in the period between 1979 and 1985. This appears to have been a low period for vessel numbers in ports across British Columbia, suggesting an overall decline due to the recession of the early 1980s, yet a more or less sizable return in tonnage. These contradictory trends — fewer vessels, more cargo — are partly to do with advances in shipping technology.[5]

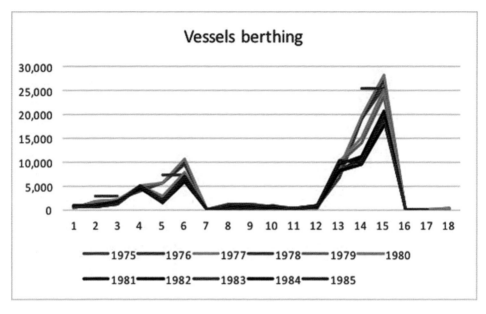

Number of vessels berthing at ports in the jurisdiction of the Fraser River Harbour Commission, formerly the New Westminster Harbour Commission (now Port Metro Vancouver), 1975–1985.
Source: Annual Reports of the New Westminster Harbour Commission/Fraser River Harbour Commission

No matter how you cut the data, the memories of longshore workers in the present tell a story about the late 1970s and early 1980s being a low point for Local 502. Work along the shore was minimal. Those longshore workers who were members might have been able to count themselves lucky, but those who were looking to become members had few prospects. Ron Noullett, then the business agent for Local 502, was quoted in the *Province* newspaper saying that for casuals in the early 1980s sometimes there would only be one day of work per week. The reasons for the decline in fortunes for those ports under the jurisdiction of Local 502 are numerous. In some ways, the moves toward mechanization and automation that were coming onstream in the 1960s and 1970s had, by the early 1980s, taken a partial toll on employment numbers, just as longshore workers had feared. The availability of work 'on the beach' was and is intimately intertwined with the desire or ability of industry to extract, sell, and move goods and raw materials. The North American economy in the late 1970s is often remembered for inflation and price and wage controls. The fortunes of Local 502 were therefore closely linked with national and global, as well as local, events. The survival and resilience of Local 502 is in many ways attributable to the ability of the local to adapt to these changing circumstances.

It is also important to consider local developments in British Columbia and specifically in the Lower Mainland. This was an era of strikes, unemployment, and inflation. From the vantage point of today, we can now look back at this period and see how those economic and social problems set the stage for events to come, such as Operation Solidarity in 1983. This was a move by the BC Federation of Labour and its member unions, together with community groups and individual citizens, to rally for political solutions to the austerity and retrenchment policies of the provincial government at that time. This was a moment in which longshore workers' memories of a bad economic reality are best understood within a wider social, economic, and political milieu that, like the times themselves, are epitomized by contradictory trends: rancorous strike threats on the waterfront and occasional strikes, though few memories of hard-fought labour battles; bitter contract negotiations and lockouts, but also cooperation and corporatism; low economic activity, but occasional spurts in growth; the continuity of old work habits, but also modernization and change; and despair, but also promise and hope.

Consolidation at the Fraser Surrey Docks and the Roberts Bank Superport (Deltaport and Westshore)

In the years between 1980 and 2010, the geography of longshore workers' labour had changed dramatically. Gone were the days when longshore workers would report for work at any number of small company-owned terminals along or near the New Westminster riverfront. The closing of the massive Pacific Coast Terminals (PCT) facilities in 1981 and its eventual dismantling in 1983 paved the way for redevelopment in New Westminster, a city that was deindustrializing though also hoping to capitalize on these structural and economic changes through urban redevelopment. It is important to keep in mind, however, this was not confined to the 1980s; rather, it was an ongoing process by the late

2000s, perhaps best epitomized by the closing of New Westminster's docks, but also its other riverside industries, including the Interfor, Canfor, and Western Forest Products mills in 2007–2008.[6]

The redevelopment of the New Westminster waterfront to make way for condominiums is something that has been remarked upon in oral histories of residents of New Westminster. Indeed, one would be hard-pressed nowadays not to sympathize with such memories: downtown New Westminster in the period prior to the 1980s seemed to have an idyllic peace between its industrial, commercial, and residential sectors. Such was the harmony between these sectors that, when longshore workers had the weekends off, the downtown core was still a vibrant place. One woman, remembering all the way back to the 1940s, noted that "Saturdays were for shopping," for example. She continued, "You couldn't walk a block without meeting half a dozen people you knew."[7] Longshore workers and other riverside workers kept the downtown core busy during the week; shoppers and residents kept it busy on the weekend.

Another resident who worked in downtown New Westminster in the early 1980s spoke about the vibrant community that existed there just prior to deindustrialization. Businesses were interconnected in a way they would no longer be after the 1980s. Indeed, downtown New Westminster and its once-lively commercial district in many ways relied on dockside industry. Some complained that the city's character had been destroyed in this period.[8] Another, and perhaps far more iconic representation of the changes in New Westminster in the 1980s, was the shuttering of the King Neptune restaurant, a waterfront institution that first opened its doors in 1953, which one observer called the city's "first elegant dining."[9] It was a very popular place, said another resident.[10] A purported impasse between the First Capital Development Company and the owners of the King Neptune over the restaurant's lease and its controversial closing to make way for new condominiums is something that many former residents mourn and many longshore workers remember.

New Westminster's deindustrialization happened for numerous reasons and was due to decisions and events that span decades. Contrary to the consensus that seems to appear in oral histories noting the vibrancy of downtown New Westminster prior to the 1980s, city reports often told a different story. An urban renewal study, commissioned by the City of

New Westminster and drafted by a three-man committee that the city appointed, highlighted certain areas of New Westminster as a "hovel." One of the neighbourhoods that was underlined as requiring particular attention, to deal with the issue of urban blight, was the Market neighbourhood, identified in the report as the heavily-industrialized western end of downtown New Westminster, where the PCT terminals and old union hall once existed. The area was described in the report as "unsuitable" and having some of the poorest quality housing in the city. This "gateway" was marred, the report suggested, by "vacant" industrial and commercial lots. The neighbourhood labelled 'Downtown' — just east of the Market neighbourhood, itself part of what would otherwise be considered downtown New Westminster — needed significant improvement in parking spots.[11] This report suggests that New Westminster City Hall desired a revamped downtown waterfront as early as the mid-1960s. By the mid-1970s, City Hall had entered into discussions with the British Columbia Development Corporation, a crown corporation, to redevelop the entire downtown waterfront. In 1979, the provincial *New Westminster Redevelopment Act* received royal assent and set out the parameters of the city's abilities to rezone or redevelop.[12]

However, according to Allen Domaas, the former CEO of the Fraser River Port Authority, the crucial thing making New Westminster less attractive for shipping, and ultimately causing its deindustrialization, was the lack of space. With modernization and mechanization came steadily larger vessels carrying greater amounts of cargo that in turn required more sizable storage facilities. As Domaas noted:

When New West was in its heyday, lumber was a big piece. Lumber came down the river from the sawmills to the outside of the ship and was loaded onto the ships. You did not need much backup land. When the CPR was bringing lumber from the interior, concentrates, or fruit, they would bring it in and load the ship from the railcar. The idea of warehousing was not in the mix. You could build a terminal with very modest backup land, maybe 5 or 6 acres. By the 1970s, with the advent of containerization, suddenly you had to receive and hold containers, and load the ships when they came because the ships, rather than coming for cargo, came on a schedule . . . the back-up land component went from 5 acres to 15 to 40 to 100 to now it is 225 acres per berth.

The closing of the PCT facilities in downtown New Westminster was one such example of a terminal which Domaas noted was perfectly suitable for perhaps the 1950s but not so for the container age. The closer proximity of the Port Coquitlam railyard and a rail terminus right next to the PCT facility in Port Moody further provided the incentive for PCT's permanent move there.[13]

A work geography once typified by a multiplicity of diverse work locations huddled primarily, though not exclusively, around New Westminster had now given way to a handful of larger centralized terminals spread along the lower Fraser River and beyond. The Fraser Surrey Docks, a container and breakbulk terminal, is representative of a gradual shift away from New Westminster. It is also emblematic of the sort of innovations that the Harbour Commission, the employer, and Local 502 were trying to accomplish. The strategy of innovating and moving with the tide of modernization was partly successful. PCT's coincidental and gradual move away from the Fraser River in this same time period meant that Public Works Canada had less incentive to invest in dredging; something that the Harbour Commission, shippers, and thus also longshore workers, correctly viewed as crucial to the continuation of shipping and longshore work along the river. The Annacis car terminals (mentioned in Chapter 4), which had opened in 1973, also shaped the river economy in the 1980s. Annacis Island became the primary choice for the location of a car terminal due to the low tidal effect on the 'ro-ro' car ship ramps.[14]

Indeed, the union itself made the move from New Westminster to Surrey when, after years of negotiations with the FRHC, the union hall moved from its location at 71 Tenth Street in New Westminster to its current location on the corner of Tannery Road and Timberland Road in North Surrey. Archival evidence shows that in joint meetings held between Local 502 and the FRHC, longshore workers kept the commission abreast of its desire to purchase or lease land on the Surrey side of the river so as to ultimately relocate its union hall closer to where the work was moving. One proposal was to lease land at the St. Mungo cannery property in North Delta, near the Alex Fraser Bridge.[15] Between 1993 and 1994, the union had revisited the issue and advised the commission that the union was looking to keep its options open.[16] In 1997, the FRHC, Local 502, and the BCMEA reached agreement on a lease for a new dispatch hall.[17] The Tenth Street hall saw the swearing-in of its last members on March 15th, 2000. The new union hall in Surrey held its first meeting on April 12th, 2000.[18]

The last new members sworn in at the old New Westminster union hall	The first members to be sworn in at the new Surrey union hall
March 2000	April 2000
D. Keeling	S. Dosen
B. Chehal	L. Tuura
B. Rougeau	R. Macpherson
S. Nolan	R. Mclellen
G. Mclean	C. Smith
B. Schultz	R. Tompson
C. Playne	K. Kalish
R. Larose	S. Morrison
T. Nannar	M. Mann
T. Blomme	

Perhaps the biggest development was the maintenance of, or continued growth in, employment at the Westshore coal terminals at the Roberts Bank superport in Delta, a development that came onstream in 1970 (see Chapter 4). This allowed Local 502 to achieve growth in members during some of the more difficult years of the 1980s. The expansion of Roberts Bank to accommodate the new Deltaport facility in 1997 was a huge development that further centralized the bulk of Local 502's work on the Delta site. Local 502's members have become geographically spread out and yet at the same time progressively more centralized at expansive, distant terminals rather than at the comparatively small urban terminals of previous decades. For some longshore workers, this had an isolating effect on the sense of fraternity that had long epitomized longshoring. Many of the retired longshore workers we interviewed noted that the work culture was just not the same anymore.

Even current longshore workers, who were hired in the period just before the ascendance of Deltaport, have noticed the change. Said one, "A lot of the times you're in a machine by yourself for eight hours . . . whereas before you'd have an eight-man gang."[19] Local 502's members noted these changes when interviewed, but tended not to describe a stark, isolating experience, just a different one:

> *All of a sudden when Deltaport opened up, that was the huge change — rubber tire gantry, rail mounted gantries, everyone was driving a bomb cart . . . Even some of the checkers were up in the tower sitting by themselves . . . You didn't have feelings of alienation . . . you're just . . . sort of out of the loop.*[20]

At the same time, even within the post-Deltaport period after 1997, Shane Johnson reported the gradual professionalization of work and a seeming decline in the fraternal and jovial nature of work that some remember. At one time, for example, longshore workers would test each other on forklifts — themselves introduced through mechanization processes — to see who could load or unload faster, but "you almost feel like a robot now, in the machines."[21]

Longshore workers nevertheless adapted to new technologies by finding ways to maintain solidarity through those same advancements in technology that otherwise caused their work to be increasingly isolated. The introduction of the cellphone, for example, allowed longshore workers quick and easy contact with fellow workers, the union hall, the business agent, and so on.[22]

The 1997 opening of Deltaport was indeed a momentous occasion for Local 502, though it was not without controversy. It raised some long-dormant questions about jurisdiction, including whether Local 502 or Local 500 was going to represent its workers. Brian Ringrose recalled that there was, in some quarters, a sentiment of "If it's ocean, it's Vancouver", or, "We handle containers in Vancouver. You guys hardly ever do."[23] This kind of thinking persisted among stevedores and longshore workers alike. Primarily though, these were comments from within industry. There was a body of opinion that, as Ringrose paraphrased, "you [Local 502] don't have total jurisdiction yet until we give it to you." The reasons for reluctance to accede jurisdiction over the Deltaport facilities to Local 502 might have been caused by Local 502's reputation for ensuring adherence to strict safety standards, but also because, as Ringrose put it, "they didn't have faith in us doing the job . . . not enough people, not enough skilled people."[24] Local 502, however, did become the ILWU representatives of Deltaport's workers, thus furthering the trend not only of work and workers moving away from New Westminster to Surrey but also, eventually, away from both and further down the river towards Delta.

Labour Strife or Labour Cooperation?

There were relatively few strikes between 1980 and 2010, and the local began to adopt a newly cooperative approach toward the employer in the same time period. The union however had little interest in abdicating its traditional role or its zealous defence of the strike as a tool. By the 1980s, the possibility of a strike along the BC coast was enough to send wide swaths of the provincial and national economies into a state of panic. Longshore workers and employers alike, as well as key actors in other parts of the local economy, had a memory of the tumultuous strikes of 1969 and 1970, as well as labour conflict in 1972 and 1975. A handful of people still had a living memory of strikes going back much further, including the strife in 1935. People knew what power the longshore workers had and the longshore workers themselves were careful about using it. A number of current longshore workers feel that the government's willingness to legislate striking workers back to work diminishes the power of threats of labour disruption.

Year	Type of Dispute
1982	Rotating Strike
1986–1987	Lockout threat; mandatory conciliation
1994	Strike

Selected industrial disputes between employers and ILWU Canada, 1980–2010.

After working without a contract for eight months, the Canadian Area of the ILWU began a revolving wave of one-day strikes across British Columbia's ports in August and September of 1982. No picket lines were set up, however. Plans to idle the waterfront were devised to allow longshore workers to meet with their union executive and discuss the union's proposal, as well as to allow the union executive a chance to hear what members wanted. On September 2nd, 1982, the Fraser Surrey docks, the Annacis marine terminal in Delta, the New Westminster dock, Fraser Wharves, and Johnson Terminals in Surrey were shut down for this purpose.[25] Reports of an "imminent shutdown of west coast ports" proved false, however, when Don Garcia, then Canadian Area president of the ILWU, noted that longshore workers were keenly aware of the economic climate of the time.[26] Also noting that both sides were closer in agreement than was generally perceived, Garcia eventually went on to sign a three-year agreement with the BCMEA. However, later in the 1980s, the two sides would be back to the bargaining table over a hotly contested issue: the 'container clause'.

Since the tumultuous strikes and negotiations of 1969–1970, ILWU's Canadian Area won a container clause in their contract. With the move toward the shipment of containerized rather than loose hand-stowed materials and goods in the 1960s, longshoremen were worried that their labour would now be replaced in an increasingly crane-filled waterfront. As such, in the 1970 contract, British Columbia's longshoremen had won a right to pack and unpack a certain number of containers, thus ensuring more work on the waterfront. This was a clause that was particularly helpful for members of Local 500 where the bulk of container shipping was then taking place. But it also affected members in Local 502. The clause would remain a source of contention between longshore workers and the employer for the remainder of its life.[27]

By 1986, negotiations over a new contract resulted in a standoff between the two sides that sent ripple effects throughout the economy. The union's unwillingness to bend on the container clause, which the BCMEA wanted to do away with, resulted in the BCMEA threatening to lock out longshore workers from the waterfront. This was part of the reason cited by the Canadian National Railway at the time for laying off more than seven hundred of its employees in Western Canada until such time as the federal Labour Minister could intervene. The confluence of the lockout threat and a simultaneous IWA strike hit the railways, and thus Western farmers, quite hard.[28] The BCMEA put the threat into action when it locked out all of the ILWU's 3,700-strong labour force in British Columbia later in October of that year.[29] By November, the federal government passed the *Maintenance of Ports Operations Act*, which ordered that companies resume business and that

> every person who is ordinarily employed in longshoring or related operations at a port on the west coast of Canada and

who, on December 30, 1985, was bound by the collective agreement to which this Act applies shall, when so required, return forthwith to the duties of his employment.[30]

This act was important because, unlike the *West Coast Port Operations Acts* of the 1970s, the *Maintenance of Ports Operations Act* did not have to be re-legislated each time there was an industrial dispute on the waterfront. In other words, the federal cabinet could, using the *Maintenance of Ports Operations Act*, just issue orders-in-council reordering striking or locked-out workers back to work, making the business of back-to-work legislation much less subject to public criticism. Retired longshore workers in Local 502 have maintained copies of the orders that they received from the federal government.

In 1987, the ILWU and BCMEA underwent conciliation before a federal commissioner, Joseph Weiler, who made a binding recommendation in July of that year that removed the container clause in exchange for compensation and a five-year work contract.[31] The ILWU responded by filing an appeal,[32] though eventually it threw in the towel when the Supreme Court of Canada "refused . . . to grant the union leave to launch an appeal" aimed at nullifying Weiler's authority as a conciliator.[33] Six months later, the *Globe and Mail* reported cheerfully that container movements were up, seeming to confirm the BCMEA's previous warnings that shipping lines were escaping to Portland, Seattle, and Tacoma, and shipping Canadian-bound product overland so as to avoid the defunct container clause.[34] The compensation packages provided for in lieu of the container clause were called the Gainshare fund and the Productivity fund. Members were given the right to vote on what to do with the two funds. Some longshore workers said that the money should be divided up and paid to active longshore workers in a lump sum. Others felt the money should only go to those ports that handled containers. Local 502 backed the ultimately successful decision of pooling the two funds and investing it into the Waterfront Industry Pension Plan.[35]

Labour strife did not rear its head again until 1994, at which time the union conducted its longest strike since the events of 1969 and 1970, walking off the job for nearly two weeks. The dispute was largely monetary, with longshore workers wanting a three-year contract with

PRIVY COUNCIL OFFICE   BUREAU DU CONSEIL PRIVÉ

CANADA

OTTAWA, K1A 0A3

September 1, 1972

Dear Mr. Breaks:

        The Prime Minister has asked me to ensure
that Officials of the British Columbia Maritime
Employers Association and the International Longshoremen's and Warehousemen's Union - Canadian Area, who
are directly concerned with the provisions of Sections
4, 5, 6 and 7 of the West Coast Ports Operations Act
are provided with copies of this legislation at the
earliest possible opportunity. I am accordingly
enclosing duly certified copies of the Act, together
with additional copies of the legislation for
distribution to the Officers in your organization.

        There is always some difficulty in distribut-
ing quickly an Act which has just been passed by
Parliament. I am, therefore, sending these to you by
special delivery for your attention. If additional
copies are required they can readily be secured through
my office or that of the Deputy Minister of Labour.

Yours sincerely,

R.G. Robertson,
Clerk of the Privy Council

Mr. Joe Breaks,
   President,
      Local 502,
         ILWU - Canadian Area,
           71 Tenth Street,
             New Westminster, B.C.

A letter by R.G. Robertson, Clerk of the Privy Council in Ottawa, to Joe Breaks, then president of Local 502, notifying Breaks and the local of the *West Coast Ports Operations Act* (1972) coming into force.
Source: Joe Breaks

a 75¢ increase in the base rate in the first two years and a 65¢ increase in the third year, as well as additional health and welfare coverage. The base rate of pay for ILWU longshore workers at the time was $21.41 per hour. Lloyd Axworthy, then the federal Minister of Human Resources, ordered the strikers back to work by invoking the *West Coast Port Operations Act,* which also forced both the ILWU and BCMEA to submit to final-offer arbitration.[36]

Source: http://www.bcmea.com/CMS_Content/CABB/39/BCMEA_LONGSHORE_ CA_FINAL.pdf, http://www.bcmea.com/pdfs/collectiveagreement99.pdf (1999– 2002), Collective agreement 1982–1984

In keeping with the theme of contradiction, it is worth noting that by 1980, Local 502 was suffering, though resilient. Many longshore workers along the Fraser River were sitting idle, waiting for work. The people most impacted by the economic slump in this period, however, were casuals for whom this period of low activity and employment meant longer and longer wait times to become a member and less income. The nature of being a casual at the time meant that many of the men who were able to attain only sporadic employment wound up leaving or pursuing jobs in fields other than longshoring. Some casuals went to Vancouver and worked when and where opportunities for work arose in those areas under the jurisdiction of Local 500. The slump affected them too; if casuals were not getting work, recruitment of new longshore workers would decline. If Local 502 did not have a steady stream of incoming casuals and eventually members, it would not be able to meet the demands of the river-based economy when the economy turned around. The availability of work and the supply of labour were mutually dependent, as were the fates of Local 502 and the river economy around New Westminster and Surrey in particular.

As such, the 1980s was a period of deep introspection for members of Local 502. Members began to ask themselves and each other about the reasons for the economic slump. They started to ask themselves about how things were going to be turned around and if there was a future in longshoring along the Fraser River. Most importantly, union members began to consider the role that, some argued, they themselves were said to have played as a union in the economic slump. This was a polarizing issue, and it was met with fierce debate in and outside the union hall. Most longshore workers disputed any notion that the practices and behaviours of their members, individually or collectively, were somehow responsible for the lack of work or for the state of the local economy. Indeed they were correct, since much of the economic slump was due to broader economic and policy changes happening at the provincial and national levels, to say nothing of wider geopolitical phenomena that had local effects. But many longshore workers in Local 502 started to conceive of ways that they themselves could contribute to making the Fraser River's ports more attractive for shipping lines and thus work. This too would not be an easy undertaking.

Modernizing the Work Culture at Local 502

One thing to understand about longshoring is that, as with jobs across the world of labour, the sorts of safety standards and workplace norms that exist in the present came about as a result of a combination of things that came to a head in the early 1980s: union activism, government legislation and regulations, and general cultural change. It was not uncommon, for example, for a longshoreman in the 1960s and 1970s to have a drink at any number of restaurants or pubs in downtown New Westminster. Oral histories of retired longshore workers are replete with fond memories of going to the Russell, Dunsmuir, or Windsor hotels in downtown New Westminster in those days, either on their lunch break or after a day's work.

Beer Parlours

During the 1960s and 1970s during lunch breaks and after work, many of the longshoremen would drink at the beer parlours in downtown New Westminster. It is claimed that during these decades New Westminster had the most beer parlours per capita in all of British Columbia. The beer parlours that longshoremen frequented were in the Terminal Hotel, Best Hotel, Dunsmuir Hotel, King Edward Hotel, the Windsor Hotel, Turf Hotel, and the Woods Hotel. A retired longshoreman recalls the ritual of drinking at beer parlours during the hour lunch break:

Always, one guy would leave early, especially near at Fraser Mills. So one guy would leave early and go to the Woods Hotel in Maillardville and sat at the table, especially at quitting time at twelve o clock at night. The table was absolutely loaded with glasses of beer, while at lunchtime beer was twenty cents. You used to be able to get ten-cent glasses at the Dunsmuir. Then they went to the beer glasses with the plimsoll line in it, and they were twenty cents. So you would get five beers for a buck at lunchtime. If you were at Overseas, you would run over to the Windsor or the King Ed and set up the table. So everyone threw in a buck, and if there were six of you, then you would have thirty beers and you're throwing these things down. You would get so good at it, pretty soon you'll be throwing out some more money and get two more. So you go from five to six or seven beers at lunch hour. By that time, you have drank so fast, when you got back to work it started to hit you . . . Like I said, it was a ritual because you worked hard, especially during the summertime, and then you run over to the beer parlour . . . a lot of the times you would carry on, and after work you would drink again.

— *Michelle La*

This was neither against the rules, nor unusual or out-of-place to longshore workers or anybody else in the wider world of working men and women. Indeed, the enjoyment of time off and the occasional drink shows us that

New Westminster's pubs, restaurants, and hotels were sites of convergence where longshore workers were economically and socially connected to the communities where their jobs, and for some their homes, were located.

However, by the 1980s, an overall change in culture that emphasized worker safety took hold. This happened in tandem with the shift towards mechanization and efficiency, as global trade networks became increasingly interconnected, a process that, as the previous chapter shows, began before the 1980s. One of the things that Local 502 realized it needed to change was the perception by some, including shipping companies and the FRHC, of alcohol abuse by some of its members. This was not something specific to Local 502, nor was it particularly high among longshore workers generally. Indeed, longshore work was comparatively well-paid labour, and those men who worked on the docks and stayed there for the rest of their working lives tended to be family men who preferred to head home after a day's work. Nevertheless, the FRHC alleged that, for example, Fraser Surrey Docks had the highest rate of firings "on the west coast" for alcohol consumption on the job.[37] Alcohol use was precisely the sort of thing that shipping companies would cite or inquire about in the 1980s, when longshore workers started participating in trade missions organized by the FRHC. Like those shipping lines, the Harbour Commission was particularly concerned about liability.[38]

Steel pipes unloaded from *Ilsabe Oldendorff* in an unsafe manner
The bundle of pipes shown here has not been slung properly. This ship, now the *Ocean Hope*, still occasionally comes to the Fraser River and Burrard Inlet.
Source: Larry Kalish

However, because the ILWU and the FRHC started holding joint meetings, this issue was resolved internally when the union reminded the Harbour Commission that it dealt with such matters in-house and that an Employee Assistance Program was available for those longshore workers with substance abuse problems. Shipping lines stated that they were concerned about the safety of their crew and their vessels, though as Ringrose stated, they also "wanted their ship in and out."[39] The twin drives toward efficiency and safety thus resulted in a massive cultural change on the docks. The days when ports were sites of relatively informal work-safety standards were long gone in the transition toward increasingly professionalized and regulated spaces.

Year	Title
1913	New Westminster Harbour Commission
1965	Fraser River Harbour Commission
1999	Fraser River Port Authority
2008	Port Metro Vancouver (encompassing all of the former Fraser River Port Authority, along with the Port of Vancouver and The North Fraser Port Authority

The evolution of the Harbour Commission/Port Authority in and around New Westminster.

It should also be noted that such concerns about alcohol use among longshore workers tended to be part and parcel with a general concern among shipping and stevedoring companies that longshore workers were not just a labour cost but, worse, a source of work disruption. Such costs were seen to be particularly onerous in the supposedly cumbersome gang structures that unions wanted to keep, strikes over contract negotiations (which, incidentally, were relatively rare in the 1980–2010 period, despite the frequent *threats* of a strike or lockout), alleged alcohol use, or any number of other issues. But the most frequent cause of concern for international shipping lines was Local 502's reputation for rigorously checking and insisting upon the safety of gear on vessels. Vessel safety was a cost for shipping lines. The longer a vessel was tied up on the dock and not being loaded or unloaded, the costlier it was for those involved in the shipment of goods or raw materials.

Local 502's members, however, had long prided themselves on their safety record. In any case, gear inspections needed the approval of someone from the federal ministry of transportation or someone designated by the ministry to certify worker-initiated safety inspections. Indeed, what longshoreman would want to load or unload an unsafe vessel? The captains of ships docking on the Fraser River would sometimes get irritated with Local 502 members. Ringrose paraphrased one ship's captain as having said, "we just came from Seattle and we worked for four days and had no problem."[40]

Most of the longshore workers interviewed for this book were keen to note that Local 502 was proud of this safety record and that it was something that made Local 502 well-known, sometimes to the chagrin of the employer. One former machinist apprentice who worked with Webb & Gifford Ltd. and was involved in verifying the safety of equipment aboard ships, spoke of Local 502's safety reputation as follows:

> . . .The Liberty ships would come in from, say the Orient, and they'd come over here and steam up the Fraser River and dock and amazingly enough, they always had a piece of paper that said that all their lifting equipment had been inspected and that it was safe, somewhere signed off . . . and Dick Wilson would go down on board, him and another cohort, and say, "all right." When you did testing of the equipment, you had to attach a plate and an up-to-date stamp. And it was a copper plate which was pinned into the heel of the boom, and the date, and the whole 'It's been safe working load tested for three tons' or whatever, and . . . the captain thought he could just get away with just the paperwork, but there would be Dick who would be looking at the heel of the boom and he'd say, "That paint hasn't been off there for five years!" Or for ten years. [laughs] The longshoremen's union was very strict on this. Unless they had lifting apparatus certification that was approved by our inspectors on the west coast here, they could not load lumber . . . Webb & Gifford would have a representative on board to say "We're prepared to lift your ship up to standards."[41]

Well before the 1980s, the issue of safety was not just something ushered in by the employer, the FRHC, or the various levels of government, but rather by the workers themselves. Longshore workers who worked in and around New Westminster and Surrey were aware of their reputation as being sticklers for safety. But Local 502's strong record for ensuring vessel safety and refusing to work aboard ships that had safety concerns was one thing that longshore workers were not willing to sacrifice in order to accommodate shipping companies' concerns about getting their ships 'in and out' of berth. It was within this setting of concerns about efficiency and safety that we can see how Local 502 was instrumental to the river economy. It is impossible to know how much business was either gained or lost in shipping on the Fraser River due to Local 502's strenuous oversight of vessel safety. Suffice it to say that their record in thoroughly monitoring their own safety and in protecting their right to do so likely not only influenced the course of economic development along the Fraser River but also saved lives.

The Trade Missions: Capitulation or Cooperation?

In the 1980s and 1990s, longshore workers began participating in trade missions to Europe and Asia. These were exciting new developments for Local 502. Until that time, the FRHC pursued foreign business opportunities without the assistance of the union. However, by the 1980s, Local 502's members came to the conclusion that in order for foreign shipping lines to have confidence in the ports and terminals where Local 502 operated, it would have to form a united front with the Harbour Commission. This was a marked departure from past practices and some longshore workers were uneasy about these developments. There was resistance among some of 502's members to reaching out to the Harbour Commission or accepting its invitations to be part of these trade missions. Harbour Commissions (or port authorities) are historically composed of government-appointed members, most often from regulatory agencies and the local business community. Although the FRHC did not receive the hostility from longshore workers that was occasionally reserved for the employers, particularly during contract negotiations, some longshore workers still thought that working with the Harbour Commission was selling out. "You have a very tough group of people that are used to doing things one way . . . 'the employer's the enemy'," remembered Ringrose about the dominant thinking at the time among Local 502's members. But the thinking changed with the dire circumstances of the 1980s. It eventually came to pass that longshore workers felt "It might pay off if we started talking to these guys."[42]

So it did come to pass that the executive of Local 502 approved participation in these trade missions, which themselves were just one of many examples of longshore workers adopting a more conciliatory and involved model than they had previously. Longshore workers remember attending several trade missions with the Harbour Commission. The 1987 mission to Asia brought longshore workers to Hong Kong, South Korea, Taiwan, and Japan for two to three days in each country. A 1989 mission to Europe involved much hastier travel and many more cities in more countries, including the Netherlands, Germany, Sweden, Finland, Denmark, and Norway. A 1993 mission brought longshore workers to a ports convention in Sydney, Australia, with a side trip to Melbourne.

One thing to know about the world of shipping is that it is the quintessential international business. Particularly for big ports on the west coast of North America, your business neighbourhood is the entire Pacific Rim trading area, or indeed the globe. This was a truth with which longshore workers had long been accustomed, having had interactions with ship's crews for as long as there was international shipping up the Fraser River. Still, those longshore workers who participated in trade missions were confronted with just how small their world was when they liaised with shipping magnates in the international corridors of power. The vessel safety issue, as it turned out, was not just something that Local 502 was known for locally. Its reputation, they discovered, was known the world over.

"We kept getting asked by shipping lines why were we shutting ships down; why were we so adamant on fixing the gear. They didn't quite understand," remembers Brian Ringrose, who participated in many of these trade missions as a representative of Local 502. Instead of adapting to the concerns of shippers by minimizing safety, longshore workers, together with members of the Harbour Commission, realized that they would need to confront this issue head-on. So, one night after a long day of consorting with shippers and realizing that delays caused by vessel safety were affecting port calls, members of the trade mission sat down and devised guidelines for which longshore workers were looking when boarding a vessel to load or unload it.

Members of those trade missions remember that the preparation and distribution of these guidelines, a list of things that Local 502 members already kept in-house, was something that was appreciated by foreign shipping lines which had hitherto been wary of shipping up the Fraser River.[43] Sometimes Local 502's reputation made for awkward encounters while overseas. At the 1993 ports convention in Sydney, Ringrose recounted that he was walking down by Sydney Harbour with Ed Kargl of the FRHC and asked the longshore workers and crew of a vessel tied up at dock if they could go aboard and take a look. They had recognized the name of the ship as one that had called at Fraser River terminals. Upon boarding, they were introduced to the ship's captain who, upon hearing they were from New Westminster, gave them the cold shoulder — it seems that he, just a few weeks prior, had had his vessel tied up for too long over safety concerns. The same thing happened when delegates from the trade mission team bumped into a ship owner in Japan who knew of New Westminster's reputation all too well. As Ringrose recalled:

> "Would you know why they shut my car ship down today?" A lot of car ships, in the early days, the ramp [off of which] you drive the cars would be decayed, rusted out, so I guess this particular one was in bad shape and they shut his car ship down. Another meeting that did not go over too well. But that's how small the world is, you just get a knock on the door, you're there visiting, and his car ship is now sitting at Annacis auto terminal, not working and he's pretty upset.[44]

Longshore workers, previously accustomed only to defending their own interest vis-à-vis the employer, were now confronted with having to perform the delicate art of foreign trade diplomacy. Indeed, that was how small the world was becoming. In such cases, longshore workers hastily made calls back home to make inquiries about the reasons why a vessel was tied up at berth and relayed those reasons to the people they were meeting. But safety was never sacrificed.

The purpose of these trips was to attract business along the Fraser River from foreign shipping lines. Whether or not they achieved that end is a trickier question. Some longshore workers reported mixed results for the trips. Nevertheless, Local 502 was in a position where it saw its interests aligning with that of the employer. Longshore workers were increasingly keen on drumming up business by signalling to foreign shipping lines that the Fraser River was ready for business. Ringrose reported that, "not all were callers [but] some were . . . that's what the port was trying to do, to say, 'We know you don't call, but here we are, come and see us.'"[45]

Commodities Linked to Globalization/Trade

Many commodities that have gone through Local 502's port were influenced by trade deals and aid agreements. During the 1960s, the Canadian government made an aid deal with India through the Colombo Plan where it would ship fertilizer but India had to supply the ships. Sherritt Gordon Mines, a Canadian mining company now known as Sherritt International, made the fertilizer from ammonium nitrate. During this time, retired Local 502 longshoremen recall spending six months loading thousands of tons of fertilizer in 112-pound bags, loading from the bottom of the ship to the very top. On a pallet, a load was thirty-five sacks. Sometimes it would take longshoremen three weeks to a month to fill up a ship. After a ship was finished, they would work on the next one.

During the 1960s and 1970s, there was also the wheat deal that Russia made with Canada — Canada sold wheat cheaply and Russia supplied the ships. This resulted in thousands upon thousands of tons of wheat being handled at the former Searle elevator at Surrey Fraser Docks. Since wheat is a seasonal commodity, Local 502 longshoremen would be loading sacks for only two to three months of the year. The rest of the time, wheat would be poured into the ship. The ship's hatches would go black because light couldn't get past the piles of wheat. Sixty longshoremen would shovel it level, then fill sacks to be placed on top of the levelled wheat to keep it from moving when at sea. The wheat dust the longshoremen were exposed to was terrible, but most of them did not wear the masks they were given because it restricted their breathing.

Another huge commodity that Local 502 handled was millions of board feet of lumber, which went around the world but mostly to the UK and Japan. Local 502 longshoremen handled 240-pound sacks of coffee at the Rice Mills and this was because the shipping company would have to pay fewer tariffs if they had less sacks going through the Panama Canal. On average, it would take two longshoremen to handle a 240-pound coffee sack, but some longshoremen were strong enough to carry a sack individually.

— *Michelle La*

The pitch that longshore workers had to make is indicative of the conundrum the Fraser River's longshore workers faced. On the one hand, in seeking out new business from shipping companies — some of which may have done business in other west coast ports — longshore workers were competing for the same economic activity that may have benefited longshore workers elsewhere within the ILWU family. On the other hand, Local 502 had made the decision to support sending its members on these trade missions precisely so that they could drum up business and in so doing, protect their own jobs.

The balance that was struck is interesting. Longshore workers were loath to attack other ports. Ringrose noted that the pitch never set up "New Westminster versus Vancouver," for example. That was not the style of the longshore workers, or indeed the FRHC itself, and would have to directly put New Westminster's longshore workers at odds with their nearby brothers. Still, it was not above these trade missions and the longshore workers involved to make their case based on very real concerns that shipping companies had about economic cost and what made sense geographically. Ringrose summarized the pitch as, "'If that product has got some business in Canada, rather than trucking it up from the States, we'd rather you try it out here' — just stuff like that, that's how we tried to sell it."[46]

This represents a very interesting and contentious development in the history of Local 502. The 1980s was a time in which longshore workers began to use their position as labourers not just to negotiate better contracts for themselves from the employer, but also to work with the employer to bring in business to the Fraser River. Although this collaboration was uneasy, it also represented a moment in which the local started to recognize that their labour was instrumental to the lifeblood of Fraser River shipping. Although the union was willing to cooperate with the commission and the employer to achieve greater business along the river, when everyone returned home, it was back to the bargaining table.

Although it was an arduous process to get longshore workers to agree to adopt this more cooperative model, the idea of economic cooperation among labour and capital on the waterfront was not new. As early as the 1970s, longshore workers toyed with the idea of lobbying for the right to participate on the Harbour Commission.

Documentary evidence suggests that in the later years of the New Westminster Harbour Commission (NWHC), which changed to the Fraser River Harbour Commission in 1965, the commission had cordial relations with Local 502. For example, it extended to Local 502 "an invitation to attend any future public meeting called to deal with harbour development."[47] It is not clear what the commission intended by inviting the union to its meetings. It is likely that the commission was inviting the union as a courtesy and for Local 502's members to simply attend and perhaps speak to certain issues, rather than vote on matters under consideration at the commission's meetings.

In 1972, the ILWU sent correspondence to the Harbour Commission requesting that its members be represented there. Though the local did not get representation on the commission, the question of representation was rekindled in the minds of some longshore workers in the 1980s when longshore workers visited Europe on a trade mission.

Ringrose reflected on witnessing Swedish and Norwegian workers being represented on their local equivalents of the FRHC:

> They had dockers representing their commission, as part of their harbour commissions, so that was very interesting to see, that they had actual workers right on the commission, giving their input . . . because here you would have businessmen, you'd have people working on the river, who were commissioners. One was a towboat company [owner], another owned a . . . marina. So those were some of the type of people they had on the commission during those years . . . so why not have a longshoreman? Never happened, but we always thought it would be a nice thing to have, to give your input, and to show that this is what we would like the Harbour Commission to look at doing, because there's a lot of things that go on: land development, dredging . . . there's a lot of things that they're involved in that have a direct impact on our work. So it was good to be at least included in their meetings . . .[48]

One of the trade-offs that the FRHC made to accommodate the growing desire of longshore workers to be more integrally involved in commission activities was to hold joint meetings, or for harbour commissioners to attend at Local 502 meetings, and vice-versa.[49]

The trade missions thus provided longshore workers with a view of the global world to which they were already connected by virtue of trade networks. This in turn happened around the same time that longshore workers' demands for representation on the commission were instead being accommodated through joint meetings and through representation on those very trade missions, themselves a cooperative endeavour. Such experiences also allowed longshore workers in Local 502 to interact with workers in other parts of the world, including fellow longshore workers, and to gain insight into the lives of those with whom they had work and class interests in common.

Women on the Waterfront

In an undated recruitment video titled *Women on the Waterfront*, jointly produced by the BCMEA and the ILWU, one female longshore worker from a different local reported that "the ILWU has opened the door for women and given them that opportunity to try [longshoring], whereas before they [didn't]."[50] This frank assessment of the union's own intransigence toward having women on the docks is an accurate depiction of the exclusivity of the ILWU's early culture of brotherhood, though it also belies the various ways in which women contributed to the vitality of longshoring and the wider waterfront. Many of the advances in women's presence on the waterfront were made in the key decades of the 1980s, 1990s, and early 2000s, though the history of women's work along the river is as old as the river economy itself.

During World War II, many of the companies that were growing from the boom in the wartime economy in and around New Westminster were in desperate need for administrative labour, including secretaries. One of the beneficiaries of this high demand for labour sat down to do an interview and told our interviewers that she found employment at Mercer Star Shipyards before she finished high school, before she could even complete what was then the equivalent of a secretarial training course.[51] Another narrator also had had her pick of jobs in the wartime/postwar economy and was able to turn down at least two good positions with some of the then-biggest companies on the riverfront.[52] Women performed a number of tasks, however, not just administrative: one woman had a number of experiences including doing office work but also specialized and general labour tasks at various former lumber mills that once dotted the New Westminster waterfront.[53]

Women played a role in union culture as well, both within Local 502 and beyond. The wives of the longshoremen set up a women's auxiliary within Local 502, though Dean Johnson remembered that it only lasted a brief period of time.[54] The purpose of the auxiliary was to organize occasional social events throughout the year. Incidentally, in the period leading up to 1980, many, though not all, longshoremen's wives were working in their own jobs.

One wife of a retired longshoreman reported learning many of her union skills from her husband's experience within the ILWU. She went on to organize at her own work through the Telephone Workers Union (TWU) at the former BC Tel. The TWU copied many of the strategies and even contract clauses from the ILWU and other unions. In this way, the wives of longshoremen were not only involved in taking care of the home and organizing social events for their husbands, but they also came to be actively involved in their own spheres of work in other labour contexts through associations with their husbands' union.[55] Longshore workers are quick to point out that despite the predominantly male character of their union, Local 502 has also organized women workers by bringing them in to the ILWU fold, by organizing the Roberts Bank office workers in 1975 to form Local 517, which they claimed was at the time 95% female.[56]

Though details about the first woman to try longshoring with Local 502 are sparse, oral histories reveal that her hiring came about as a result of tragedy. She was the widow of a longshoreman who died in an undated industrial accident in the 1970s. The president at the time "unilaterally" gave her a job working in a prime position on a car ship, after which "fifty or sixty" men walked off the job. The incident so shocked longshoremen that some of them had threatened to initiate an impeachment against the president of the local at the time. This case illustrates the apprehension many longshoremen felt about suddenly finding themselves working alongside a woman for the first time. But longshoremen's anger about this incident had more to do with the apparently sneaky means through which the president gave the widow a job, punting her ahead of casuals and members and into a plum position without her having had to work putting her way up to it.

Nevertheless, some longshoremen were resistant to the idea of women on the docks, given the perceived differences between the labour they were performing as men and the labour they felt (and some still feel) is more suitable for women. Some point out that the work requires a level of physical strength that they felt women did not possess, such as lifting of heavy sacks that weighed in excess of a hundred pounds. This sort of attitude, however, was not specific just to longshoremen. For example, other workers in and around the New Westminster river economy in the 1970s also described similar changing attitudes about women working in carpentry and millwork at this time.[57] A few retired longshoremen to this day remain opposed or cautiously supportive of women working in the rough and tumble world of longshoring, though most are supportive.[58]

Though some male longshore workers stressed that Local 502 itself never actively resisted the changing demography on the docks — whether it be the increase of women or monorities — female longshore workers[59] themselves were frank about the frosty reception they got in the early years. Denise Block was the first woman to register for work with Local 502 in November 1994 and, eight years later in November 2002, she finally became its first female member. Block remembered a time when casuals had to put their names "in the bucket," and names would randomly then be pulled from the bucket by the dispatcher for a job. Even so, she noted, her name never got picked when other people's names did. She remembered waiting in the dispatch hall for a job, but then noticing everyone in the hall had stepped outside. After a while, she stepped outside for a minute, returned back into the hall, and found that suddenly, she had missed her chance at a job.

There exists a misconception that women have found a place in Local 502 and in longshoring generally with the rise of mechanization. This notion suggests that as work becomes less manual and physically demanding, more highly skilled and technical, women are more able to find a place in longshoring. One current male longshore worker suggested that the big change was when Deltaport opened up in 1997. Due to the new availability of machine jobs and checker jobs, one did not "have to be really physical to work at Deltaport."[60] Women who work in Local 502 pointed out that that is not the case. As one Local 502 member aptly put it, "Women came into longshoring not because the jobs changed, but because the world changed."[61]

Regardless of their sex, new entrants into longshoring work did not and do not get their pick of jobs. Most jobs for casuals just starting out, including women, are very physically demanding. Whereas many new, male longshore workers have difficulty with some of the physical demands of the job, for women, that difficulty is immediately assumed, and so they must go above and beyond to prove themselves. Nevertheless, Block remembered cases in her early days where she claimed she did not have the same strength as many of her male coworkers. For example, she was not able to throw heavy sacks over her shoulder with the same ease as some of her male coworkers. This affected her ability to meet her quotas, which often were missed in the early days.

One current male longshore worker noted that when he started working in 1987, there were no women doing any longshoring in the areas under Local 502's jurisdiction, either as casuals or members. He also reported that when he first started seeing women on the docks, it would likely have been a wife or sister of someone who already worked there, but, he laughed, the reaction would still be "Whoa! Who are you?" whereas nowadays it is so common that men on the waterfront hardly notice the number of women on the docks.[62]

Notably, as one female longshore worker in Local 502 pointed out, ironically, it was within the occasional male reluctance to accept women on the job that women found ways to flourish. When a new longshore worker is being trained on the job, he or she is the protégé of his or her trainer or trainers. No one wants to be faulted for training someone poorly. One Local 502 woman, working one of her first lashing jobs at Deltaport, was partnered with a senior Vancouver member who was wolfing there. On the ship, he said, "if you're going to be a lasher, I'm going to show you how to be a good one." He proceeded to show her the ins and outs of 'lashing'. She joked that this was better to hear than "if you're going to be here, fine, just stay out of the way." The interdependence of senior and junior longshore workers for training has in the past three decades acted as an important mode of contact for new female employees but also served as the means through which they are often able to learn, train, and prove themselves.[63]

The Late 1990s and Beyond

On May 1, 1999, as a result of the *Canada Marine Act* having been proclaimed a year prior, the Fraser River Harbour Commission became a Canada Port Authority, the Fraser River Port Authority (FRPA). Likewise, the Port of Vancouver, which oversaw the Roberts Bank Terminals where Local 502's members worked, was also designated a Canada Port Authority. These legislative changes were intended by the federal government at the time to modernize port governance, to cede some federal control over appointments to the new port authorities to local private interests, and to encourage ports to commercialize and raise their own capital.[64]

Such changes were happening in advance of major federal infrastructure and spending plans aimed at modernizing shipping and Lower Mainland transportation networks to better accommodate the new containerized shipping economy that some critics noted was increasingly disconnected from the cities they once served.[65] The Asia-Pacific Gateway and Corridor Initiative, or the Pacific Gateway project, was and is a massive undertaking aimed at facilitating the anticipated increase in trade that such policy and economic changes from terminal expansion and containerization would bring. One example of an initiative that comprises part of the Gateway project is the South Fraser Perimeter Road or SFPR, which runs adjacent to the Fraser River and thus weakens the use of the river. Local 502 endorsed the project,[66] owing to its workers' reliance on a streamlined transportation corridor connecting them to their chief employers at Roberts Bank, as well as to traditional employment hubs along the Fraser River running adjacent to the SFPR, such as Fraser Surrey Docks.

In more recent times, one of the most important developments in Lower Mainland port history happened in 2008 when the Port of Vancouver, the Fraser River Port Authority, and the North Fraser Port Authority were merged into the Vancouver Fraser Port Authority (VFPA), more frequently branded as Port Metro Vancouver (PMV). In this new arrangement, all port affairs throughout the Lower Mainland of British Columbia come under the jurisdiction of the PMV. Amalgamation, which had been floated previously, was seen as a way to more efficiently manage Lower Mainland shipping and to avoid competition.[67] However, the merger resulted in a weakening of the close connection that Local 502 had fostered with the original port authorities. The independent dealings that Local 502 used to have (primarily) with the former FRHC, including community members who were on the Harbour Commission, are now, as many complained, part of a larger unit that is in many ways disconnected. Ringrose remembered that it was ". . . kind of sad when they amalgamated with the Vancouver port. We weren't too keen on that happening but there was nothing we could do about it."[68]

In many ways, the period between 1980–2010 was the culmination of key economic, structural, and technological processes that had long preceded it. Mechanization, automation, and containerization are all processes that began long before 1980. Still, it was in those later decades that we see what a mechanized, automated and containerized waterfront looked like. For one, it would no longer be in New Westminster, the local's former home, despite the fact that many still to this day refer to Local 502 as the "New Westminster local", despite the fact that no longshore workers work there anymore or as the "River Rats", despite a sizable majority of the work now being done on an artificial peninsula sticking out into the Georgia Strait. Secondly, for Local 502, the challenge was to maintain the union's commitment to its members, to good-paying jobs and benefits for its members, and to the sense of brotherhood (and eventually sisterhood) in the face of an increasingly fractured and autonomous workplace.

Conclusion

The era from 1980 to 2010 was a period in which Local 502 cemented many of the gains its members had made in the years prior. However, it was also a period of deep contradiction. Local 502 was beginning to send its members on international trade missions where they had to stand alongside employers in a united front in order to attract foreign investment. Yet as soon as those members came home, it was back to the bargaining table.

The decline of New Westminster as a regional hub for shipping was buffered by that city's own adaptations to deindustrialization. The decline of New Westminster as a base of operations for longshore workers was also counteracted by a rise in and consolidation of bigger terminals elsewhere along the Fraser River (especially Surrey) and beyond, including most prominently the expansive port facilities at Roberts Bank in Delta.

The consensus among many longshore workers who remember this period was that this was an era of cultural as well as technological modernization. While some members lamented a perceived decline in solidarity, fraternity, and overall connectedness among members, the local also saw its first long-term female members getting their feet in the door in the 1990s. The local was also known as having had a strict safety standard for ships, yet occasionally stood accused of having lackadaisical standards in some other respects. Navigating these changes and contradictions required reforms to the culture of Local 502, a project that was not easy, but one that members nevertheless took up out of their own volition. Finally, the busy work of negotiating contracts also became a changed business in this period. Over this period, longshore workers worked under progressively longer contracts, such that by 2008, ILWU members endorsed an eight-year collective agreement taking them up to 2018. With such changes afoot, what does the future hold for Local 502?

Chapter Notes

1 Harvey Schwartz, "Harry Bridges and the Scholars: Looking at History's Verdict," *California History* 59, no. 1 (Spring, 1980), 70n12.

2 Library and Archives Canada, FRHC minutes (1991), RG 66, Acc. no. V-2011-00173-0, file number A71-04-02, file 1991, box 9.

3 Wayne Harding, "New Westminster: City of Paradox," *The Columbian* (27 January 1966), 15.

4 "Buying Dockside Peace Could Trigger Inflation Round," *The Columbian* (2 January 1979).

5 Data compiled from multiple annual reports of the Fraser River Harbour Commission and New Westminster Harbour Commission; thank you to Andreas Qvale Hovland and Kristianne Hendricks for compiling commodity data.

6 Theresa McManus, "Union Holds Rally: Event Marks 'Grand Closing' of Interfor's Queensborough Mill," *The Record* [New Westminster] (30 August 2008).

7 Helen Hughan interview, 8 January 2014.

8 Spider Wilson interview, 13 August 2013.

9 Tom Mark interview, 14 February 2014.

10 Helen Hughan interview, 8 January 2014.

11 Wayne Harding, "New Westminster: City of Paradox," *The Columbian* (27 January 1966), 15.

12 Supreme Court of Canada, *British Columbia Development Corporation v. Friedmann* (Ombudsman), [1984] 2 S.C.R. 447, 22 November 1984 https://scc-csc.lexum.com/scc-csc/scc-csc/en/item/5282/index.do

13 Allen Domaas interview, 11 August 2014.

14 *Ibid.*

15 Library and Archives Canada, Joint FRHC-ILWU Local 502 meeting minutes, 19 September 1989, RG 66, Acc no. V-2011-00173-0, file number A71-04-02, file 1989, box 9.

16 Library and Archives Canada, Joint FRHC-ILWU Local 502 meeting minutes, 16 February 1993, and FRHC minutes 18 May 1994, RG 66, Acc no. V-2011-00173-0, file number A71-04-02, files 1993 and 1994, box 10.

17 Library and Archives Canada, undated FRHC meeting minutes, RG 66, Acc. No. V-2011-00173-0, file number A71-04-02, file 1997, Box 11.

18 Gerry White, personal communication, 6 March 2015.

19 Shane Johnson interview, 7 October 2014.

20 *Ibid.*

21 *Ibid.*

22 *Ibid.*

23 Brian Ringrose interview, 19 June 2014.

24 *Ibid.*

25 "Royal City Faces Port Shutdown," *The Columbian* (30 August 1982), 1.

26 Terry Glavin, "Longshoremen Reject Strike," *The Columbian* (10 September 1982), 3.

27 See for example "West Coast Longshoremen End Strike, Accept $1.85 Raise in 2-Year Pact," where it was reported that "the container clause was the most contentious of the non-monetary issues, and the terms of the settlement represent a victory for the union," *Globe and Mail* (17 March 1975).

28 Jennifer Hunter, "Minister Tries to Keep Port Operating," *Globe and Mail* (14 November 1986), B1–B2.

29 John Cruickshank and Carey French, "B.C. Lockout Closes Ports, Idles 3,700," *Globe and Mail* (7 October 1986), A1–A2.

30 Maintenance of Ports Operations Act, 1986 (Canada), accessed 10 November 2015, at http://laws-lois.justice.gc.ca/eng/acts/M-0.25/FullText.html

31 "Longshoremen's Challenge to Save Clause is Stymied," *Globe and Mail* (9 December 1987).

32 "Longshoremen's Union Fights Container Ruling," *Globe and Mail* (18 July 1987).

33 "Longshoremen's Challenge to Save Clause is Stymied," *Globe and Mail* (9 December 1987).

34 "End of Container Clause Perks up Vancouver Port," *Globe and Mail* (19 July 1988).

35 Peter Haines, "The Container Gainshare Money versus the Container Clause," 18 July 2005, 3, accessed 15 April 2015, http://ilwu500.org/wp-content/uploads/2013/11/Gainshare.pdf; also Joe Breaks, personal communication, 24 March 2015.

36 "Bill Passed to End Dock Dispute," *Globe and Mail* (9 February 1994).

37 RG 66, Acc. No. V-2011-00173-0, File number A71-04-02, File: 1986, Box 8, 1 January 1979 to 31 December 1986.

38 *Ibid.*

39 Brian Ringrose interview, 19 June 2014.

40 *Ibid.*

41 Geoff Clayton interview, 27 June 2013.

42 Brian Ringrose interview, 19 June 2014.

43 Brian Ringrose interview 1 of 2, 11 June 2013.

44 *Ibid.*

45 Brian Ringrose interview, 19 June 2014.

46 *Ibid.*

47 Library and Archives Canada, undated FRHC meeting minutes, RG 66, Acc. no. V2011-00173-0, file number A71-04-02, file 1960, Box 5.

48 Brian Ringrose interview, 19 June 2014.

49 Library and Archives Canada, various FRHC meeting minutes, including

17 March 1987, 1 April 1987, and others, RG 66, Acc no. V-2011-00173-0, file number A71-04-02, file 1987, box 9.

50 "Women on the Waterfront," BCMEA website, accessed 10 November 2014, http://www.bcmea.com/women_on_the_waterfront.aspx?page=hr womenwaterfront&section=hr#.

51 Helen Hughan interview, 8 January 2014.

52 Elve Morrison interview, 22 February 2013.

53 Alice LaRose interview, 30 July 2013.

54 Dean Johnson interview, 23 July 2013.

55 Fiona White interview, 2 July 2013.

56 Joe Breaks, Dean Johnson, Ron Noullett, Brian Ringrose, Gerry White, Tracey Noullett, personal communication, 30 March 2015.

57 Bill Zander interview, 21 March 2013.

58 Gerry White interview, 2 July 2013; Bruce Briggs interview, 23 May 2013; and Ron Noullett interview, 29 January 2013.

59 Some female members of ILWU Local 502 who were interviewed for this book tended to prefer the term 'longshoremen', and not 'longshorewomen', viewing the former as sufficiently neutral. In 1997, the official name of the union was changed from International Longshoremen's and Warehousemen's Union to the International Longshore and Warehouse Union as a result of a resolution passed at that year's international convention of the ILWU. This chapter uses the term 'longshore workers' where appropriate to reflect the spirit of that resolution.

60 Shane Johnson interview, 7 October 2014.

61 Anonymous interview, 30 March 2015.

62 Shane Johnson interview, 7 October 2014.

63 Anonymous interview, personal communication, 30 March 2015.

64 Alan Daniels, "Port Ready to Call Its Own Shots," *Vancouver Sun* (23 February 1999).

65 Peter V. Hall, "Connecting, Disconnecting and Reconnecting: Port Logistics and Vancouver's Fraser River," *L'Espace géographique* 41 (2012–2013): 223–235; and Peter V. Hall and Anthony Clark, "Maritime Ports and the Politics of Reconnection," in *Transforming Urban Waterfronts: Fixity and Flow*, edited by Gene Desfor, Jennefer Laidley, Quentin Stevens and Dirk Schubert (London: Routledge, 2010), 17–34;

66 Library and Archives Canada, FRHC meeting minutes 18 May 1994, RG 66, Acc. no. V-2011-00173-0, file number A71-04-02, file 1994, box 10.

67 "Container Docks in Surrey Idle After $190m Expansion," *Vancouver Sun* (21 June 2006).

68 Brian Ringrose interview, 19 June 2014.

Chapter 6

Looking to the Future

Recording and celebrating the history of ILWU Local 502 is important in and of itself. It is a story worth sharing! But the importance of history is not just about the past; it is also to provide guidance and education for current and future challenges. The conclusion to this book looks to the future in two sections.

The first section contains the reflections on the prospects for Local 502, written by Peter Hall with Joe Breaks, Gerry White, Brian Ringrose, Ron Noullett, Dean Johnson, and Tracey Noullett. They conclude that the education of current and future members is a key objective for the local. Also, that education can and should extend beyond workers to the community, and to the next generations.

Thus the second section, written by Susan O'Neill and Sue Dyer, is a record of an intergenerational arts project in New Westminster schools. We include it here as inspiration for ongoing efforts to create the next chapters in the story of *Longshoring on the Fraser*.

Reflections and Prospects

The history of Local 502 in New Westminster and on the Fraser River is a story of survival and growth despite many global changes in longshoring and ports, a process that is still ongoing. It is easy to forget today that longshoring was once a very difficult job. The work was much more dangerous, irregular, and poorly paid until workers organized themselves into a union. The training and technology that allowed for high productivity and hence good wages, generous pensions, and other benefits, and a predictable and fair system of allocating work did not happen automatically. It took organizing, occasional industrial action, and constant democratic reflection within the union about the best way forward.

As the geography of work changed — as the terminals moved away from New Westminster across and down the river — Local 502 made the difficult choice to follow the work. If it had stayed in New Westminster, it probably would have withered away like so many other unions in former industrial places. In hindsight, Local 502 took some difficult but important decisions in the late 1960s that have allowed it to thrive in the container age.

In the late 1960s, when Johnson Terminals took over the Fraser Surrey terminal, Local 502 made an agreement to take four Teamsters as members into the ILWU and admitted one Teamster as a casual on the spare board. This meant that some ILWU casuals who had served their time were delayed in becoming members, thereby losing seniority to those former Teamsters for the rest of their working lives, so this was not an easy decision. However, it allowed Local 502 to secure the jurisdiction of the Fraser Surrey terminal. In this way, the local moved across the river with the Harbour Commission. Fraser Surrey has never been a large or successful container terminal, but the move also provided early exposure to what was then a new technology.

At about the same time, Local 502 agreed to sign a separate agreement with Kaiser Resources to handle coal at Roberts Bank. Harry Bridges helped negotiate this deal by talking directly to Edgar Kaiser at his headquarters in Oakland, California. This was another difficult and risky decision for the local — Kaiser was a big company and Japanese demand for resources was booming, but the coal terminal could have been a failure. Also, it was an agreement with an employer outside of the BC Maritime Employers Association. The BCMEA was not happy! Local 502 could easily have chosen instead to give up that work to the Operating Engineers or even to a non-union shop. Ultimately it was the right decision because it secured the work at Westshore, and ultimately Deltaport, for Local 502.

During the same period, Local 502, in a signed agreement with Local 500, formalized its geographic jurisdiction. It went from Hatzic down the Fraser, then along the middle of the Fraser's north arm to the river's mouth, turning south to the United States border. This jurisdiction was already established in the founding charter of the local, but was then confirmed by near-unanimous decision at an ILWU convention.

Local 502 picnic in 1983 at Cultus Lake
From left: Bill McKay, Henry Clifford, George Bershansky, Andy Andresen (seated), Howard McIntyre, Victor Ely, and Al Hunt.
Source: Ron Noullett

The lesson from each of these difficult decisions is that Local 502 chose to defend, build, and organize its jurisdiction. There was short-term pain for long-term gain.

Over the years, Local 502 has also chosen to work with employers to allow these terminals to succeed and to implement new technologies. Technology continues to be a major challenge for the union — we may expect the new Terminal 2 to be fully automated. Will Local 502 be ready to fill the repair, maintenance, and information technology jobs that will replace some current on-dock jobs? As the workplace continues to change, how will Local 502 maintain the bonds of solidarity that have been a source of strength throughout its history? First and foremost is the solidarity amongst the members, but we also need to remember how a broader sense of solidarity and connections with others have helped the local over the decades. This includes solidarity with other longshore workers in Vancouver, in BC, along the North American west coast, and around the world, but also with the seafarers, truckers, and warehouse workers who are part of the same supply chains that longshore workers serve.

Longshore workers also need to explain their value and connections to the communities that host Vancouver's port operations. At the time of the writing of this book, the future is looking bright for both ILWU Local 502 and the City of New Westminster. The local continues to take in new members, expansions at Deltaport Terminal 2 and Fraser Surrey Docks are on the horizon, and key marine terminals are enjoying record throughput, including Deltaport-GCT, Westshore, and Annacis. The city continues to attract new residents and is governed by a progressive and inclusive coalition. Indeed, some parts of the city, including waterfront areas, are experiencing a property development boom.

All this urban growth brings its own challenges — for the union and for the community. Industrial lands, especially lands with access to the waterfront, are under continuous pressure for redevelopment. Road and rail traffic, whether generated in the community or simply passing through, remain the most complained-about facts of life in the Royal City. Much of this traffic is a legacy of the port's relationship to the city. The rail lines that connected and still connect marine terminals to the intercontinental railyards are not going away, so their daily interface with the city must be managed. Likewise, when waterfront land is converted from industrial to non-industrial uses, the displaced industrial activity generates additional traffic. Industrial businesses continue to choose trucks rather than water-based transport and they will continue to do so until the alternatives of river-barging and short-sea shipping become cost-competitive, which includes making truck transport not rock-bottom cheap. For this reason, the ongoing efforts by container truckers to improve their working conditions and wages deserve the support of both longshore workers and the residents of communities such as New Westminster.

The challenges of growth for Local 502 are a good problem to have. Still, that does mean that there is a pressing need to educate new members about the history and culture of the union. As can be learned from the experiences of including women and successive waves of immigrants, the inclusion of new members is not always easy, but if it is done right, the new members add ideas and energy to the union. Everyone needs to be involved in meeting this challenge: pensioners, who lived the history discussed in this book, can pass on their knowledge and experience, younger rank-and-file members can bring their enthusiasm and expertise in digital media technology to share these stories and lessons, and the leadership can support these activities with guidance and resources. Finally, it is important not to forget the casual workers in these efforts — they are the members of tomorrow.

New inductees take coffee break in a steel ship
Back — left to right, Dane Mudrunic, Ben MacDonald.
Front — left to right Candace Usak, Jas Dhaliwal, Derek Langill.
Source: Judy Wallace

(Re)Claiming the New Westminster Waterfront: Intergenerational Arts Program for Schools

There are few opportunities in the school curriculum for students to learn directly from those in our community who have lived the history and experienced the places and events that are studied in the classroom. Intergenerational collaboration provides opportunities for 'real world practical' learning about work issues that define a community as well as opportunities for relationship building and enhanced communication between generations.

With these aims in mind, Dr. Susan O'Neill from the Faculty of Education at Simon Fraser University, developed an intergenerational arts/civic history educational program as part of the (Re)Claiming the New Westminster Waterfront research partnership led by Dr. Peter Hall from Urban Studies at SFU. The program is designed to bring together longshore workers, who spent their working lives on the waterfront, with children and young adults who are learning about the history of the waterfront. As the longshore workers share their experiences of working on the waterfront, the students gain a stronger sense of the history and importance of the waterfront in their community. A series of art projects were coordinated and taught by art teacher and SFU research assistant, Sue Dyer, in collaboration with researchers and teachers at the elementary and secondary school level. The volunteer retired members of Local 502 of the International Longshore and Warehouse Union participated in the arts projects with the students and shared their experiences and stories from their working lives on the waterfront.

Description of Program Activities

In spring 2012, an eight-week pilot project took place with students in Grades 5–6 from the New Westminster Homelearners' Program (HLP), School District 40. A highlight of this project involved a field trip where the children joined retired longshore worker Joe Breaks, who led a guided walk along the waterfront. The children were each given a disposable camera to take photos that they compared to photos of the waterfront from the past. In subsequent weeks, they created

Loading lumber from scow and dock, Berths 7/8, Fraser Surrey Docks.
Source: Port Metro Vancouver

Work on Pacific Coast Terminals 1B dock, showing a forklift (Hyster model), dollies with bagged goods. Note the terminal's steam engine in front of the PCT main terminal building.
Source: Port Metro Vancouver

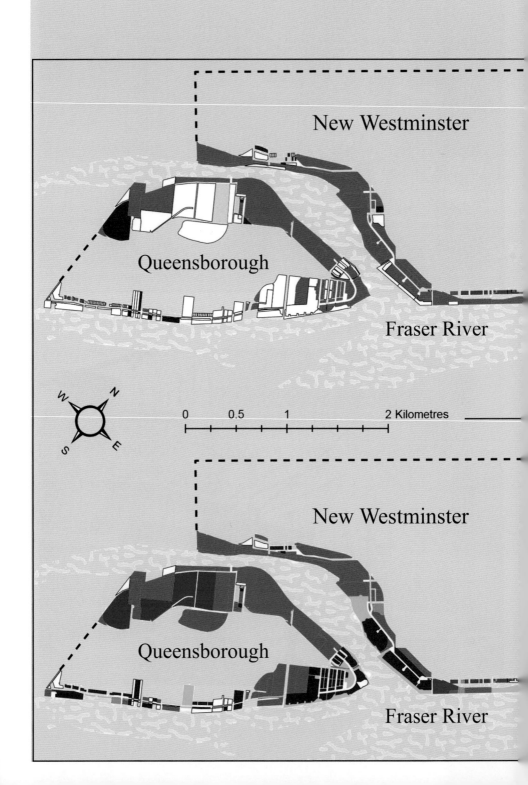

New Westminster

Queensborough

Fraser River

W N
E
S

0   0.5   1   2 Kilometres

New Westminster

Queensborough

Fraser River

Changes in land use on the central New Westminster waterfront

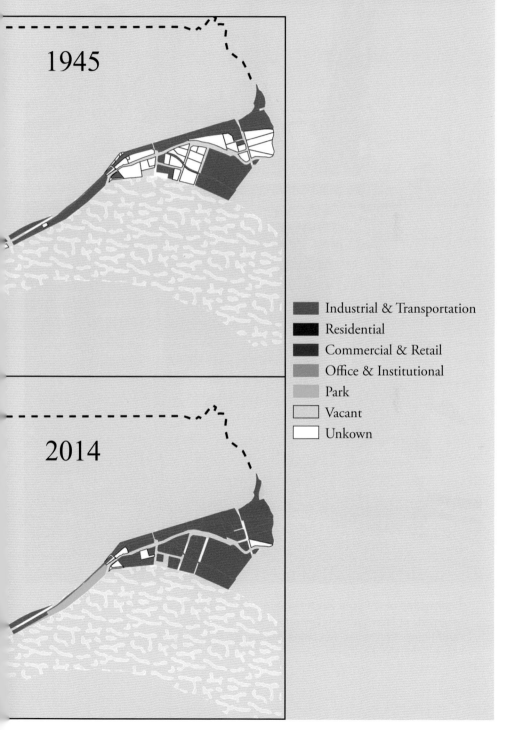

1945

2014

Industrial & Transportation
Residential
Commercial & Retail
Office & Institutional
Park
Vacant
Unkown

Stern ramp on a Pacific Australia Direct (PAD) ship. The PAD ships, which called regularly at New Westminster and Fraser Surrey Docks, were ro-ro ships with a stern ramp for loading and unloading cargo.
Source: Port Metro Vancouver

Container ship at Fraser Surrey Docks, being loaded by the gantry crane installed in the early 1970s. The first 502 members trained as gantry (container crane) drivers were Freddy Stopple and Jack Labinsky Sr., who became the trainers after that. Frank Pyatt was the electrical engineer who installed the first gantry. Note this vessel is only 5 containers wide; while the newest ships are over 20 containers wide.
Source: Ron Noullett

Ford trucks damaged in transit, offloaded at Fraser Wharves. The lower decks on the carship carrying these imports flooded, causing some trucks to break loose and get smashed up.
Source: Ron Noullett

Wilf Hinshaw (L) and Richard 'Stretch' Johnson (R), rebuilding a broken package of lumber at Fraser Surrey Dock. In the background, the MacGregor hatch covers on the ship which fold open are visible.
Source: Wilf Hinshaw

Offloading motor vehicles from the *Orient*.
Source: Ron Noullett

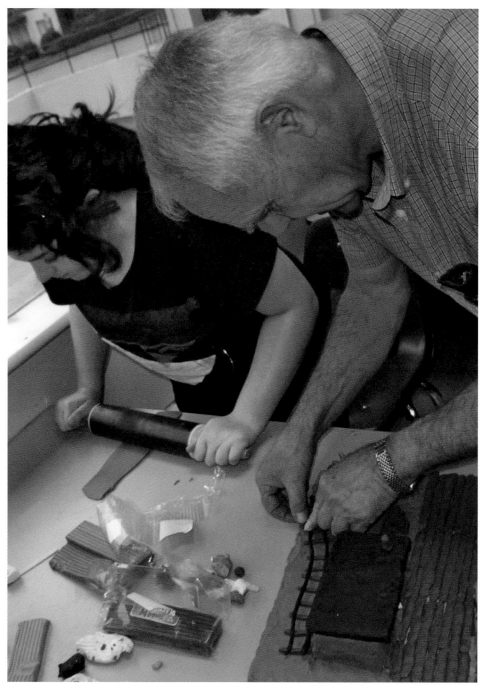

Joe Breaks helping a student with a project for the Intergenerational Arts Program for Schools, some of which were exhibited in the Anvil Centre.
Source: Susan O'Neill

Top: Joe Breaks works hands-on with other students.
Bottom: Gerry White is also highly involved with the Intergenerational Arts Program for Schools.
Source: Susan O'Neill

clay sculptures that represented different aspects of working life on the waterfront in partnership with Joe Breaks, Gerry White, and other retired longshore workers who attended the art classes taught by Sue Dyer. The students also created drawings of what they imagined the waterfront to be like in the future and a celebration display of their art projects took place with parents, teachers, students, SFU project collaborators and invited members of the community attending.

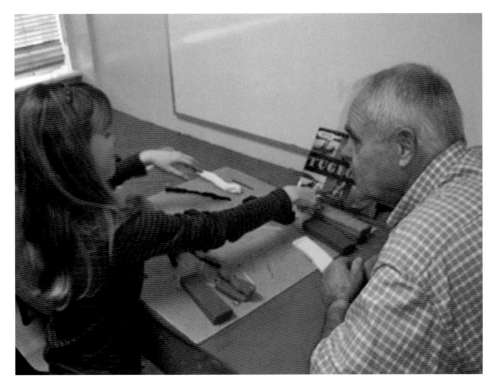

Joe Breaks helps children with elaborate multiple art craft projects.
Source: Susan O'Neill

In spring of 2013, a second project was conducted by Sue Dyer with Matthew Sol's class of students in Grades 3–4 at F. W. Howay Elementary School in New Westminster and longshore worker retirees Joe Breaks, Gerry White, and Brian Ringrose. This project followed a similar model as the pilot project and illustrated the benefits of how intergenerational sharing of lived experiences can enhance classroom learning and provide a social and generative opportunity for the retirees.

Classroom learning about the past, present, and future of the waterfront was enhanced by the intergenerational relationships developed, and the children and longshore workers collaborated on the creation of art projects that included clay sculptures, mask making, painting, drawing, and wire sculpture, as well as puppet shows and comic book creations using an iPad. A highlight was the celebration day, when the students shared their work and experiences with other students and teachers in the school, continuing the oral history tradition.

A third project was conducted in May 2013, with Grade 10 students in Pat Dyer's Social Studies class at New Westminster Secondary School. This project involved students working in small groups together with retired longshore workers in the creation of short 'documentary' films exploring the history of the working waterfront using everyday technology available to the students such as smart phones and computers. The longshore workers (Joe Breaks, Gerry White, Brian Ringrose, Ken Bauder, Dean Johnson, Ron Noullett) shared stories with the students about the evolution over time of the community, working conditions, and the improvements that were made through ILWU and government labour laws. Using storytelling, photography, film, and music the students and longshore workers created films that communicated meaningful messages about past and present work on the New Westminster waterfront. These short films were viewed and celebrated with the students and retirees by current working members of the longshore workers' union, communicating to them the value of this work recording their local history.

Voices of Program Participants

What some of the children had to say about the program:

- *We had no clue before we started and when the retirees went on the walk along the waterfront with us they could tell us what it was like before.*
- *They helped us by showing what went where. They helped us get the shape of the boat, they helped to flatten out the clay to shape it.*
- *They gave us all the details on the little things, what the door would have been, what the roof would have been and these little details*

are important for a clay model. They helped us to make it look realistic and this makes it look so much better because people can get the idea better of what we are trying to show them. We like to capture all the little details because it's not just a landscape — it's a scene. And it made it more realistic. They were so helpful and we would not know even half as much without them here.

- *They know a lot more than we do because they worked there. You can ask them questions and you can't ask questions of a book or even the internet. It isn't easy to get answers to the questions you have. We could see what it used to look like better by matching up the old photo. It helped our imagination because we could imagine even more.*
- *It was fun working with them. I will miss them.*

What some of the retirees had to say about the program:

Joe Breaks (Local 502, ILWU Retired Longshore Worker): We were impressed by how fast they learned the information and how keen they were. It was easy to relate to the students. It was easy to work with them. Once we learned what they were doing with the iPads, we were just as able to join in and connect with the students.

Gerry White (Local 502, ILWU Retired Longshore Worker): I've enjoyed all sessions, the kids were excellent. I find it all interesting and entertaining. It was quite a lot of fun; I didn't think I was artistically inclined.

Brian Ringrose (Local 502, ILWU Retired Longshore Worker): I thought it was cute the way they interviewed us for the comic book. I got a kick out of the questions they asked at Howay.

Ken Bauder (Local 502, ILWU Retired Longshore Worker): Stereotypes and generalization can be the currency of young growing minds. How can we change the way of assimilating information about the workers on the waterfront? This story is about a very young lad in a pilot project and his epiphany that holds my mind with the hope for a change in societal attitudes through intergenerational collaborations using teachers, art, education, and communication as vehicles for change. The first pilot project had a group of elementary students working with a group of retired longshore workers. The task was to have the retirees explain through walks on the docks, photos past and present, and oral history to the students who would then recreate models in clay of the working environment — a daunting task. The underpinning of this task was how to establish a communication method for the exchange of information about that work. A young lad who was part of the student cohort in the first project was overheard at the very beginning of the project saying to another student that "longshore workers are rednecks," something that was undoubtly presented to him by the outside world. Still, through the discussion, seeing the photos, and creating the clay model, which he worked on with the retiree, the student had changed his attitude and was left with a new respect for the longshore industry and retirees. I always will always remember this epiphany as a life-changing moment for the student.

Gerry White gets/gives a lesson in making art about the working waterfront.
Source: Susan O'Neill

What the teachers had to say about the program:

Sue Dyer, Art teacher: The students very quickly became comfortable with the retirees, and enjoyed the interaction. The students were enthusiastic toward asking questions and listening to the retiree's responses; the dialogue was very dynamic. The students and retirees worked incredibly well together. After the first four sessions, the project took on a life of its own as the retirees and the students collaborated creating the art pieces. I watched the intergenerational connections being made as they worked together. The students enjoyed working with the arts media and spending time with the retirees. I was very surprised by how well the students with learning disabilities thrived in this project. They were completely absorbed in it. They were able to contribute and work equally with their peers without needing any support or being isolated, even taking a leadership role. It was encouraging to see the students so enthusiastic toward sharing their work with other students; this was a highlight of the project. I watched the students continuing the oral history telling as they explained the project to their peers. I observed which art medium best supported the intergenerational connections: the clay by far encouraged the most continuous interaction. Both the retirees and the students benefited from this exchange. As the projects progressed the retirees became more confident with their artistic abilities and with their interaction with the class. One retiree, who wouldn't draw during the first project, was actively drawing toward the end of the second project. He was also hesitant to talk to the entire class at first, and during the second project asked if he could address the whole class with some information.

Matthew Sol, Grade 3–4 teacher: I was surprised at how easily the students connected with the retirees, I thought they would be more reluctant and would hesitate to include them. I was very surprised how quickly these connections were made. I think this was due to how the retirees interacted with the students, they let the students lead and answered their questions; they were just willing to share whatever the students were interested in knowing. For me, the highlight of the project was the students sharing with the other children in the school so willingly and with such enthusiasm that it surprised me. With so many curriculum requirements, I wondered if the time required is feasible for this project, but when looked at deeply, the curriculum requirements are included, just in a different way. I think the success of this project for all students is due to how open it is. There are many ways a student can work with this.

Pat Dyer, Grade 10 Social Studies teacher: I would like to do something like this again in the future. The interaction between the parties involved is just too powerful not to use again. To have the people who really did the work tell their stories reaches students in a way no book and few teachers can. The waterfront visit was the highlight of the whole project. When we debriefed back at school it was clear everyone had enjoyed the trip and had learned a lot. We were all quite excited to see how the filmmaking process would unfold. The students discussed with the retirees what they had remembered from the waterfront visit and they searched together for more images. Several students really shined working with the retirees, showing them how to find images on the computer, and the retirees were great at asking questions and being a receptive audience. Searching for music for their films with the retirees became a highlight for the groups. The students took an active role in walking the retirees through the different music searches or uploading music a retiree had brought. I saw some excellent work being done and was surprised by the students becoming teachers and the retirees being students.

Special Education Assistant (grade 3–4 students): I think the students gained some compassion for how dangerous the job really was for the longshore worker.

Community Engagement

Artwork produced during the various projects was placed on display at the New Westminster's Homelearners' site in March 2012, F. W. Howay Elementary in May 2013, New Westminster Secondary School in June 2013, New Westminster City Hall in June 2013, Place des Arts Community Arts Centre in Coquitlam in Sept. 2013, and was featured prominently in a poster display about the entire Reclaiming project at the Canadian History Association Conference in Victoria in May 2013. Displays were also featured at the Discovery Centre, during RiverFest celebrations in September 2014, and for the "Our Working Waterfront" museum exhibit at the New Westminster Museum.

(Re)Claiming the New Westminster Waterfront Intergenerational Arts Program is anticipated to continue in the future.

Longshore Glossary Terms

Michelle La

Assassinator: The nickname of the machine that was used when packaged lumber was first loaded into wings of ships.

The assassinator was the first machine that was used by Local 502 longshoremen to load packaged lumber onto ships. The name 'assassinator' was a nickname that the longshoremen gave to this machine because some men got hurt using it. It was a metal machine with four rollers on the bottom, four on top, and a lock on the side. It was three feet long, eight inches high, and had a twenty-foot rope attached to it. A longshoreman would put packaged lumber in the centre of the assassinator and when it was pushed into place, one gang member unlocked it, then pulled it out from under the load with an attached rope. The packaged lumber would come shooting out.

Automation: The use of various control systems for operating equipment, such as machinery, to lessen handling by hand.

The surge of automation occurred on the New Westminster waterfront during the 1960s.

The Bar: At times, one of the first things longshoremen did was to build a beverage bar with the cargo they were loading. They would check the hatches for any hidden alcohol.

Barge: A large flat-bottomed vessel used to carry cargo from a port to shallow-draft waterways. Barges are sometimes motorized or self-propelled. A single standard barge can hold 1,500 tons of cargo or as much as either fifteen railroad cars or sixty trucks can carry. A typical barge is 200 feet long, 35 feet wide and has a draft of 9 feet. Barges carry dry bulk (grain, coal, lumber, gravel, etc.) and liquid bulk (petroleum, vegetable oils, molasses, etc.). *See also* scow.

Berth: The wharf space where a ship docks. A wharf may have two or more berths, depending on the length of incoming ships.

Board of Commissioners: The members of the governing board of a port authority are called commissioners. Members of a Board of Commissioners can be elected or appointed and usually serve for several years. When the port authority was a commission, the members were called Commissioners. Now, members in port authorities are called board members.

Bombcart: A machine that is driven around the docks. It is used for transporting heavy cargo and loading/unloading of containers, as well as cargo such as lumber.

Boom: The boom, similar to a crane, is used for lifting cargo on and off a ship. A swinging stick boom located in the centre of a hatch, much like a crane used for heavier lifts, moved over the dock or the scow.

Box: Slang term for a shipping container. *See also* can.

Breakbulk Cargo: Loose, non-containerized cargo.

Bulk Cargo: Cargo that is not shipped in packages or containers. It is shipped loose in the hold of a ship, such as grain, coal, and sulphur, or as liquid bulk shipped in tankers, such as oil and LNG. It is also known as bulk freight.

Bulkhead: A structure used to protect against shifting cargo and/or to separate the cargo.

Bulkhead Stow: A type of cargo used to divide the hold of a ship into two separate stows, usually sacked cargo, such as flour, fertilizer, or coffee. The bulkhead stow is much like building a brick wall with a strong face that would not collapse when one end of the hold was unloaded.

Bulk Loaders: Ships without decks.

Bullion Slings: Slings made of wire rope used for loading lead or zinc.

Business Agent: The Local 502 executive who is the workplace representative of the longshoremen.

Butting Out: There was often limited space between the first plank of lumber and the second one that was laid down in a ship's hatch. A gang member judged the length of space remaining and would go to the load to pick a piece would fit that space. If gang members did not pick the right plank, the side-runner would tell them to redo it. Over time, the longshoremen got used to judging the perfect plank sizes. It was similar to creating a laminate floor but the longshoremen did not have a saw to customize the sizes; instead they started with the longest pieces first and created layers of lumber on top of each other.

Can: Slang term for a shipping container. *See also* box.

The Canary: An eight-foot quarter-inch steel rod with a small hook at one end and a handle at the other. This tool was needed to wrap slings around loads when unloading steel wire used for making nails. The canary was useful when things were out of reach. The tool is needed to reach for the slings and acts like a long extension to one's arm.

The Cant Hook: A peavey, but without the spike at the end tip of the tool. When a longshoreman's partner is at one end of a plank of wood and the longshoreman wants to pick it up, the partner will twist (or cant) it so that it is easy for the longshoreman to pick up.

Cargo Winches: Power-driven machines used to lift, lower, or move cargo. Winches are classified according to their source of power (e.g. steam, hydraulic, and electric). Electric winches are standard equipment on most vessels today.

Chains: Used for slinging steel beams or for lashing down deck loads of logs or lumber. Also used to secure cargo in a hatch.

Cones: A device that locks containers together.

Container: A rectangular steel box that is made to withstand shipment, storage, and handling. It can be detached from the chassis for loading into a vessel or railcar or stacked in a container depot. Containers may be ventilated, insulated, refrigerated, flat rack, vehicle rack, open top, bulk liquid, or equipped with interior devices. *See also* box, can, flat rack and vehicle rack.

Container Crane: Usually, a rail-mounted gantry crane located on a wharf for the purpose of loading and unloading containers on vessels.

Container Terminal: A specialized facility where ocean container vessels dock to discharge and load containers. These terminals' cranes are equipped with a safe lifting capacity of 35–40 tonnes that have booms with an outreach of up to 120 feet in order to reach the outside cells of vessels. Most terminals have direct rail access and container storage areas and are served by highway carriers.

Containerization: The technique of using a container to store, protect, and handle cargo while it is in transit. This shipping method has both greatly expedited the speed at which cargo was moved from origin to destination and lowered shipping costs. Containerization was first introduced to Local 502 longshoremen in the early 1970s.

Corner Hook: A special hook that is put in a corner of the hatch, so that a gang member could pull the runner, a wire/rope/cable from one winch into the hook, and then the load could be put in the corner of the hatch. This hook helped the gang down below when they were working the cargo, as they used it to swing the cargo closer. This was only used when there was standing gear. The corner hook was not considered safe or legal.

Crane: A mechanical lifting device that lifts or lowers cargo into or out of ships.

Creosote and Non-Creosote Ties: A chemical wood preserver (creosote) used on railway ties that longshoremen handled with a tool called a picaroon. One would drive a picaroon into the wood and drag the tie. Longshoremen would evenly organize these railway ties to cover the floor of the hatch, which is known as 'flooring off'. The longshoremen carried the ties with one man at each end. Due to the chemical wood preserver, handling these ties would bother and burn longshoremen's eyes and skin.

Decasualization: When casual workers, who face uncertain and irregular jobs, become permanent employees.

Work on the waterfront was notorious for being casual and organized through the shape-up system before unionization. One of the main achievements of the ILWU on the west coast of Canada and the United States was decasualization by creating a system to allocate the available jobs fairly and reliably. Decasualization does not mean that workers always have full-time work, but it does mean that the available jobs are allocated according to a fair and reliable system.

Deck Loads: This is a term used to describe when hatches are full of cargo and the deck space is needed to load the rest of the cargo. Before containers, lumber and logs were the only cargo stowed on the deck. To hold the cargo on deck, there were chains every ten feet holding the cargo to the deck of the ship.

Deep Tanks: These are ballast tanks with removable lids that were emptied to store cargo. The opening of the ballast tank was approximately four by eight feet. When a gang member went down the hatch to stow cargo in the deep tank, they had to choke the load with one sling when handling cargo such as loose lumber to tip the end of the load. When the load was coming down, the longshoremen had to get as far as away from the opening of the tank as they could because the load often spilled all over the deep tank. If the longshoremen were handling lumber, they stacked it and assembled it until the floor was so high they could not get down the hatch.

Derrick: Used for lifting cargo on and off a ship, similar to a crane. This is a swinging stick boom located in the centre of a hatch, much like a crane used for heavier lifts, moved over the dock or the scow.

Dispatch: The method by which longshoremen are assigned jobs.

Dock: *(verb)* To bring in a vessel to tie up at a wharf berth.

(noun) A dock is a structure built along, or at an angle from, a navigable waterway so that vessels may lie alongside to receive or discharge cargo. Sometimes, the whole wharf is informally called a dock.

Dock Worker: The dockworkers worked and did the maintenance on the dock. ILWU Local 511 was a separate local for dockworkers and Local 502 was a separate local for deep-sea workers until the two locals amalgamated in the early 1960s.

Dockage: A charge by a port authority for the length of water frontage used by a vessel tied up at a wharf.

Dolly: Dollies used on the waterfront were made of steel, with hard rubber tires and a four-foot-long steering handle. They were very heavy and were made to hold five or more tons. One longshoreman could push an empty dolly, but two to three longshoremen were needed to push a full one. Dollies were pulled by jitneys. *See also* jitney.

Dry Bulk: Minerals or grains stored in loose piles. Examples are industrial sands, potash, wheat, soybeans, coal, sulphur, and peanuts. *See also* Bulk Cargo.

Elevator Ship: A car ship that had an elevator in it. This was one of the methods of unloading car ships. The longshoremen would drive the car into the elevator, press a button to go to the top deck, and then drive it down a ramp attached to the ship onto the dock. After parking the vehicle, the longshoreman would walk back to the ship, take the elevator down the ship, and repeat the process.

False Decking: Temporary decks created to have more storage for any commodity.

First Point of Rest: This is where documentation of unloaded cargo is confirmed.

Flat Rack: A container with collapsible end wall and without side walls to allow the loading of cargoes of irregular sizes and shapes. Once the end walls are restored, a regular container crane and other handling equipment can lift them. *See also* container and vehicle rack.

Fletchers: Six-inch thick lumber of any length or width.

Floor off: Stowing cargo in a ship evenly, covering the floor of a ship's hold. This was the most space-efficient method of stowing cargo, as layers of cargo could evenly be stored on top of another. Sacks and loose lumber were commonly stowed in a hatch this way.

Foreman: The foreman supervises and directs the work of longshoremen. There was a foreman for each hatch and one head foreman for the ship. Foremen have their own Local 514, and they are not a part of the longshore gang structure.

Forklift: A machine used to lift and transport cargo.

Freight: Merchandise hauled by transportation lines.

Frisco Face: Once in a while when the gang got tired of stowing cargo, they would leave an unfilled cargo space, instead of taking the cargo all the way into the wing to stow it. This effectively left unused hatch space in the ship. If the foreman got down to the hatch, leaned against the frisco face, and it tumbled, the gang had to clean it up and redo it properly. Hand-stowed lumber and sacks were the cargo which gangs would usually make a frisco face with. The name may have derived from San Francisco.

Gang: A working group of longshoremen.

Gantry Crane: A track-mounted shoreside crane utilized in the loading and unloading of breakbulk cargo, containers, and heavy lift cargo. Today, there are ship gantries and dock gantries and both are used for the discharge of various cargos.

General Cargo: Consists of both containerized and breakbulk goods, in contrast to bulk cargo. General cargo operations produce more jobs than bulk handling.

Grabs (clamps): Any equipment that grabbed and held anything. For instance, these are on cranes that would grab metal, pick it up, and place it somewhere. These are used in the loading and unloading of steel plates and are commonly known as clamps today.

Grain Elevator: A facility where bulk grain is unloaded from railcars into silos where it is weighed, cleaned, and blended. In longshore work, sometimes the grain is poured into a ship.

Gross Tonnage: The sum of container, breakbulk, and bulk spaces into which cargo can be loaded onto a waterborne conveyor.

Guy: Rope or wire used to keep the booms in place.

'The Hall': Before moving to Surrey, Local 502's union hall building was located at the east foot of Tenth Street, north of Carnarvon Street, at 71 Tenth Street, New Westminster. Longshore workers referred to it simply as 'the hall'. It was a two-storey wooden building and the top floor was reserved for union members. The bottom floor was where the office was located. On the west side of the hall was the treasurer's office and on the east side was the job dispatcher's office. There were three ten-foot tables so the longshore workers could play cards while waiting for a job.

Hand Truck: A two-wheeled truck used for sacks or cases.

'Hanging the Hook': A term used to describe when a crew stowed their load faster than the hook (lifting gear) could bring them another load. Then they would have a rest while waiting.

Hatch: An opening in the ship through which the cargo is stowed in the ship's hold.

Hatch Tender: The leader of the gang. His responsibilities were to give directions to the winch drivers by hand signals and to look out for the safety of the crew.

'Heads Up': What longshoremen would say to each other to watch for loads coming into or out of the ship's hatch.

Heavy Lift: Very heavy cargoes require specialized equipment to move the products to and from ship, truck, rail, barge, and terminals. Heavy lift machines are installed aboard a ship that is designed just for transporting heavy cargo.

Hopper: A large bin that the Gradall excavator poured ore into. The hopper would be on the end of the conveyor and it could be set to regulate the flow of the ore going to the ship.

Jitney: A small tractor device which could pull multiple dollies at once. *See also* dolly.

Johnson Bar: A four-foot bar that the winch driver moved to change a winch's direction.

Landlord Port: At a landlord port, the port authority builds the wharves, which it then rents or leases to a terminal operator (usually a stevedoring company or steamship line). The operator invests in cargo-handling equipment (forklifts, cranes, etc.), hires longshore labourers to operate such lift machinery, and negotiates contracts with ocean carriers to handle the unloading and loading of ship cargoes.

Lasher: A longshoreman who uses lash bars (long steel rods) to tighten a container and various types of cargo before they leave a port. It is used to ensure cargo is secure enough to handle rough sea conditions.

Liberty Ships: Cargo ships built in the United States during World War II. These ships were purchased by shipping companies after World War II to import and export cargo. These ships had standing gear, steam winches, electric winches, and hydraulic winches. In Canada, these were technically known as Victory Ships.

Loading Bulk Ore: This term refers to the ore that came to Pacific Coast Terminals, New Westminster, in open railcars with fibreglass covers. Dockworkers took the covers off with the help of a forklift. The railcars were shunted under a frame that the Gradall excavator was sitting on. In general, only Gradall excavators were used. The excavator took the ore out of the railcars and dumped it loose into the warehouse. A front-end loader inside the warehouse scooped up the ore and created a big pile. When it came time to load it aboard a ship, the front-end loader scooped the bulk ore into a big hopper. From the hopper, a conveyer belt took the ore to the hatch of the ship and dropped it in. *See also* hopper.

Loading Hides by Hand: Cow hides were a cargo which was manually handled in the 1960s and 1970s in New Westminster and Vancouver. They were raw animal skins which generally were covered with maggots and had a horrible stench. If the slime got onto the longshoremen's clothes, the smell could not be washed off. The hides were folded inside-out, into two-by-three-foot bundles that weighed approximately 80 pounds. The longshoremen had to carry them off the pallet and stow them in the wing of the ship. Working with the hides was considered the worst job on the waterfront and many longshoremen would vomit handling them.

Loading Lead and Zinc by Hand: Lead came in 112-pound bars and zinc in 60-pound bars. A single lift of cargo had 45 bars per load. Two longshoremen set the load on a dolly and began stowing by hand. Four longshoremen would take alternating shifts of loading and resting because it was such heavy lifting. They worked two to a load and stowed the metal faster than they brought it aboard.

Loading Plywood by Hand: Plywood was mostly stowed in the tween deck of a hatch. The plywood came down the hatch, twelve or more bundles at a time, and was put on a dolly. The bundles were four inches high. The plywood was wrapped in thick brown waxed paper, which made it easier for it to slide into place. Then it was pushed into the wing of a hatch. Four men in each corner picked up a bundle and stowed it onto the floor that was prepared for it with two-by-four dunnage. Longshoremen then piled these bundles on top of each other until they reached the top of the hatch. The bundles had four half-inch bands holding the bundle together. When the longshoremen slid the bundle into place, they had to watch that the bands did not break, as they could cut the longshoremen very easily. *See also* tween deck.

Loading Pulp by Hand: Each bale of pulp weighed 450 pounds and came down to the hatches eight bales at a time. Longshoremen would put a bale on a hand truck and wheel it to where they wanted it, then flip it into place.

Loading Sacks by Hand: Each fertilizer, flour, or grain sack weighed 112 pounds and coffee sacks weighed up to 250 pounds. The fertilizer sacks were made out of strong paper. Flour, grain, and coffee sacks were made out of burlap. Sacks were shipped with thirty-five sacks on a pallet and were brought down the hatch to be loaded. Longshoremen had to work their way up the hatch storing them and they would often twist their ankles due to the difficulty of manoeuvring them. While handling nitraprills, longshoremen had to build trenches and bulkhead them. Because nitraprills are explosive, it was considered a dangerous job and the longshoremen got paid ten cents more an hour.

Longshoreman: An individual employed in a port to load and unload ships. In the United States, most longshoremen are unionized members of the ILWU (International Longshore and Warehouse Union) or the ILA (International Longshoremen's Association). The ILWU operates on the west coast of Canada and the United States. The ILA operates on the east and Gulf coasts.

Mark-off Paint: Used on a loose lumber stow to differentiate between different ports of call, mark-off paint quite often consisted of coloured powder mixed with water and applied with a brush made of short pieces of rope or rags tied to a stick. When all the cargo for one port was loaded, lines were painted across the top of the cargo to separate it from the next port's cargo on the ships.

Mechanization: The development of increasingly technologically-advanced ways of handling cargo. In many cases, this often meant machines replacing the labour of longshoremen. The shift became widespread in the 1960s.

Mud Ships: Ships that carried bulk ore from Pacific Coast Terminals in New Westminster.

Mud Shed: The nickname of the warehouse at Pacific Coast Terminals that held piles of bulk ore until it was loaded onto ships.

Nautical Bollard: A rotating drum on the winch. It was used to pull the ship's line tight.

Nelly's Locker/Nellie's Locker: The room between two bulkheads on a ship. If a ship had two bulkheads, longshoremen would often fill Nellie's Locker with lumber.

Net Slings: Rope woven in the form of a net for loading cargo.

Nickel and Copper Ore: During the 1960s, nickel and copper matte was loaded and unloaded by hand. The pieces were broken off from a large ingot and weighed approximately 50–60 pounds apiece. The longshoremen had to bend down and pick up the pieces from the floor, then put them into a skiff to be taken out to the dock. They were very jagged pieces and the longshoremen often cut and smashed their fingers. This was a job longshoremen particularly did not enjoy.

On-dock Rail: Direct shipside rail service that includes the ability to load and unload containers/breakbulk directly from railcar to vessel.

Ore: *See also* loading bulk ore, and nickel and copper ore.

PAD Ship: These were ships that came from Australia. 'PAD' came from the official name of the operator Pacific Australia Direct Line. It was also the acronym from the first letters of the ships that went that regular route: Paralla, Allunga, and Dilkara.

Pad Eye: A large metal ring welded on the deck used for attachment of things to the ship.

Pallet: A short wooden, metal, or plastic platform on which packaged cargo is placed and handled by a forklift truck.

Panamax: Term for the size limits for ships travelling through the Panama Canal.

Peavey: A tool that had a four-foot wooden handle with a steel point and a moveable hook that was set for moving timber. If the timber was too big, the men lifted it with a peavey, put a steel roller underneath, and rolled the timber into place.

Penalty Time: During the 1960s, if certain cargo could not be finished loading in a shift, longshoremen would go into 'penalty time', which was paid as double time. This had a maximum of up to a four-hour extension and could only be used if there were no other gangs available. The other condition of 'penalty time' was that the vessel had to be finished to sail. Penalty time was eight to nine dollars an hour and the employer had to supply the longshoremen with dinner.

Rail Mounted Gantry (RMG): An electrically-powered machine mounted on rail tracks that is used to move containers.

Rib Stow: Sometimes the ship's captain wanted more lumber on board, and the captain told the ship foreman to 'rib stow'. Longshoremen had to floor off loose lumber until they were halfway up the hatch. This would be done in the space between the ribs of the ship, the side of the cargo, and the skin of the ship would be filled up with loose lumber.

Captains made extra money due to rib stow, as they were contracted for a certain amount of lumber and any extra lumber was left for them to sell. On some ships, every space was filled with cargo. This was hard work that longshoremen particularly did not enjoy.

Robots: A cage frame that was used for eliminating the need to use slings or slingmen.

'Ro-ro' ships: Shortening of the term roll on/roll off. These ships have ramps which allowed wheeled vehicles to load and discharge cargo without the use of cranes.

Romeos: Slip-on leatherwork shoes that the longshoremen wore. These had rubber soles with oilproof and waterproof foot construction.

Rubber-Tired Gantry (RTG): A diesel-powered motorized machine on rubber tires that is used to stack and move containers in a yard or to trucks.

Saveall: This was a forty-foot-long and twenty-foot-wide net made out of one-inch rope. It was a safety catch-all to save any cargo that might fall while the loading was taking place. It was tied from the rail of the ship to the dock. Longshoremen would not board ships unless the save-all was tied up correctly to a gangplank.

Scab: Scab is a derogatory term for a person who works despite an ongoing strike or is a strike-breaker. Scabs and scabbing have a special significance in the history of longshoring in British Columbia. The term '35 scab refers to an individual who was a strike-breaker during the 1935 Ballantyne Pier strike in Vancouver, British Columbia. The defeat of the 1935 strike by scabs and employers laid the ground for the successful creation of the locals that eventually became ILWU Canada.

Scow: Like a barge but not motorized. Longshoremen use scows mostly to move steel, pipe, and lumber.

Shape-up: The system of hiring longshore (and other) workers who are casual employees. Under the shape-up, workers assemble in a place and are chosen to work for that day by the employer. The system destroys solidarity amongst workers because they are forced to compete directly with each other for every job. Decasualization replaced the shape-up with a fair and reliable system for longshore workers on the west coast of Canada and the United States.

Shipper: The person or company who is usually the supplier or owner of commodities shipped.

Shop Steward: An employee of an organization or company who represents and defends the interests of his/her fellow employees and who is also a labour union official.

Side-Runner: In a gang, there were two side-runners, one on each side of the hatch, and they were in charge of where and how cargo was stored. Due to this responsibility, they were paid a higher salary. If they thought a gang member was not doing their share, the side-runner could fire them or tell the foreman to do so.

Slider: Any cargo that accidently slides loose out of a load.

Slingman: A longshoreman who hooks and unhooks cargo that goes on and off ships.

Slings: Wire or rope used for lifting or lowering cargo.

Slip Boards: Boards that were used to help move heavy cargo into a ship that could easily slide on the boards, such as bundles of cotton.

Specialty Gangs: Gangs of varying sizes who were appropriate for individual types of cargoes and ships. For example, a specialty gang would be employed to load wheat. Certain ships had special lifting devices that required a specialty longshore gang to operate.

Splitting Bar: A piece of steel that was two-and-a-half inches wide, half an inch thick, and five feet long. On one end, it had a one-inch square hole. The other end was flattened like a chisel. This tool was often used when cargo was too heavy. By putting the splitting bar in the middle, the peavey held it down to make a two-inch gap and then slings were used. For example, the splitting bar would be used to move 450-pound bales of pulp. Wires were wrapped around the bale and the splitting bar would be used to give the bale a two to three-inch lift.

Spud: A long handle made of wood that came to a rounded point. It was a tool used by longshoremen to help move cargo. The spud would be placed into crevasses of cargo, such as paper and pulp, which would have been damaged if a peavey was used instead.

Standing Gear: The ship's loading gear that was located between hatches. Ships had two large steel posts called Samson posts between each hatch. The rigging gear that held up the booms was attached to each of the Samson posts. A cable ran from the winches through a pulley block at the heel of the boom, then up a pulley at the top of the boom, and then down, where it was connected to the hook. The cable that came from the other winch was also connected to the hook. This way, the hook could travel from the dock or scow to the bottom of the hatch.

Stevedores: Labour management companies that provide equipment and hire workers to transfer cargo between ships and docks. Stevedore companies may also serve as terminal operators. The labourers hired by the stevedoring firms are called stevedores or longshoremen.

Stook: A variation of blackjack that the longshoremen would play at the union hall in the early years of longshoring, while waiting for dispatch and after getting their weekly paycheques. Longshoremen played for money.

Straddle Carriers or 'Strads': Machines used when the length of the load was longer than the width of the dock face. The loads were put in special blocks built especially for straddle carriers which were a foot wider than the load. They were built so they could go over a load five-and-a-half feet wide and six feet high, with long grabs at the bottom that could expand out sideways and up a few inches to pick up a block. A straddle carrier picked up the load and took it to the ship's hatch. Straddle carriers were often used at Pacific Coast Terminals and Overseas Transport docks in New Westminster. The PAD ships had their own strads. These were bigger than a regular strad and had forks that swivelled under them. These could pick up two loads of lumber at a time.

Sweat Boards: Used to keep the cargo away from the steel ribs of the ship's hold, to eliminate the moisture transfer. They were two by six-inch wide boards of various lengths, attached horizontally to the ribs using removable steel brackets.

Swinging Stick: Is a boom attached to the ship between two Samson posts with cables attached to the boom and posts. This allows the boom to swing from hatch to dock or hatch to scow to load or unload cargo. The cables made the swinging stick sloppy and dangerous to use.

Tag Line: Additional rope tied to a large object that is being moved by crane. A longshoreman on the dock holds the tag line to ensure that the object does not swing when being moved.

Tarps: A canvas or polyester covering for cargo or hatches.

The Tent: A tent would need to be set up over the hatch to prevent certain cargo from getting wet while loading. A hatch tent was used to cover the hatch at night and could be set up or torn down quickly.

Timbers: Square-cut lumber that came in three sizes, but most were twelve by twelve inches. Some were eighteen by eighteen inches and, very rarely, some were twenty-four by twenty-four inches.

Trade Missions: During the 1980s and 1990s, Local 502 executives went with the Fraser River Harbour Commission on trade missions to Asia and Europe to promote the port and its facilities.

Travelling Cards: Up until the early 1960s, longshoremen were able to get travelling cards that permitted them to travel to other ILWU ports on the west coast of North America for three months in a year.

Terminal: An assigned area where containers are prepared for loading into a vessel or are stacked immediately after discharge from the vessel.

Terminal Operator: The company that operates cargo handling activities on a wharf. A terminal operator oversees unloading cargo from ship to dock, checking the quantity of cargoes versus the manifest, storing the cargo, checking documents authorizing a trucker to pick up cargo, overseeing the loading/unloading of railroad cars, etc.

TEU: Twenty-foot equivalent unit, a standard linear measure used to quantify container flows. Containers generally come in three sizes; twenty, forty, and forty-five feet.

Toplift: A piece of equipment similar to a forklift that lifts from above rather than below. It is used to move containers in the storage yard to and from storage stacks, trucks, and railcars.

Trainship: On Thursdays, the train ships would come from Whittier, Alaska, to Fraser Surrey Docks with empty containers. The longshoremen would unload railcars. It was usually a two-shift job during the day and afternoon shifts.

Transshipment: The unloading of cargo at a port or point where it is then reloaded, sometimes into another mode of transportation, for transfer to a final destination.

Trim Boards: Used in conjunction with the ship winches to level or trim bulk cargoes such as grains (wheat), sulphur, and potash.

Turn Buckle: Used to tighten chain or cable lashing on deck loads of logs or lumber, or to secure cargo in a ship's hold. Used for machinery, large crates, or containers.

Tween Deck: Deck between the main deck and lower hold: each hatch of a liberty ship would have a tween deck. On the liberty ships, the tween decks would be about eight feet high. This was a place where the longshoremen also stored cargo.

Uncovering the Hatch: After setting the gear, the longshoremen uncovered the hatch by first knocking the wedges that held quarter-inch by two-inch by twenty-foot bars. These bars held down the tarps that covered the hatch covers to keep water from getting in. Next, the longshoremen got on top of the hatch and pulled the tarps off, sometimes three or more.

The hatch covers were made of wood and were about two feet by four feet long with handles. When they got the hatch covers off and stacked them on the deck away from the work site, the longshoremen would take off the beams that held the hatch covers in place. The longshoremen did this by first hooking up the bridle to the centre beam and then the gear would put the beam on deck. Longshoremen would go back and get the next beam until all the beams were out.

Vehicle Rack: A rack or frame that allows up to three motor vehicles to be loaded into a single (40-foot-high cube) container. This technology is only used for luxury and small-volume vehicle shipments.

Most imported vehicles handled by Local 502 longshoremen at Annacis Island and Fraser Wharves are transported in car ships, and loaded via ramps. *See also* container and flat rack.

Walking Boards: Longshoremen would put walking boards in the ship's hatch if there was a large crack in the floor or if it was uneven. The longshoremen would put sheets of plywood to ensure they would not fall into the cracks when they were hauling sacks.

Wharf: The place where ships tie up to unload and load cargo. The wharf typically has front and rear loading docks (aprons), a transit shed, open (unshedded) storage areas, truck bays, and rail tracks.

Wharfage: A charge assessed by a terminal operator, dock owner, or port authority, against freight handled over the dock or against a steamship company using the dock.

White List: A list of people who are qualified to work at Westshore Terminals as spare longshoremen.

Winches: A machine for lifting cargo in and out of the ship. A longshoreman drives a double winch because there are two linked together and can be operated by one man. Single winches have one operator per winch. Winches can be steam, electric, friction, or hydraulic.

Wolfing: 1) When you went out of your home port to another port to seek work, e.g. going to Vancouver.

2) When steady workers on a scheduled day off would go to the hall and take a job anyway. The term may have derived from a longshoreman who used to call this "Keeping the wolf away from the door."

Bibliography

"10 Union Officials Choose Jail Over Fines." *Globe and Mail* (18 June 1966).

"14 Pickets Arrested at City Docks." *British Columbian* (3 September 1935).

"A Study of a Dispute in B.C. Ports 1969–1970." *Business Quarterly* 35, no. 3, Autumn 1970.

"A. F. of L. Organizer Heatherton a Busy Man." *BC Federationist* (3 October 1913).

"Agreement Near in Waterfront Strike?" *British Columbian* (28 August 1935).

"Al Currie." *Gang Plank* no. 27, June 1960.

"Ald. Sullivan Questioned in Dock Strike." *British Columbian* (16 January 1936).

"All City Docks Occupied as Ten Freighters Load Cargo." *British Columbian* (9 January 1940).

"Another Riot Almost Precipitated at Noon Today — Veterans Visit the Longshoremen's Hall — Ugly Situation Saved by Mayor." *Vancouver Daily World* (3 August 1918).

"Another Ship Loading at City Docks." *British Columbian* (25 June 1935).

1050 CHUM Timeline. "CHUM Hit Parade, 1960." Accessed 6 August 2015. http://chumtribute.ca/timeline/.

"B.C. District Council is Established." *The Dispatcher* vol. 4 no. 1 (11 January 1946).

"B.C. Longshoremen Agree to Arbitration." *Globe and Mail* (28 March 1972).

BC Studies no. 162, Summer 2009.

"Bennett Attacks Ottawa Policies on Roberts Bank." *Globe and Mail* (8 May 1968).

Billboard Charts Archive. "The Hot 100 — 1960 Archive." Accessed 6 August 2015. http://www.billboard.com/archive/charts/1960/hot-100.

"Bill on Gain Shipping Panned." *Globe and Mail* (24 February 1997).

"Bill Passed to End Dock Dispute." *Globe and Mail* (9 February 1994).

Bjarnason, Emil. "Mechanisation and Collective Bargaining in the British Columbia Longshore Industry." Ph.D. dissertation, Burnaby: Simon Fraser University, 1975.

Black, Lawrence and Hugh Pemberton, eds. "An Affluent Society?: Britain's Post-War 'Golden Age' Revisited." Burlington: Ashgate, 2004.

"Blake Named as Candidate by City C.C.F." *British Columbian* (26 April 1937).

Bonthius, Andrew. "Origins of the International Longshoremen's and Warehousemen's Union." *Southern California Quarterly*, vol. 59 no. 4, Winter 1977.

Boyer, Harold. "Canada and Cuba: A Study in International Relations." Ph.D. Thesis, Simon Fraser University, 1972

British Columbia Maritime Employers Association. "Women on the Waterfront." Accessed 10 November 2014. http://www.bcmea.com/women_on_the_waterfront.aspx?page=hrwomenwaterfront&section=hr#.

"Buying Dockside Peace Could Trigger Inflation Round." *The Columbian* (2 January 1979).

Cairncross, Alec and Frances Cairncross, eds. "The Legacy of the Golden Age: The 1960s and Their Consequences." London: Routledge, 1992.

ILWU Canada Waterfront News (5 October 1966).

"Captain John Macmillan." *Gang Plank* no. 41, September 1961.

"CLC Official Praises British Columbia Longshoremen for Social Conscience." *Globe and Mail* (10 October 1969).

"Container Docks in Surrey Idle After $190m Expansion." *Vancouver Sun* (21 June 2006).

Cruickshank, John and Carey French. "B.C. Lockout Closes Ports, Idles 3,700." *Globe and Mail* (7 October 1986).

Daniels, Alan. "Port Ready to Call Its Own Shots." *Vancouver Sun* (23 February 1999).

"Davis Blames Longshoremen: Complete Text of Davis Report on Waterfront Probe." *Vancouver Sun* (28 October 1935).

Department of Labour Canada. Fifteenth Annual Report on Labour Organization in Canada (For the Calendar Year 1925), Ottawa: F.A. Acland, 1926.

Department of Labour Canada. Seventeenth Annual Report of Labour Organization in Canada (For the Calendar Year 1927), Ottawa: F.A. Acland, 1928.

"Difficult to Fill the Gap." *British Columbian* (18 June 1913).

"Dock Pickets Case Delayed Till Tuesday." *British Columbian* (11 September 1935).

"Dock Strike Inquiry Opens in Vancouver." *British Columbian* (17 September 1935).

"Dock Workers in City Ready to Join Strike." *British Columbian* (10 June 1935).

"Dynamite is Found under Dockers' Hall." *British Columbian* (14 December 1936).

Eliel, Paul. *The Waterfront and General Strikes, San Francisco, 1934; A Brief History.* Hooper Printing, 1934.

Electoral History of British Columbia 1871–1986, Elections British Columbia, Victoria: Queen's Printer for British Columbia, 1988.

"End of Container Clause Perks up Vancouver Port." *Globe and Mail* (19 July 1988).

Foster, John Bellamy. "On the Waterfront: Longshoring in Canada." *On the Job: Confronting the Labour Process in Canada*, edited by Craig Heron and Robert Storey, Montreal and Kingston: McGill-Queen's University Press, 1986.

Frank, Dana. *Purchasing Power: Consumer Organizing, Gender and the Seattle Labor Movement, 1919–1929.* New York: Cambridge University, 1994.

"Fred Hume and Harry Sullivan Answer Anonymous Letter Writers." *British Columbian* (10 January 1934).

"General Tie-up of All Shipping on Pacific." *BC Federationist* (12 March 1915).

Glavin, Terry. "Longshoremen Reject Strike." *The Columbian* (10 September 1982).

"Gordon J. Kelly is Near Death." *Daily Colonist* (9 November 1918).

"Government Aid to Settle Dock Strike Sought." *British Columbian* (17 June 1935).

Gresko, Jacqueline and Richard Howard, eds. *Fraser Port: Freightway to the Pacific.* Victoria: Sono Nis Press, 1986.

Haines, Peter, "The Container Gainshare Money versus the Container

Clause." 18 July 2005. Accessed 15 April 2015. http://ilwu500.org/wp-content/uploads/2013/11/Gainshare.pdf.

Hall, Peter V. "Connecting, Disconnecting and Reconnecting: Port Logistics and Vancouver's Fraser River." *L'Espace géographique* 41, 2012-2013.

Hall, Peter V. and Anthony Clark, "Maritime Ports and the Politics of Reconnecting." *Transforming Urban Waterfronts: Fixity and Flow*, Gene Desfor, Jennefer Laidley, Quentin Stevens, and Dirk Schubert, eds. New York: Routledge, 2010.

Harding, Wayne, "New Westminster: City of Paradox." *The Columbian* (27 January 1966).

Harris, Jr., James Clinton, "A Study of the Pacific Coast Longshore Industry with Special Reference to Collective Bargaining and its Influence on the Stabilisation and Equalization of Longshoremen's Income." MA thesis, University of Oregon, Eugene: Knight Library, 1942.

Harry Bridges Center for Labor Studies, University of Washington. "Waterfront Workers History Project — Harry Bridges: Life and Legacy." Accessed 6 August 2015. http://depts.washington.edu/dock/Harry_Bridges_intro.shtml.

Harry Bridges Center for Labor Studies, University of Washington. "Waterfront Workers History Project — Harry Bridges: Life and Legacy." Accessed 6 August 2015. http://depts.washington.edu/dock/Harry_Bridges_intro.shtml.

Hick, W.B.M. *Canada's Pacific Gateways: Realizing the Vision.* Prince Rupert: Prince Rupert Port Authority, 2011.

Howay, F.W. and E.O.S. Scholefield, *British Columbia from the Earliest Times to the Present* vol. IV. Vancouver: S.J. Clarke Publishing Co., 1914.

"Hume Seeking Settlement in Dock Impasse." *British Columbian* (9 April 1936).

Hunter, Jennifer. "Minister Tries to Keep Port Operating." *Globe and Mail* (14 November 1986).

"Increased Pay Announced for Longshoremen." *British Columbian* (8 April 1937).

"Injunction Allows Ships to be Loaded." *Vancouver Sun* (6 September 1958).

Jackson and Cope v. Shipping Federation of British Columbia, 1954.

Jones et al v. Shipping Federation of British Columbia, *1963 Dominion Law Reports* (2nd).

"Kaiser Coal Completes $650 Million Deal with Japanese for Coking Coal

Exports." *Globe and Mail* (1 February 1968).

Kealey, Gregory S. "The Early Years of State Surveillance of Labour and the Left in Canada: The Institutional Framework of the Royal Canadian Mounted Police Security and Intelligence Apparatus, 1918–26." *Intelligence and National Security* vol. 8 no. 3, 1993.

Keller, Marvel. "Decasualization of Longshore Work in San Francisco." Report No. L-2 Works Progress Administration, National Research Project, April 1939.

La, Michelle. "The Effects of Automation, Mechanization, and Formalization on Camaraderie within ILWU Local 502, from the 1960s to Present." Undergraduate thesis, Simon Fraser University, 2014.

Labour Gazette vol. 1, 1900–1901.

Labour Gazette vol. 2, 1901–1902.

Labour Gazette vol. 7, 1906–1907.

Labour Gazette vol. 20, 1920.

Labour Gazette vol. 36, 1936.

Labour Gazette vol. 60, 1955.

"Labor Leader Laid to Rest." *Vancouver Daily World* (13 November 1918).

"L. & W.T.W. of C is Dissolved." *Ship and Dock* vol. 1 no. 21, 11 March 1936.

Leier, Mark. *Where the Fraser River Flows: The Industrial Workers of the World in British Columbia.* Vancouver: New Star Books, 1990.

"Longshore Decision Reserved." *The Columbian* (26 July 1972).

"Longshoremen Buy Property for New Hall." *British Columbian* (5 February 1936).

ILWU Canada Waterfront News, Centennial Edition, November 1971.

"Longshoremen Charged with Carrying Gun." *British Columbian* (3 August 1935).

"Longshoremen Get Increase." *BC Federationist* (29 August 1919). *Labour Gazette* vol. 19, 1919.

"Longshoremen in BC Okay Shipments to Cuba." *The Province* (9 December 1960).

"Longshoremen in Convention." *BC Federationist* (9 May 1919).

"Longshoremen Lose in Judge's Report." *British Columbian* (28 October 1935).

"Longshoremen Meet Tonight: May Boycott Dutch Freighters." *The Columbian* (4 August 1947).

"Longshoremen Seeking Higher Scale of Pay." *British Columbian* (13 February 1935).

"Longshoremen's Challenge to Save Clause is Stymied." *Globe and Mail* (9 December 1987).

"Longshoremen's Convention." *BC Federationist* (23 May 1913).

"Longshoremen's Pacific Coast Difficulties." *BC Federationist* (20 August 1915).

"Longshoremen's Strike along Pacific Coast." *BC Federationist* (21 July 1916).

"Longshoremen's Union Fights Container Ruling." *Globe and Mail* (18 July 1987).

"Longshoremen's Vote Insufficient to Authorize Strike." *British Columbian* (14 May 1934).

"Longshoremen's Wages." *Daily Colonist* (7 March 1901).

Louis Goldblatt and Otto Hagel introduced by Harry Bridges and J. Paul St. Sure. *Men and Machines: A Story About Longshoring on the West Coast Waterfront*, San Francisco: International Longshoremen's and Warehousemen's Union Pacific Maritime Association, 1963.

MacDonald, Sandy. *The Halifax Longshoremen's Association 1907–2007: Celebrating 100 Years*. Halifax: ILA Local 269, 2007.

Magden, Ronald and A.D. Martinson. *The Working Waterfront: The Story of Tacoma's Ships and Men*. Tacoma: ILWU Local 23, 1982.

Magden, Ronald E. *A History of Seattle Waterfront Workers 1884–1934*. Seattle: International Longshore and Warehouse Union Local 19, 1991.

Maintenance of Ports Operations Act, 1986 (Canada), Accessed 10 November 2015. http://laws-lois.justice.gc.ca/eng/acts/M-0.25/FullText.html.

Man Along the Shore! The Story of the Vancouver Waterfront as told by Longshoremen Themselves 1860's–1975. Vancouver: ILWU Local 500 Pensioners, 1975.

Marine and Dock Labor: Work, Wages and Industrial Relations during the Period of the War, Report of the Director of the Marine and Dock Industrial Relations Division. United States Shipping Board, Washington, D.C.: Government Printing Office, 1922.

Mather, Barry and Margaret McDonald. *New Westminster: The Royal City*. Vancouver: J.M. Dent & Sons, 1958.

"Mayor Beth Wood." New Westminster Parks, Culture & Recreation, Accessed 6 August 2015. http://www.newwestpcr.ca/database/files/library/Mayor_Beth_Wood.pdf.

"Mayor Hume Wins Sweeping Endorsement in City Voting; Retiring Aldermen Re-elected." *British Columbian* (16 December 1938).

Mayse, Susan, *Ginger: The Life and Death of Albert Goodwin.* Madeira Park: Harbour Publishing, 1990.

McCandless, R.C. "Vancouver's 'Red Menace' of 1935: The Waterfront Situation." *BC Studies* no. 22, Summer 1974.

McCaugherty, Jack. "On the Labor Front: Pay Hike This Week for Longshoremen." *Vancouver Daily Province* (20 September 1950).

McInnis, Peter S. "Harnessing Labour Confrontation: Shaping the Postwar Settlement in Canada, 1943–1950." Toronto: University of Toronto Press, 2002.

McLean, Bruce. "Strike Idles Docks." *The Columbian* (22 August 1958).

McManus, Theresa, "Union Holds Rally: Event Marks 'Grand Closing' of Interfor's Queensborough Mill." *The Record* [New Westminster] (30 August 2008).

Mills, Herb. "The San Francisco Water Front: The Social Consequences of Industrial Modernization, Part One: 'The Good Old Days'." *Journal of Contemporary Ethnography* 5, July 1976.

Ministry of Forests, Lands & Natural Resource Operations. "Population of British Columbia, 1800–2006." Accessed 6 August 2015. http://www.for.gov.bc.ca/hfp/sof/2006/figures/fig06.pdf.

Monk, H.A.J. and John Stewart, *History of Coquitlam and Fraser Mills, 1858–1958.* Coquitlam: District of Coquitlam-Fraser Mills Centennial Commission, 1958.

"Mr. Average Longshoreman." *The Columbian* (8 September 1958).

"Mr. Taylor Talks of General Strike." *Daily Colonist* (25 May 1919).

Neill, William J. and Ted Matthews. *Ministerial Review of Ports Policing in Lower Mainland Seaports.* Vancouver: Ministry of Attorney General, 1997.

Nelson, Bruce. *Workers on the Waterfront: Seamen, Longshoremen, and Unionism in the 1930s.* Urbana and Chicago: University of Illinois Press, 1990.

"New Plans to Improve Fraser." *British Columbian* (18 October 1919).

New Westminster & District Labour Council. "About Us." Accessed 6 August 2015. http://www.nwdlc.ca/aboutnwdlc.html.

New Westminster Heritage. "Mayors of New Westminster." Accessed 6 August 2015. http://www.nwheritage.org/heritagesite/history/content/mayors.htm.

"New Westminster Record Meeting to Receive Charter." *The Dispatcher* vol. 2

no. 16 (28 July 1944).

"[New] Westminster Welcomes Workers." *BC Federationist* (27 December 1912).

"No Longshore Gangs Brought to Work Here." *British Columbian* (9 March 1936).

"No Need to Bluff, with Province's High Cards: B.C.-owned Super-Port Proposed Answer to Crow's Nest Coal Impasse." *Globe and Mail* (28 March 1967).

"Opinion of the Attorney General in re Water Frontage New Westminster 8th April 1872." RG 13 A-2 vol. 2138 file 1872-746, LAC.

"Ottawa's Port Decision Shows Lack of Rapport with B.C. Government." *Globe and Mail* (21 October 1967).

"Pacific Coast District, No. 38, I.L.A." *BC Federationist* (29 May 1914).

Pacific Coast Terminals. "PCT Newsletter: Channels, Spring 2005, Vol. 21, No. 1." Accessed 6 August 2015. http://pct.ca/wp-content/uploads/2014/12/PCTNewsletterSpring2005.pdf.

Parnaby, Andrew. "'The best men that ever worked the lumber': Aboriginal Longshoremen on Burrard Inlet, BC, 1863–1939." *Canadian Historical Review* vol. 87 no. 1, 2006.

Parnaby, Andrew. *Citizen Docker: Making a New Deal on the Vancouver Waterfront 1919–1939.* Toronto: University of Toronto Press, 2008.

Pathy, Alexander C. Waterfront Blues: Labour Strife at the Port of Montreal, 1960–1978. Toronto: University of Toronto Press, 2004.

Pensions on the Waterfront: The Climax of an Era of ILWU Progress. San Francisco: International Longshoremen's and Warehousemen's Union, 1952.

Philpott, Stuart B. "The Union Hiring Hall as a Labour Market: A Sociological Analysis." *British Journal of Industrial Relations* vol. 3 no. 1, March 1965.

"Police Ban Pickets at City Docks." *British Columbian* (22 August 1935).

"Police Guarding Workers." *Montreal Gazette* (25 June 1935).

"President Labinsky report on Conciliation." *Gang Plank* no. 3, June 1958.

"Proclamation Issued by Mayor in City Dock Strike." *British Columbian* (22 June 1935).

"Rail Strike Won't Close Ocean Port." *Vancouver Daily Province* (24 August 1950).

Report on Labour Organization in Canada 1913. Department of Labour Canada, Ottawa: Government Printing Bureau, 1914.

"Royal City Faces Port Shutdown." *The Columbian* (30 August 1982).

Russell, Maud. *Men Along the Shore*. New York: Brussel and Brussel, 1966.

Safford, Jeffrey J. "The Pacific Coast Maritime Strike of 1936: Another View." *Pacific Historical Review* vol. 77 no. 4, 2008.

Sanford, Barrie. *Royal Metal: The People, Times and Trains of New Westminster Bridge*. Vancouver: National Railway Historical Society, 2004.

Schwantes, Carlos A. *Radical Heritage: Labor, Socialism and Reform in Washington and British Columbia 1885–1917*. Seattle: University of Washington Press, 1979.

Schwartz, Harvey. "Solidarity Stories: An Oral History of the ILWU." Seattle: University of Washington Press, 2009.

Schwartz, Harvey. "Harry Bridges and the Scholars: Looking at History's Verdict." *California History* 59, no. 1, Spring 1980.

Seager, Allen., "Workers, Class, and Industrial Conflict in New Westminster, 1900–1930." *Workers, Capital, and the State in British Columbia: Selected Papers*, Vancouver: University of British Columbia Press, 1988.

Smith, Roy. "Vancouver Longshoremen, Resilient Solidarity, and the 1935 Interruption: Company Unionism 1923–1945." MA thesis. Burnaby: Simon Fraser University, 2013.

"Statement is Issued by City Dock Workers." *British Columbian* (18 June 1935).

"Strike Fear Grows on Waterfront." *Vancouver Sun* (9 August 1958).

"Strike of City Dock Workers Believed Ended." *British Columbian* (27 November 1935).

"Strike Outlay at Royal City Fully Repaid." *Vancouver News-Herald* (12 August 1935).

"Strike Will Tie Up Shipping." *Daily Colonist (*1 June 1916).

Taft, Philip. "Labor Politics American Style: The California State Federation of Labor." Cambridge: Harvard University Press, 1968.

"Terms of Settlement." *Gang Plank* no. 7, October 1958.

"The Longshoremen's Strike: A Brief Historical Sketch of the Strike inaugurated on 1 June 1916, in Pacific Coast Ports of the United States.", Waterfront Workers' Federation, San Francisco, California, 23 August 1916.

The Truth About the Waterfront: The I.L.A. States its Case to the Public. San Francisco: International Longshoremen's Association Local 38-79, 1935. Oakland Public Library History Room, Oakland, California.

Torigian, Michael. "Work on the Waterfront: Communist Politics and the ILWU during the Second World War." *Labor History* vol. 30 no. 3, July 1989.

Towers, Brian. *Waterfront Blues: The Rise and Fall of Liverpool's Dockland.* Lancaster: Carnegie Publishing, 2011.

Tucker, Warren. "Pacific Mechanization Contract Delights U.S. Dockers, Shippers." *Globe and Mail* (26 March 1963).

"U.S. Marine Unions Lift Ban From New Westminster: Port Now Open to American Ships." *British Columbian* (5 March 1937).

"U.S. Strike is Not Affecting City Shipping." *British Columbian* (17 May 1934).

"Victoria Close for Convention." *Daily Colonist* (14 May 1912).

"Victoria Stevedores Win." *BC Federationist* (5 April 1912).

Walsh, Victor Anthony. "The International Longshoremen's Association: Rebirth of a Union." MA thesis, San Francisco State College, 1972, San Francisco Public Library History Center.

Webber, Jeremy. "The Malaise of Compulsory Conciliation: Strike Prevention in Canada during World War II." *Labour/Le travail* vol. 15, Spring 1985.

Webber, Michael J. and David L. Rigby. *The Golden Age Illusion: Rethinking Postwar Capitalism.* New York: The Guildford Press, 1996.

"West Coast Longshoremean End Strike, Accept $1.85 Raise in 2-year Pact." *Globe and Mail* (17 March 1975).

"Westminster on Fair List." *The Province* (5 March 1937).

Woodsworth, J.S. *On the Waterfront.* Ottawa: Mutual Press, 1927.

Yarmie, Andrew. "The Right to Manage: Vancouver Employers' Associations, 1900–1923." *BC Studies* no. 90, Summer 1991.

Yarmie, Andrew. "The State and Employers' Associations in British Columbia: 1900–1932." *Labour/Le travail* vol. 45, Spring 2000.

"Youths Admit Burning Fiery Cross." *British Columbian* (23 October 1935).

Acknowledgements

This book has been made possible by the generous contributions, dedication, and hard work of many individuals and committees, both those listed below and others who are too many to name.

The members of the ILWU Local 502 Book Committee, which brought overall direction to the book project, consisted of Joe Breaks, Gerry White, Brian Ringrose, Ron Noullett, Dean Johnson, and Tracey Noullett.

ILWU Local 502 provided resources and support for the book, through the leadership of Tim Farrell, Lorne Pennell, Tom Doran, and other elected officeholders, as well as through the support of the wider membership.

Key individuals in the leadership of ILWU Canada offered inspiration and support for the project, including Tom Dufresne, Mark Gordienko, Frank Kennedy and Dave Lomas.

Generous funding from the Social Sciences and Humanities Research Council of Canada made the (Re)Claiming the New Westminster Waterfront Research Partnership possible. Financial and in-kind contributions were also provided by ILWU Local 502, the New Westminster Museum and Archives, and Simon Fraser University.

The (Re)Claiming the New Westminster Waterfront Research Partnership was governed by a Steering Committee consisting of Peter Hall, Willeen Keough, Rob McCollough, Oana Capota, Joe Breaks, Gerry White, Brian Ringrose, Ken Bauder, and Sue Dyer.

The staff of the New Westminster Museum and Archives, in particular archivist Barry Dykes, provided research support to the authors.

Over 100 people, from the longshore industry as well as many others, told their stories about work on the New Westminster waterfront and the Fraser River. These oral histories are available to the public as part of the permanent collection of the New Westminster Archives. A large team identified, collected, summarized, and curated the oral histories: Pamela Stern provided overall leadership of this activity, Willeen Keough provided training for interviewers, Andrea Walisser coordinated and conducted many interviews, Dean Johnson conducted numerous longshore interviews, Michelle La conducted and summarized many interviews, and Bailey Garden handled the digital audio recordings. Others who contributed to this research activity included Oana Capota, Kate Petrusa, Peter Hall, Liam O'Flaherty, Barry Dykes, Andreas Hovland, Mark McKenzie, Leigha Smith, Joe Breaks, Gerry White, Brian Ringrose, Ron Noullett, Ken Bauder, Dave Lomas, Colin Osmond, Jackie Gootee, Courtney Manlove, Jane French, Annika Airas, Kristianne Hendricks, Mary-Ellen Kelm, and Rob McCullough.

Chris Madsen was a SSHRC collaborator on the community partnership project. Jacqueline Gresko, Mark Leier, Earl Noah, and Barry Dykes offered assistance and materials for the writing of Chapters 1, 2, and 3. Robin Walker at the ILWU Library and Archives in San Francisco humoured a persistent researcher. Permission was given from the British Columbia Maritime Employers Association to access the Shipping Federation of British Columbia fonds at the City of Vancouver Archives, and the University of Oregon Special Collections and University Archives opened the International Longshoremen's Association Pacific District collection to us. Chapter 3 was presented at the Canadian Nautical Research Society Conference in Ottawa, June 2015. Parts of Chapter 2 were presented at the *BC Studies* Conference in New Westminster, May 2013 and the North American Society for

Oceanic History Conference in Monterey, California, May 2015. Parts of Chapter 1 have been developed into a research note introducing James Shaver Woodsworth's *On the Waterfront* appearing in *The Northern Mariner/Le marin du nord*. The Royal Military College of Canada and Department of National Defence granted sabbatical leave for a year of writing. Research in Ottawa was done in-between visits to Lieutenant-General Stuart Beare and his joint staffs at DND Star Top while working a special tasking for Canadian Joint Operations Command. Colonel Steve Moritsugu is singled out for his encouragement and professionalism. Integrity and leadership underscore academics at the Canadian Forces College, Professor Madsen's home institution.

The following people helped to make the World of Work on the Waterfront Intergenerational Arts Program possible: Dr. Susan O'Neill, Project Director; Dr. Peter Hall, Partnership Director; Sue Dyer, Deanna Peluso, Elisa Vandenborn, and Claire Carolan, Graduate Research Assistants; Rose Dyer, Youth Research Assistant; Matthew Sol of F. W. Howay Elementary School and Pat Dyer of New Westminster Secondary School, Teacher Affiliates; Joe Breaks, Gerry White, Brian Ringrose, Ken Bauder, Dean Johnson, and Ron Noullett, retired longshore workers; and students in the New Westminster School District.

The staff of Granville Island Publishing, including Jo Blackmore, Kyle Hawke, and Victor D. Colmont, were responsible for editing, layout, and design, bringing parts of the book from different authors to final publication.

Index

longshore workers, xiv, 276n59
Longshoremen's Union of the Pacific, 11, 13
longshoremen/longshore workers, 5, 87, 103, 159, 165, 192, 233, 281
  American, 19–20, 102
  arrests, 90
  card men, 203–4
  collective bargaining, 65
  and the community, xviii
  decasualization, 292
  defined, 296
  earnings and payrolls, 126, 168–69
  interactions with sailors and crewmen, 231–33
  old-timers, 188–91, 229–30
  preferred casuals list, 125–26, 202–3
  ratings, 199–200
  work conditions/culture, 5, 188–91
  workers, 276n59, xiv
lumber, 6, 27, 125
  export, 3–5, 21–22, 125, 194, 247
  handling, xvii, 12, 47, 154b, 154c, 282a, 282f
  packaged, xvii, 194, 197–98, 289
  plywood, 269
  See also trade, export/import
lumber mills/sawmills, 3, 4, 5, 6, 8, 15
Lynch, B., 41
Lynch, John, 41, 90
Lynch, L., 39

MacDonald, Ben, 281
Macdonald, John A., 208
Mackie, Laing, 211–12
Macpherson, R., 249
Madsen, James, 16
Mahaney, Rowland, 19
Maidens, H., 39
Maintenance of Port Operations Act, 252–53
Man Along the Shore!, 188–89, 191, 204

Mann, M., 249
Manson, Alexander, 164, 166
Marine Association of BC, 15, 21–22, 47–49
  See also BC Maritime Employers Association; Shipping Federation of BC
Maritime Federation of the Pacific Coast, 102
Martin, Arthur, 81
Mason, Dave, 211–12
Matthes, R., 41
Matthews, Jack, 90
McCormack, J.M., 39
McDade, J., 41
McIlwaine, S., 41
McIntyre, Howard, 279
McKay, William 'Bill,' 81, 279
McKee, George, 132, 143, 144, 153, 164, 167, 170–71
McKenzie, Stewart, 143–44
McKinnie, John, 71–73
Mclean, G., 249
McLean, R., 39
Mclellen, R., 249
mechanization and modernization (M&M), 62, 199, 282e, 282f, 296–97
  anxiety about, 214, 234
  changing waterfront work, 8–9, 196–98, 272
  containerization, xvii, 247
  containers/containerization, xvii, 218, 247–48, 252–53, 271–72, 291
  and declining employment, xii, 196, 244
  defined, 296–97
  and the gang system, 191–201, 204
  M&M agreement, 188, 195–96
Meehan, Matt, 104
military veterans, 36, 38–39, 163, 229–30

Authors

Chris Madsen is a professor in the Department of Defence Studies at the Canadian Forces College and Royal Military College of Canada in Toronto, where he teaches senior and mid-rank officers in the area of military planning and operations. He finds creative ways to put adversaries into impossible situations. Professor Madsen is president of the Canadian Nautical Research Society. He was a visiting scholar in the Urban Studies Program at Simon Fraser University and academic collaborator on the Social Studies and Humanities Research Council community partnership project during 2014/15.

Liam O'Flaherty is a Master's student in the History department at Simon Fraser University and a research assistant on the (Re)Claiming the New Westminster Waterfront project. He holds a Bachelor of Arts (Honours) in political science and history from Memorial University of Newfoundland and a Master of Arts in political science from the University of British Columbia. His thesis research is about sectarianism within the Newfoundland and Labrador labour movement in the early 20th Century. Liam is also engaged in other oral history/public history projects and is currently teaching a Canadian History survey course at Fraser International College.

Michelle La completed her undergraduate degree (with honours) in sociology and anthropology and a Certificate in Social Justice at Simon Fraser University. She is a research assistant for the (Re)Claiming the New Westminster Waterfront project. She currently works as a research assistant on a global maternal health project called PRE-EMPT (Pre-eclampsia & Eclampsia Monitoring, Prevention and Treatment), funded by the Bill & Melinda Gates Foundation, at the Department of Obstetrics and Gynaecology at the University of British Columbia. She is looking forward to pursuing a Master's degree in the field of anthropology focusing on the utilization of mHealth technology in low-resourced settings. In addition, Michelle is an active member of the Vietnamese in North America community that advocates for social justice on issues that pertain to human rights violations in Vietnam.

Peter Hall is professor of Urban Studies at Simon Fraser University in Vancouver, where he teaches economic development, research methods, and transportation geography. He received his doctorate in city and regional planning from the University of California at Berkeley. His research examines the connections between port cities, seaports, and logistics, as well as community, local economic, and employment development. His publications include the co-edited *Integrating Seaports and Trade Corridors* (Ashgate, 2011) and *Cities, Regions and Flow* (Routledge, 2013), as well as numerous journal articles, book chapters, and reports. He is an Associate Editor of the *Journal of Transport Geography*, and was director of the (Re)Claiming the New Westminster Waterfront Research Partnership.